J. EDGAR
THOMSON

J. Edgar Thomson

Thomson retained his striking intensity late into his career as this etching illustrates. Courtesy of the John Edgar Thomson Foundation.

J. EDGAR THOMSON

MASTER OF THE PENNSYLVANIA

James A. Ward

Contributions in Economics and Economic History, Number 33

GREENWOOD PRESS

WESTPORT, CONNECTICUT ● LONDON, ENGLAND

Grateful acknowledgment is made to the following:

Business History Review for permission to reprint portions of James A. Ward, "Power and Accountability on the Pennsylvania Railroad, 1846–1878," Spring 1975.

Railroad History for permission to reprint portions of James A. Ward, "Pioneer Railroading in the South; J. Edgar Thomson and the Georgia Railroad, 1834–37," Spring 1976, pp. 4–33.

Pennsylvania Historical and Museum Commission, Harrisburg, Pennsylvania.

The John Edgar Thomson Foundation, Philadelphia, Pennsylvania.

Library of Congress Cataloging in Publication Data

Ward, James Arthur, 1941–
    J. Edgar Thomson.

    (Contributions in economics and economic history; no. 33 ISSN 0084–9235)
    Bibliography: p.
    Includes index.
    1. Thomson, Edgar, 1808–1874. 2. Pennsylvania Railroad—History. 3. Businessmen—United States—Biography.
HE2754.T53W37   385'.092'4 [B]   79–6569
ISBN 0–313–22095–6 lib. bdg.

Library of Congress Catalog Card Number: 79–6569
ISBN: 0–313–22095–6
ISSN: 0084–9235

First published in 1980

Greenwood Press
A division of Congressional Information Service, Inc.
88 Post Road West, Westport, Connecticut 06880

Printed in the United States of America

10 9 8 7 6 5 4 3 2 1

For my mother, Rose Ward Heburn, and
in the memory of
James A Ward
and
Clark J. Heburn

CONTENTS

ILLUSTRATIONS

MAPS

PREFACE

Biographers are a strange breed. While they create, destroy, and otherwise mangle their subjects' reputations, playing God with the lives of others and sometimes living vicariously through greater men, they inevitably begin their books with an apologia for yet another version of their subject's life. Mercifully, I am spared such a task, not because I am not guilty of all the foregoing, but for the simple reason that J. Edgar Thomson has no other treatment. Having lived with the man for about a decade now, reading his correspondence, checking innumerable details of his busy and varied career, and in general just poking my nose into his business—pursuits I am sure were he alive he would resist with all his fiber—I have become convinced that J. Edgar did not want anyone to write his biography. He certainly did nothing to promote it or for that matter to make it an iota easier; no notes to some mysterious beauty, no enigmatic letters discussing large amounts of money and prominent politicians connected with "the topic last discussed," as was Tom Scott's style, no half-finished novel or notebooks full of poetry in his crabbed hand; in fact, he left no collection of letters at all. None at least that I have turned up. By a conservative estimate Thomson must have written about 10,000 letters over his lifetime and received perhaps twice as many. A well-organized man, he kept copies of his outgoing correspondence and filed his incoming mail—he was that type. But it has all disappeared, perhaps destroyed as was Scott's, or maybe still hidden in some fifth cousin's attic.

Such a dearth of material discouraged those who earlier considered writing his biography, as it did me numerous times throughout the project. Newspapers were of almost no use because Thomson was an extremely private man, and he either planted the items that did reach the dailies, or they were purely conjectural. The number of times reporters directly quoted him can be counted on one hand. So I had to reach Thomson the hard way—through surviving letters that he sent to others; undoubtedly, there are many more of his missives squirreled away in collections I missed or was too "thick" to recognize as possibilities. Almost all of his surviving letters deal with business affairs and are typically cold and formal. While they help outline what he did, they singularly fail to indicate why he did it. He was not the kind of man to reveal his inner feelings to anyone anyway and certainly would not have put them down on paper. Any biographer longs to know something about his subject's dreams, hopes, and passions; in Thomson's case I do not even know if he smoked (I suspect he did), drank (again yes—in moderation), or, for example, whether he liked grapes. So the story on the following pages is really, as Julius Grodinsky subtitled his masterful biography of Jay Gould, "His Business Career." It cannot be helped; Thomson did not cooperate.

From that restricted vantage point, I am tempted to label Thomson a transitional figure, but to do that is, I think, to miss the significance of his life and times. He did not simply span the disparate periods separated by the internecine bloodletting; his life was an example of the sinews that bound the eras together—he and men like him helped to shape the early part of the century into what it later became. He did not have to wrestle a rural nation kicking and struggling into a new, glittering, and oftentimes brutal industrial world; he helped harness forces already abroad in the land. Such spirits had prompted the young nation's political leaders, many of whom were still alive at Thomson's birth, to join Alexander Hamilton and others who enthusiastically touted the delights of industrialization. That path once chosen almost guaranteed that Americans would worship progress measured in terms of material growth. Thomson's noteworthiness was that he was in the vanguard that reshaped those impulses into the institutional embodiments they ultimately assumed, which are so familiar to us today.

In the process Thomson was forced to grapple with the fact that as an engineer fascinated by things mechanical, a man who intrinsically understood and revered objects and what they could do, he was, as he prospered, increasingly obliged to deal more with people than with things. He was always much more comfortable with a locomotive than with most people. He intuitively understood machines; he constantly doubted his own estimation of people. From 1852 on, however, he was more concerned with organizing, managing, and financing corporate creations than with their actual construction. He discovered that personalities and money were irrevocably intertwined. In his business world men were no better than their assets, no more secure than their holdings; one man's million dollars was worth a great deal more than another's. The secret was to divine which men were the more trustworthy, and Thomson quickly learned to withhold judgment as long as practicable and to work as much as possible only with close intimates. He undoubtedly appreciated the irony inherent in a situation where the more he succeeded in his chosen field of expertise the more he was propelled into pursuits for which he knew he was tempermentally unsuited.

I have remarked, at least 100 times over the last few years, that the next time I attempt a biography, if I ever do, I am going to "do" somebody exciting, a derring-do; a person with a sense of humor, a couple of mistresses, and a glorious finale. Thomson enjoyed none of these things. In fact, according to his contemporaries, he was a dull man. But the longer I lived with him, I must admit, the more I came to respect and later to genuinely like the man; I sensed an inner force under that stolid exterior, a self-recognition of who and what he was and, more importantly, what he was not—a trait that I find admirable in people. He possessed a confidence and optimism that his ponderous personality stifled, but which shone through in his deeds. I do not know that I would have liked to spend a very long time alone with Thomson on a desert island, but I do suspect that he could have discoursed intelligently, if I could have prompted him to speak at all, on a wide variety of subjects. He was an interesting, if not exciting, man who was a vital force in American business development; if the following pages convey that fact alone, I have succeeded; if they also convey a sense of Thomson the man, I have won.

ACKNOWLEDGMENTS

Writing a book consumes prodigious amounts of time and money. Three timely grants, one from the American Philosophical Society and two from the University of Tennessee at Chattanooga Faculty Research Committee, funded numerous research trips and considerably eased my financial burdens. The University of Chattanooga Foundation generously aided the project with a sabbatical in 1977 that enabled me to write the bulk of the book free from the daily cares of teaching. The remaining expenses came out of my own pocket, an investment Thomson undoubtedly would have frowned upon.

Part of the fun of putting together a book is the opportunities it provides to meet, talk, and correspond with a host of people who preserve and care for historical records. Every individual was friendly, helpful, and knowledgeable. Rather than risk omitting anyone, I would simply like to express my appreciation to all the staff members with whom I dealt at the Library of Congress, The Historical Society of Pennsylvania, The Pennsylvania Historical and Museum Commission, The Historical Society of Western Pennsylvania, The Kansas Historical Society, Sterling Library, The Association of American Railroads Library, Dauphin County Historical Society, the Georgia University Libraries, the Maryland Historical Society, The New York Public Library, and the Huntington Library.

At the University of Tennessee at Chattanooga's library, I have to thank Wikki Carter, who cowered every time she saw me stride across the reference room trailing sheaves of interlibrary loan requests in my wake, but good-humoredly always found copies of what I needed. Her colleague, Neal Coulter, is a veritable wizard at locating esoterica. I have yet to stump him.

Several other people deserve special mention. Philip S. Klein, recently retired from Pennsylvania State University, was instrumental in securing permission from the trustees of the Penn Central for me to use the minute books of the PRR's board of directors. Employees in the Office of the Secretary of the Penn Central in Philadelphia were most helpful in furnishing pleasant working accommodations and copying services. Helen S. Drinkhouse and later Gilda Verstein, directors of the John Edgar Thomson Foundation, gladly made available the Thomson family materials they had and spent considerable hours tracking down detailed information that I requested. The art work on the maps speaks for Lydia Reynold's manifold talents, and I deeply appreciate her contribution to the book. My colleague, James M. Russell, deserves a special note of thanks for pointing out the Thomson material at the Atlanta Historical Society. Franklin Garrett and Richard Eltzroth located everything they had at the Society and extended every courtesy to the author. John N. McLaurin, Jr., vice president of the Georgia Railroad & Banking Company, belied the image of a stuffy corporate official always peering at the bottom line. Enthusiastically, he provided a wealth of information on Thomson and the antebellum history of the Georgia Railroad and gave me free access to all the company's records remaining from the era. After United States Steel officials refused permission to use their archives, Joseph Wall, Andrew Carnegie's biographer, in the best scholarly tradition, sent me his notes on the joint ventures undertaken by Carnegie and Thomson. Thanks are also due to Albro Martin, editor of the *Business History Review*, for permission to reprint portions of my article.

The worst part of writing a book is the editing, typing, and proofreading. For the last two I am indebted to Diana Powell, Pat Taylor, and Elke Lawson, who know how to make IBM Selectrics talk. The burdens of the editing and the index, however, were borne by my wife, who is my best and severest critic. Moreover, it was she who attended to the daily minutiae that allowed me, gnomelike at times, to scratch off reams of flat prose, most of which justifiably ended up in the wastebasket. All I can say to Roberta is thank you.

J. EDGAR
THOMSON

1

THE BASIC THOMSON

Employees at the Pennsylvania Railroad's headquarters frequently quipped that their boss, John Edgar Thomson, spoke only twice a day. John A. Wright, a Pennsylvania Railroad director, liked to illustrate the depth of Thomson's habitual terseness with an anecdote about the time a friend, William Parker, entered Thomson's presidential office and proffered a cheery "good morning, Thomson," whereupon Thomson lifted his eyes from his work and bid his friend likewise. The two sat in absolute silence for thirty minutes. Parker arose, they exchanged good mornings, and he departed. Obviously Parker, no voluble individual himself, accepted Thomson's peculiarity. Many others, however, found it disquieting. When Herman Haupt, an early business associate, recalled his first meeting with Thomson in 1847, he remembered leaving in disgust. "I found Thomson so taciturn," Haupt wrote to Samuel Mifflin, "that I could get nothing out of him. He was noncommital in everything." Mifflin, Thomson's principal assistant engineer, admitted in reply: "I know Thomson intimately. He is a queer fish."[1]

To many people he was a "queer fish," because as an intensely shy man, he took great care to preserve his privacy. His most overt personal defenses were his brusque, abrupt, and aloof public mannerisms. While these were difficult to breach, they served him well in business dealings, for they lent him the flavor of a forbidding character. Moreover, his tight control over his personal feelings and emotions added to his wary image. Frequently petitioners, sometimes even close personal friends, left his presence without the shred of an idea where Thomson stood on the issue under consideration.

To those who pierced his reserved exterior, however, he was capable of intense friendship and loyalty. Although there were not many so honored, those who were long cherished his friendship and association. Haupt, who broke with Thomson over business dealings in the late 1850s, intimated something of the hold Thomson still exercised when he wrote his former employer in 1861 that "if there is a man living for whom I have labored more than any other, that man is J. Edgar Thomson . . . In this I was influenced not by hope of reward but by considerations of personal regard." William Hassell Wilson, a close friend of Thomson's after 1827, later reminisced that Thomson "evinced no disposition to extend his acquaintance, but to those to whom he gave his friendship he manifested strong regard and appeared to take pleasure in rendering them acts of kindness." Wilson's observation was supported by that of General Isaac J. Wistar, another Thomson intimate, who characterized his friend as "slow to give his confidence to individuals, but once given he was a rock of refuge to his friends." Wilson was careful, however, to add "while his confidence in them existed, but when this failed he dropped them at once."[2]

Thomson's ability to attract and cultivate the respect and allegiance of others was of unquestionable importance to him as president of the world's largest corporation. Over the two decades that he held that office, he welded together a management team composed of such independent and talented personalities as Thomas A. Scott, Andrew Carnegie, Herman Haupt, George Roberts, and A. J. Cassatt. He nurtured their egos, delegated much responsibility to them, and, in turn, derived the benefits of their expertise. These gifted men, however, who forged their own national business reputations, never eclipsed their mentor in the councils of the company. In his quiet composed manner, Thomson determined the road's strategy, oversaw its day-to-day affairs, and dominated its strong personalities. In this he was the equal of his two more famous contemporaries: John D. Rockefeller, who towered over Stephen Harkness, Henry Flagler, and Samuel Andrews; and J. P. Morgan, who overshadowed his own partners, Charles H. Coster, George S. Bowdoin, and J. Hood Wright.

Through incredibly hard work Thomson achieved and maintained his position as president and chairman of the board of directors of the

Keystone line. It is not an overstatement to say that he wrecked his health with overwork. In later years, never robust and frequently ill enough to be confined to bed, he brought the office with all its attendant problems to his home. Although he died at sixty-six, a more than generous life span in the nineteenth century, he had ignored warnings of a breakdown from the late 1850s until he collapsed under the accumulated strains of the 1873 panic. And the pace he set at the road's headquarters was infectious; the Pennsylvania came to share with J. P. Morgan and Company the dubious honor of being an executive killer. More than a fair proportion of both companies' officers died prematurely.

The Pennsylvania Railroad (PRR) was the center of Thomson's life. He tended the corporation as if it were an organic entity. His own outside business ventures revolved around it and were usually chosen with an eye to aid it in securing traffic, blocking competitors, expanding its influence, and upgrading its physical plant, as well as for personal profit. His extraneous interests were confined to technical matters, particularly to new ideas that might have some applicability to the railroad industry. General Wistar once described Thomson as "bred to the profession of surveying and engineering;" it was an affinity he never lost. Wilson also recalled that even after Thomson became president of the road, when presented with a technical problem, "he would drop all other business and immediately proceed to an examination, entering into all the details with the spirit of an old war horse going into battle." His obsessive fascination with the practical was both an avocation and a responsibility of his office as he conceived it. Not surprisingly his railroad garnered a well-deserved reputation as a technological pacesetter, pioneering in the use of coal-burning locomotives, steel rails, steel bridges, and air brakes.[3]

Thomson's enthusiasm for mechanical things was an outward manifestation of his noted reserve. Dealing with known quantities, facts, stresses, and strengths was much more reliable than doing business with people who were apt not to be what they represented. Moreover, the empirical Thomson may have really felt comfortable only in the presence of a complex technical problem wholly dependent upon his own resources for solution. For Thomson approached life in essentially the same practical manner; he rarely acted on impulse or on the basis of personal entreaties without first investigating the proposition. A great stickler for facts, he often gave the appearance of excessive caution, and the delays occasioned by his methodical approach sometimes exasperated his friends and associates. Wilson, however, noted that when Thomson "was satisfied upon all points, he was not slow to act." His correspondence neatly manifested his personality traits; it was usually brief, blunt, to the point, and his thoughts normally flowed with a Euclidian precision. He simply omitted the normal nineteenth-century florid prose, as well as most formal punctuation marks. Thomson apparently wrote as he thought, in short, terse bursts. Curiously, the PRR's employees adopted this same peculiarity in their own letters, which stand in stark contrast to correspondence on the rival Baltimore and Ohio (B&O) with its carefully composed missives evidencing much revision and rewriting.[4]

The physical appearance of this practical, unobtrusive Philadelphian who ruled a rail empire heightened his public image. Invariably dressed in a dark suit with a matching waistcoat crossed by a massive gold watch chain and topped off with a white cravat, he appeared at first glance to be a highly respectable undertaker, or as J. Elfreth Watkins, the PRR's biographer, described him, a prosperous clergyman. His physical features only accentuated his conservative dress. Standing five feet, nine inches tall and given to portliness later in life, his overlarge head was crowned by a protruding forehead and topped with thinning dark hair. A succession of pictures revealed that the further his hairline receded, the lower he allowed his sideburns to grow, until they disappeared under his collar. His bushy eyebrows framed large gray eyes that appeared to bore inveterately for interminable periods into those about him with the disquieting habit of seeming to anticipate their thoughts. A fleshy nose bulged out over tight thin lips that were rather too small for the size of his head, accentuating the visage of a wary, careful man, not easily given to risibility.[5]

Thomson's private life confirmed this impression. His house, for the last sixteen years of his life, was designed in the Greek revival style so popular during the 1850s. It was located at the corner of Eighteenth and Spruce Streets in the fashionable Rittenhouse Square district and was both commodious and plain. Outwardly it did not advertise that its owner possessed millions of dollars. Rather, with its spacious yard, two-story ells, and a minimum of the usual decorative addenda, it exhibited in mute form Thomson's distaste for the garish style of some of his *nouveau riche* contemporaries. Its furnishings reflected the same temperate tastes. At Thomson's death, the total valuation of his personal assets within the Spruce Street house, including his wife's silver plate, was only $20,000. Unlike some of his associates, who invested heavily in artwork to acquire a patina of respectable European culture, Thomson's paintings in 1874 were appraised at only $6,000. Furthermore, as befitting a practical mind with little time or inclination for leisure, his entire library was estimated to be worth only $500. Because his home was located sixteen blocks from his office, he frequently commuted to work in his carriage. Even here, his tastes were moderate. His carriage, valued at $1,300, must have been a substantial vehicle, but he certainly was not fascinated by blooded horses. He owned only two, neither a candidate for show honors, worth a grand $100 each. Like many men of moderate wealth in the period, he employed numerous household servants and probably a coachman as well.[6]

Although Thomson resided at the center of the fashionable Rittenhouse Square society, he does not seem to have been an active participant in its social swirl. This was partially due to the fact that he felt ill at ease in large gatherings. Wilson remembered that Thomson's aversion to social affairs was of long duration. As a young man, Wilson reported, Thomson "enjoyed society in a quiet way, but gave little or no attention to the amusements generally indulged in by men of his age." Later in life he much preferred a peaceful evening at home with his family and a few friends, with good conversation that invariably turned to business affairs and acquaintances. His distaste for social events also arose from his inability to justify his attention to them in the face of his official duties. Living an incredibly burdened existence and with a methodical approach to life, Thomson was simply unable to perceive either utility or profit in the gala world of Philadelphia society. Moreover, he had no urgent need to maintain a public social standing. More often than not he was in the enviable position of having others approach him for business favors, and if they wished to do so, he was available in his office at least twelve hours a day.[7]

His personality traits, devotion to work, practical and unphilosophical outlook, and rather plain life-style, mark Thomson as an embodiment of the protestant ethic, or given the demographic context of

Philadelphia and Thomson's own antecedents, of what the historian Frederick B. Tolles has called, a "wet Quaker." Thomson could trace his genealogy from the English dissenters who crossed the Atlantic with William Penn in 1682 to his parents, both born plain people, who inexplicably were married at the Second Presbyterian Church in Philadelphia and later expelled from the Chester Meeting. Although a practicing Episcopalian, Thomson's Quaker legacy burned in him with an intensity he never consciously realized. His forebears, disciples of George Fox, had fled persecution at home to found a Quaker utopia in the wilderness, where they would be free to follow their "inner light" through which God spoke personally to each person. Believing themselves possessed of first-hand knowledge of God's will, the Quakers maintained a high degree of self-confidence in their abilities to translate His truths into everyday secular matters.[8]

In a practical sense, Quakerism was a separatist expression of the left wing of protestantism, sharing many theological and exterior manifestations with Puritanism. Both sects revered a personal deity who spoke directly to His believers; they diverged in that the plain people believed God spoke to all willing to listen, while the Puritans disdained this idea of immediate revelation. Instead, Puritans held that God chose to whom he would speak and, while awaiting the Word, believers were bound to emulate God's design by living a Scripturally faithful life. The functional result of this difference was to make the Quakers a more worldly sect, devoid of the usual biblical quibbling and with less need for an emphasis on education and metaphysical disputation; their specific problem was to put into practice the Truths of their inner lights. One important commonality of both groups, however, was their emphasis upon the importance of duty. If, as George Fox declared, "Christ has come to teach His people Himself," it was the responsibility of each person so honored to carry out Christ's injunctions faithfully. Both sects translated the primacy of duty into an emphasis on the industrious application to task, a concept that had a profound effect on Thomson's personality and motivations. Idleness was an effront to the glory of God and led to vice and sin. Work, therefore, was a divinely ordained, fundamental duty. The Quakers, moreover, with their belief that every man had equal access to God's will, stressed the inherent equality of all men and the irrelevance and artificiality of all social distinctions. They also exhibited a penchant for silence, patiently waiting for others eventually to grasp the Truth. A seventeenth-century critic of the plain people perhaps best summed up the outward evidence of the Quakers' reliance on their inner lights:

They are generally Merchants and Mechanicks, and are observ'd to be very punctual in their Dealings, Men of few Words in a Bargain, modest and compos'd in their Deportment, temperate in their Lives, and using great Frugality in all Things. In a Word, they are singularly Industrious, sparing no Labor or Pains to increase their Wealth; and so subtle and inventive, that they would, if possible, extract Gold out of Ashes.[9]

The Thomson family's inner lights had grown dim by J. Edgar's generation, but the behavior of his more pious Quaker forebears remained as simple habit to account for many of Thomson's noted personal peculiarities. For essentially he was a plain person in deed, if not in the theological sense. He was a man driven by an inner compulsion to work, but to attribute his primary motivation to an uncontrollable urge to "extract Gold out of Ashes" seems overly simplistic. It leaves too many of his actions unexplained.

While it is undeniable that Thomson, as a businessman and entrepreneur, possessed his full measure of acquisitiveness, he was also inexorably driven by several other elements of his Quaker heritage. He appears to have been convinced that the only rightful application of his energies and talents was toward his job in the broadest context of its duties and responsibilities—any other activities were suspect. A century earlier this attitude was readily accepted as tangible proof that the Friends were practicing the Truth, but as they accumulated worldly goods through their fidelity to God's will, the outward manifestations became more important than the underlying Truth. This Truth was later translated by worldly philosophers, such as Benjamin Franklin with his famous maxims, into a duty totally devoid of religious underpinnings. Thomson worshiped and apparently never questioned Duty in this sense, and it sparked his intensity of purpose.

Thomson also evidenced a variation of the older Quaker concept of community that sometimes pushed him in odd directions. Belief in an inner light was an extremely individualistic notion that imbued the plain people with centrifugal tendencies. Offsetting these, however, was the persecution and general obloquy they faced in their everyday dealings due to their bold religious convictions and the positive, unifying power of their perceived Truth, common to all who heeded their inner light. These factors lent the Friends a widely recognized spirit of community that they displayed most noticeably in their willingness to aid any Quaker in distress. Thomson, by the mid-nineteenth century, felt no such communal religious pressures, but just as the Friends' world revolved about the meetinghouse, whose values they reaffirmed and enforced, so Thomson's existence revolved around the headquarters of the Pennsylvania Railroad. The railroad was the family Thomson never had; he cared for it as he would have an adopted son. Given the constantly shifting alliances in his business world, he demonstrated a remarkable tendency to favor members of his corporate family. Even when officers left the road, they found it difficult to break their ties with the Pennsylvania Railroad's fellowship. The experiences of John Covode, John A. Wright, Samuel Morse Felton, George Washington Cass, Herman Haupt, and Andrew Carnegie were all ample testimony to this fact. Thomson exhibited his ingrained affinity for the corporate community as a substitute for the lost Quaker communal spirit most demonstrably in his last will and testament. In an era before large-scale philanthropy was fashionable, he bequeathed the bulk of his fortune "to the education and maintenance of female orphans of Pennsylvania railway employees whose fathers may have been killed while in the discharge of their duties."[10]

If Thomson was basically a Quaker in deed, he acquired his ideas of what that entailed from his father, with whom he was unusually close. John Thomson owned and worked a small farm on the Baltimore Post Road about ten miles from Philadelphia; the property had been in the family since the first Thomson came over with William Penn. It was here that John Edgar was born on February 10, 1808, of Sarah Levis and John Thomson. Their homestead, nestled in the heavily Quaker region of the Delaware Valley, obviously invoked nostalgic memories for Thomson later in life. In 1842 when the farm was sold out of the family for the first time, the outwardly unsentimental and practical John Edgar, then located in Georgia, promptly repurchased the land and held it until his death in 1874. During the intervening years he ran a few cattle and horses on the homestead, perhaps to justify his possession of it.[11]

The elder Thomson was something of a multifaceted man who ostensibly made his living from farming, but who also had an itch to travel and a fascination for mechanical things. While employed as a surveyor by the Holland Land Company in 1795, he and a friend set out from Delaware County, walked to Presque Isle where they constructed an eighteen-foot sloop, and sailed eastward. Using teams of oxen, they hauled the craft around Niagara Falls, sailed up Lake Ontario to Oswego, New York, up the Manokin River into Oneida Lake, portaged to the Mohawk River, and floated down to the Hudson River and New York City. From there they sailed their frail craft out into the Atlantic to Philadelphia. Certainly something of John Thomson's initiative was passed to his son.[12]

After the trip the elder Thomson kept busy in eastern Pennsylvania settling personal boundary disputes and platting unsettled portions of the state. He also became an early advocate of improved transportation and may have constructed the first commercial railway in the United States. In May 1809, Thomas Leiper hit upon the idea of using rails to haul stone three-quarters of a mile from his quarry to Crum Creek, and the following October he employed the elder Thomson to construct the road for him at a cost of a little over $1,500. In 1873 John Edgar donated a map drawn by his father in 1809 to the Delaware County Institute of Science to substantiate the claim that Leiper's railway was the first such experiment in the country. At the time of John Edgar's birth, his father was a well-known civil engineer much in demand for local, internal improvement projects.[13]

Despite his father's reputation and the eventual prominence to which young Thomson rose, very little information about the latter's early years survived. What few facts did were collected in the 1890s by J. Elfreth Watkins from Thomson's surviving intimates, especially William H. Wilson, Herman Haupt, Isaac Wistar, and his wife Lavinia, for his definitive history of the PRR. But even to these close friends, Thomson related only the bare outlines of his first twenty years, and many of his fragmentary reminiscences were of a general and contradictory nature.

Thomson obviously cared little about revealing information concerning his early childhood and homelife. His basically ahistorical attitude, however, was quite understandable. As a Quaker in deed, he emphasized accommodation to the present and focused his attention on contemporary problems. Furthermore, the fact that he never had

the luxury of retirement to reflect upon his successes and failures discouraged any autobiographical recounting. He even lacked pressures
from children and grandchildren for a narrative of his past on which
they could focus their own identities; Thomson sired no offspring and
only adopted his wife's niece on his deathbed. Because his personal
and corporate lives were so inextricably intertwined, he undoubtedly
saw his business achievements as living monuments. Their history in
effect became his history. Finally, given Thomson's personality and
penchant for anonymity, it was not surprising that he made no effort to
preserve his personal papers or that he shrank from personal questions; his demeanor discouraged asking them anyway.

Nevertheless, it is possible to construct a reasonable facsimile of
what the young John Edgar's life must have been like. The Thomson
household consisted of two daughters, Anna and Mary Adeline, and
two sons, John Edgar and an elder brother, Levis P. Dominated by a
strict, exacting father, acutely conscious of his standing in the neigh-
borhood, the children were infused with his bourgeois Quaker values
from an early age. His namesake, young John, was quite probably his
father's favorite and viewed his sire with mixed emotions of awe, fear,
and a yearning for recognition. Evidence of their unusually close relationship abounds in both the remembrances of friends and young
John's actions. The young Thomson accompanied his father on
several long journeys to surveying jobs in the West, where father and
son in isolation shared experiences that brought them closer together.
These prolonged trips also must have opened, at least unconsciously,
the younger man's eyes to the vastness and potential of the fledgling
nation that he would do so much in later years to develop.[14]

In a more subtle sense John Edgar evinced admiration for his father
through emulation; he adopted the elder Thomson's enthusiasm for
mechanics and for the excitement of the practical challenge posed by
engineering problems. Moreover, Thomson seems not to have exhibited that common late adolescent rebelliousness that has pervaded
biographical literature since Socrates. None of the usual avenues for
emotional outlet, so common in the new nation, apparently attracted
John Edgar's fancy. He never considered running away to sea, disap-
pearing into the uncharted West, or even joining the rowdies of his
own age in tasting the forbidden pleasures of the nearby port city.
Instead, the young Thomson showed the traits that would later harden

into his singular personality. He imitated his father, adopted his profession, stayed near home for his first twenty-four years, and used his father's connections to gain his first employment. That sense of moderate asceticism that marked his later life must have been nurtured in the family-centeredness of his first quarter century.

Several accounts relate that Thomson was self-educated with only a modicum of formal schooling. Watkins heard that, "save for mathematics he showed little aptitude for study while at school." If true, he must have acquired his facility for computations from working on his father's surveys. Yet, if Thomson was taught at home, he was taught unusually well. From his earliest extant correspondence in 1831, he showed an ability to write prose that was concise, logical, and structually sound, which indicates a good deal of practice, if not any formal training. Furthermore, it demonstrated none of the biblical rhythm so frequently found in the writings of the self-taught or the Quaker style still in common usage in the middle of the century. While Thomson's spelling was sometimes odd, such as addiction to "proffit," a word he used frequently, the early nineteenth century tolerated spelling variations among all classes, and John Edgar's seem to have been less at variance with Noah Webster's pronouncements than a cross section of incoming letters received by one of Pennsylvania's more crafty politicos, Simon Cameron. It is also interesting to note that like many other things, Thomson's writing style changed little over his lifetime.[15]

Numerous sources noted that Thomson harbored a passionate desire to attend West Point, then the only school training civil engineers, but because his family was in straitened financial circumstances he was forced to defer his dream and seek employment. Several facts, however, contradict this notion. As the nation's only military school, West Point was free to any boy who could wangle a congressional appointment; a feat that should not have been too difficult as the elder Thomson had enough political clout in 1827 to arrange for his son's employment on the state works. Even Haupt secured an appointment to the military academy in 1829 when his widowed mother supported the family running a small store selling laces and trimmings. If lack of political influence did not explain John Edgar's deferred dream, neither did the tale that he had to sacrifice his own education to support his family. His first known employment commenced in 1827 when he was nineteen, an age when many cadets graduated, and rather late for a destitute boy to enter the world to seek his future. If for some reason his father was incapacitated by 1827, fifteen years before he died, young Thomson probably would have worked the farm, and there is no evidence he did so. If his brother took over the chores instead, there was no reason to put the entire estate on the market immediately after the elder Thomson's death. And if the family was in such dire financial straits around 1827, the obvious solution would have been to sell the valuable farm.[16]

A more credible explanation for Thomson's failure to attend West Point, assuming he really desired to go, lies in his Quaker heritage. That sect historically had de-emphasized the value of higher education. As a successful practicing civil engineer in the mid-1820s, it was quite possible that the elder Thomson doubted the necessity for his son's formal training when he could, through everyday experience, teach him all he needed to know to carry on what was then essentially still a craft. With most engineers trained on internal improvement projects such as the Erie Canal, his father certainly cannot be faulted for not anticipating the ascendancy of the university-trained graduate and the rapid professionalization of his craft. Moreover, West Point's responsibility to train future army officers may well have offended the family's Quaker pacifist sympathies.[17]

Two other plausible explanations may account for Thomson's failure to attend West Point: his inability to meet its entrance requirements and his own personality. The Point required each prospective cadet to take a rigorous and comprehensive entrance examination. The test included a proficiency exam in French which may well have killed the randomly educated Thomson's chances. And John Edgar, with his close ties to father and home, shy and probably introverted, must have feared the long journey up the Hudson for a four-year stint among strangers. He certainly evidenced no adolescent inclinations to break away from his immediate family circle.

Thomson's personality traits also help to explain his lack of serious romantic entanglements until late in life. He seemed to have had either an emotional inability to relate to women or simply a lack of interest in them. His early remembrances, scanty as they were, pertained solely to his father; not a single mention of his mother has survived. In addition, his correspondence dating from the period prior to his marriage showed no evidence of any interest in the opposite sex. His indifferent attitude was in stark contrast to his young associates, who filled their letters to him with the latest romantic gossip and strong indications of their own amorous interests. Thomson only mentioned his own marital status once, and it was a curious comment. In an 1846 letter to Lemeul P. Grant, his associate on the Georgia Railroad, Thomson reported a mutual friend's engagement and added, "I shall soon be left alone in the Georgia Rail Road Bachelor Club—I shall prove true to the Standard however and fight off Hymen until death shall end our guards"; he continued in the next sentence with a discussion of chilled cast wheels.[18] Such bravado coming from a man of Thomson's disposition and temperament rings false. But undoubtedly he meant exactly what he said and may well have been expressing a personal moral standard. Certainly, the abruptness and rather brusque manner of the observation, sandwiched as it was between two other topics, implied that he was expressing an ingrained attitude.

His disinterest in affairs of the heart probably arose from his noticeable shyness and reticence, his dislike for social gatherings, and his deep dedication to a vocation that was exclusively masculine. Until 1852, Thomson's jobs required a great deal of travel and outdoor work. Prolonged contacts with women must have been very infrequent. His uncommon devotion to work as a duty served as an outlet for his sexual energies, just as his long attachment to the Pennsylvania Railroad and to a lesser extent the Georgia Railroad served him as a substitute for marriage and family. Only after his Pennsylvania settled into something like a routine, did Thomson appear to need new outlets and sources of affection. Finally, Thomson's Quaker heritage, replete with his personal exaggerations, may have precluded an intense interest in the opposite sex, particularly in light of his empiricism, fascination for mechanics, and few intimate friends of either sex. If he was a man who was extremely wary of others in the transitory world of business, the thought of a lifetime contract with someone else must have thoroughly frightened the young man.

Finally, John Edgar's early years were marked with a sense of provinciality imparted by his father and family. Although he traveled widely in the United States and Europe, he always felt strong ties to the Philadelphia region. He was lucky that his boyhood was spent outside that city and his horizons rose above those of the merchant-moneylender classes. Although an urban and urbane man, Thomson always responded to the lure of land. Many of his investments were in real estate, and he viewed them with the eyes of a farmer's son as well as through a surveyor's transit. He never cared to actually work the land, probably because the forces that ultimately determined its output were so capricious, but the lure was there nonetheless, and it drew him back to the Delaware Valley again and again. It was no accident that he died ten miles from his birthplace.[19]

It was about the same distance from the family farm that he began his professional career on the Philadelphia and Columbia Railroad (P&C). The enterprise was the brain child of Philadelphians who reacted to the challenge posed by New York City in the fierce competition for the rapidly growing western trade. Pennsylvanians had watched energetic citizens north of their border stake their credit on "Clinton's folly" and by the mid-1820s had become alarmed at the undreamed of riches bypassing the commonwealth and enriching the Empire State at the expense of Pennsylvania's port city.[20]

The New Yorkers' bold stroke finally prompted Quaker City citizens in 1823 to agitate for a canal across the Keystone State to redress the growing economic imbalance. The state legislature responded the following year with an act establishing a board of three commissioners to explore possible routes. To goad the legislature, the Pennsylvania Society for the Promotion of Internal Improvements in the Commonwealth was formed in 1824; it raised a fund of over $5,000 and dispatched an engineer the following March to England and Scotland to examine canal and railway technology there. The society also created a blue-ribbon public relations committee loaded with Philadelphia notables that included Thomas Leiper, the elder Thomson's friend. Public meetings were held across the state to pressure legislators, who quickly responded by passing an act in 1825 that created a five-member canal commission. During that summer the commission ran rough surveys across the state and compiled preliminary cost estimates for the legislature. In February 1826, that body passed the enabling legislation to construct the Pennsylvania Canal as a state project. While the act concentrated on building between Harrisburg and Pittsburgh, the following year its scope was expanded to start work east of the Susquehanna. The more favorable topography there prompted the canal commissioners to order a survey run to determine whether a canal or railroad would be more feasible to connect Philadelphia with the eastern end of the Pennsylvania Canal. This decision launched young Thomson's career.[21]

An undertaking as large and complex as the state works required many civil engineers to survey routes, choose the final location, draw up cost estimates, let contracts, oversee construction, and make the final adjustments so the entire system could be operated by untrained civil servants. Skilled engineers were hard to find in the 1820s, and the ones available commanded premium salaries for their services. In 1825 a chief engineer could earn about $3,000 per year, an assistant almost $1,300, and the lesser ranks about one-half that. Increasing demand for technical advice during the period made it possible by the mid-1830s for a chief engineer of a major project to command up to $6,000 annually. By contrast, a clerk earned about $400 per year, a skilled laborer between $1.25 and $1.75 a day, while a typical factory operative took home something less than $300 a year.[22]

Thomson aspired to enter a profession with unlimited potential and yet one in which practical experience alone could raise him to the forefront. He could expect substantial financial rewards and easy entrance into a social class where the appellation, "Esquire," was naturally attached to one's signature. Moreover, his timing was auspicious. He came of age just as the economic doldrums following the 1819 depression were lifting and a full decade before the 1837 panic brought everything to an abrupt halt. During this decade he had ample opportunity to develop his skills and establish a reputation. He was also fortunate in that his native state embarked on a massive improvement program in his immediate vicinity and that his father had both political and professional contacts with influential people. Undoubtedly, the elder Thomson was "correct" politically, because from the first, the state put a premium on political reliability as a prerequisite for employment, even for engineers. Whatever his specific connections, in June 1827, at the age of nineteen, young Thomson reported for work at Valley Forge as a neophyte engineer.[23]

He was attached as a $30-a-month rodman to a survey crew composed of a chief engineer, surveyor, leveler, two chainmen, and a couple of axemen. The men worked westward examining the countryside to decide whether to recommend a canal or a railroad. After several weeks, during which the corps made its way up to Mine Ridge that divided the Chester and Conestoga valleys, the chief engineer decided that a railway was a far more sensible investment. The party then proceeded to Middletown, on the Susquehanna about ten miles below Harrisburg, and began a survey for an eighteen-mile canal to Columbia. Thomson and the crew finished this task by August and started locating the railroad from Columbia to Philadelphia when everyone caught malaria, and they had to suspend the work for several weeks. Thomson's bout with the "ague," as it was popularly called, may have made him more susceptible to recurrences of the disease; later he was felled several times in the field with fever and chills. Constant exposure to the elements made Thomson's occupation a hazardous one.[24]

When the survey resumed, the corps made rapid progress toward Philadelphia, and by January 1828 the canal commissioners were able to present its railway proposal to the legislature. Two months later that body authorized the location and letting of contracts for one-half of the estimated eighty-one miles. To please as many constituents as possible, the lawmakers stipulated that twenty-mile sections at each end of the railway should be built first. Thomson and the engineering crew were sent back into the field to make closer surveys and draw the profile maps from which construction costs could be estimated. By fall, the canal commissioners had let contracts for the grading and bridging at both ends.[25]

While attached to the survey party, Thomson came to the attention of the P&C's chief engineer, Major John Wilson, who did much to promote Thomson's subsequent career. Wilson was born to the profession; his grandfather had been a prominent engineer and architect in Stirling, Scotland and his father had been an officer in the Highlanders' 71st Regiment, serving during the American Revolution at Charleston and Savannah with the royal engineers. The major, born in Scotland, and graduated from Edinburgh, came to Charleston where he was put in charge of the city's fortifications during the war of 1812 and was commissioned as a U.S. topographical engineer. In 1818 he was appointed chief engineer of the South Carolina Board of Public Works from which he resigned several years later due to ill health. The canal commissioners hired Wilson to supervise the eastern location, and during its progress he was quick to note young Thomson's aptitude and diligence. Perhaps Thomson's overall demeanor appealed to the Scotsman, for he took the younger man under his care. Thomson later repaid Wilson's kindness by bringing both his son and grandson into the PRR's engineering department.[26]

Early in 1829 Wilson promoted Thomson to principal assistant engineer and put him in charge of constructing the first twenty miles out of Philadelphia. Thomson broke the division down into two subdivisions and cannily appointed William Hassel Wilson, the major's son, as his subassistant. Thomson's segment was a difficult one, for the road started at Vine and Broad streets, crossed the Schuykill River on a viaduct 984 feet long, and then climbed 187 feet up the side of the valley in a distance of only 2,805 feet, creating the need until 1850 for an inclined plane to inch cars over the summit. But by late 1829, Thomson had the twenty miles graded and ready for the superstructure.[27]

He was denied the satisfaction, however, of completing the job. The state had resorted to wholesale borrowing to finance the work and had made inadequate provisions to insure payment of interest on its bonds. Thus, there were no takers when Pennsylvania placed a $2.2 million loan on the market in April 1829. The failure of the bond issue left the state with over $1.3 million due contractors and no means of payment. Commonwealth officials prudently refused to assume any further contractual obligations and stopped Thomson from letting bids for timber and iron on his division. Furthermore, the canal commission drastically cut its engineering force, and in the spring of 1830 Thomson found himself out of work. Over a year later the state finally raised the necessary funds to complete Thomson's division, and the P&C was opened to traffic in October 1834. Twenty-three years later, as president of the Pennsylvania Railroad, Thomson stood up at a public auction and purchased the whole improvement.[28]

Thomson was not long unemployed. Wilson, who had gone to New Jersey to locate the Camden and Amboy Railroad (C&A), came to Thomson's rescue that summer and hired him as chief engineer of one of the locating parties. The C&A had been chartered in 1830 to connect South Amboy, across the river from New York City, with Camden, opposite Philadelphia, a distance of sixty-two miles. Thomson's duties extended to locating and surveying the thirty-six-mile eastern division of the road from Bordentown, where he was headquartered, to South Amboy. He confronted no unusual obstacles and probably completed the location and estimates by the end of 1830 or early in 1831. Although Thomson's stint on the C&A was brief, less than a year certainly, he gained more valuable experience and demonstrated that he could be safely entrusted with managerial responsibilities.[29]

He also met Robert L. Stevens, president of the C&A, who had recently returned from inspecting English railway practices. Like Wilson, Stevens was from a prominent engineering family. His father, Colonel John Stevens, was an inventor and engineer, who has been called the "father of American railroads." Something of a dreamer, the colonel tried to wring a railway charter from New Jersey as early as 1811 and failing in that, he raised his horizons and petitioned Congress to construct a national railway. Again rebuffed, he later built the first successful steam engine to operate on rails in America. His son inherited the father's genius, and in 1830 or 1831 he invented the first "T" rail, which eventually became standard in the United States. Moreover, Stevens has been credited with the idea of spiking rails directly to crossties rather than following the usual English methods of fastening flat iron bars to granite sills or to wooden stringers nailed into spaced stone blocks, as Thomson was familiar with on the P&C. Engineers soon discovered through experience that a rigid roadbed invited frequent breaks and high maintenance costs. A more flexible arrangement of ballasted ties and iron T rail proved more practical, and the English techniques were soon discarded in America.[30]

Thomson's New Jersey experiences gave him a keen sense for the diffusion of technology between the old and new worlds. Quite by accident, he had found himself on the cutting edge of the American modification of European railway practices that could only have whetted his desire to visit England to record first-hand its advances. More fundamentally, Thomson took away from the C&A a thorough knowledge of the basic rudiments of modern track-laying techniques. In all his known subsequent surveys, he recommended either Steven's idea of the T-rail or, to save money, the use of bar iron laid on wooden stringers attached to ballasted ties. Thomson may also have noted Steven's experiments with a cowcatcher mounted on the front of a locomotive. Thomson later introduced this innovation on the Georgia Railroad, where the problem of free-roaming livestock was acute.[31]

After leaving the C&A, Thomson accepted an assignment from

Samuel Dickey, President of the Oxford Railroad Company, to locate, survey, and estimate the cost of a railway from the P&C to Port Deposit on the Susquehanna and thence to Baltimore. Thomson's final report, dated May 30, 1831, revealed a maturity and self-confidence that belied the fact that he had just turned twenty-three. In a professional manner he compared the gradients on his proposed location with those found on the Liverpool and Manchester Railway and on the C&A, demonstrating his detailed knowledge of railway locations elsewhere. Dickey was undecided whether to terminate his road at the river and depend for traffic on the local limestone trade or build to Baltimore to form an important eastern trunk line. In his conclusion Thomson left no doubt about where he stood on the question; he would always be in favor of capturing through business: "the position of this rail way, situated as it is, between two of the largest commercial cities of the Union . . . gives it a character of national importance." Thomson had learned early that his profession had two distinct and sometimes contradictory components, one technical and the other promotional, and by 1831 he had mastered both. His discussion of location and cost estimates was entirely understandable to the untrained layman and potential investor. To entice the latter, he listed all the important connections that would guarantee the proposed line a large, profitable business and confidently predicted "that its completion will fully repay those whose enterprise may urge them to the undertaking, even were its cost ultimately to exceed the present estimate."[32]

Perhaps frightened by Thomson's estimated total cost of over $1 million, capitalists shied away from the project, and it lay dormant for twenty years. The two cities were instead connected in 1838 by the Philadelphia, Wilmington & Baltimore Railroad. Dickey, however, continued to pursue his dream, and finally in 1853 he won authorization from both states to construct his Philadelphia & Baltimore Central, which he completed by 1860. He followed generally Thomson's recommendations, particularly in the area around the town of Oxford, although the finished road ran in a somewhat more northeasterly to southwesterly direction than Thomson had earlier suggested.[33]

Information about Thomson's activities between June 1831 and November 1834 is sketchy. Most traditional accounts indicate that he made a trip to England and Scotland sometime in 1831 and/or 1832, quite possibly at Stevens' prompting, to investigate railway practices there. Watkins contended that "to the experiences gathered during this brief absence from America he frequently referred in afterlife," although no such mentions have survived. Undoubtedly, Thomson carefully watched experiments using steam engines on railroads, for his knowledge in this area was minimal; cars on the Philadelphia & Columbia were horse-drawn. Quite possibly he witnessed the inaugural run of the *John Bull* on the Camden and Amboy in November 1831. That year Americans took several other important steps toward the adoption of steam technology that Thomson could not have failed to notice. The *Best Friend of Charleston* wheezed over the Charleston and Hamburg's (C&H) tracks on January 15. The *DeWitt Clinton* entered service on the Mohawk and Hudson on August 9. Matthias Baldwin, a Philadelphia watch manufacturer, built his first locomotive that prompted him to establish a company whose products Thomson long favored, and William Norris organized his American Steam Carriage Company.[34] Thomson was definitely back in the United States by the fall of 1832. His only surviving letter of the period indicated that he was hired to make a survey, quite possibly for the Schuykill Navigation Company, to locate a cross-cut canal to the Schuykill River in Philadelphia.

We know little of Thomson's activities for the next two years. William H. Wilson claimed that he did not rejoin the state works, and it was equally doubtful that he returned to the Camden and Amboy; his old eastern division had been completed in 1832, and Major Wilson, his mentor on the project, died the following February. It was also unlikely that Thomson returned to the family farm during this period, for the early 1830s witnessed the beginning of a great boom in which the demand for capable civil engineers far outweighed the supply. In addition, a great number of local projects were coming off the drawing boards: the Philadelphia and Delaware County (1831), the Philadelphia, Germantown & Norristown (1830), the Little Schuykill and Susquehanna (1831), and the Norristown and Mt. Carbon railroads (1833, 1834). Thomson probably worked on various of these improvements, shaping his skills and building up his professional reputation. Looking back later, he remembered that "I was as much respected at twenty-four as I ever was at the height of my reputation."[35]

He had served his apprenticeship; he was knowledgeable in location techniques, cost estimates, and the intricacies of drawing construction contracts. Moreover, he knew of the latest European railway experiments and their American modifications. He was no longer a provincial lad; he had been abroad, and over eight years had met or corresponded with many of the best known civil engineers in the country. Major Wilson had clearly been a great help to the young novice, and Thomson's abilities had more than upheld Wilson's glowing recommendations. Finally, Thomson had gained a good deal of self-confidence; by 1834 he was ready for larger responsibilities.

2

JOURNEYMAN IN GEORGIA

When William Makepeace Thackeray visited Georgia in 1856, he was pleased by "snug little Augusta" where the citizens were, he reported, "much pleasanter to be with than the daring go ahead northern people."[1] Thackeray's "snug little" village had more than doubled its population since Thomson, one of those ubiquitous "northern people," had arrived there twenty-two years earlier. Then an upriver and backcountry entrepôt dominated by Charleston and Savannah, Augusta slumbered along the banks of the usually placid Savannah River and prospered moderately as a transshipment point for cotton and other upcountry agricultural products going downriver by steamboat, or across the waterway to Hamburg, the terminus of the Charleston & Hamburg Railroad since 1833.[2]

Leading Augustians, long accustomed to their dominance of the northeastern Georgia river trade, bestirred themselves little to improve communications with their backcountry markets until the decade of the 1840s. And then the impetus originated in the lively, progressive little university community of Athens. The "classical city," as it dubbed itself, home of the state university and, by the end of the 1830s, a budding manufacturing center as well, with two cotton factories and the only paper mill south of the Potomac River, needed more reliable transportation to Augusta and Savannah. Legend relates that in the unusually wet winter of 1832–33, a gaping mudhole captured an entire wagon train of cotton textile machinery bound for Athens and held it fast until the following spring. True or not, in June 1833, Asbury Hull, a leading citizen of the classical city, chaired a public meeting to organize support to petition the state legislature for a railway charter. Four days before Christmas of that year, the legislature chartered the Georgia Railroad Company and conferred upon it "powers to construct a Rail or Turnpike Road from the City of Augusta, with Branches Extending to the towns of Eatonton, Madison, in Morgan County, and Athens; to be carried beyond these places at the direction of said Company."[3]

Armed with this broad authority a group of prominent Athenians met on March 10, 1834, at the home of James Camak to accept the charter and select directors. Perhaps in thanks for his hospitality, they elected Camak the line's first president. By the end of the month they were prepared to embark upon the project in earnest; the directors resolved to ask the Army Corps of Engineers for help and decided to select a design for a corporate seal embodying "in the center some appropriate Vehicle of conveyance appurtaining to Rail Roads." William Dearing, a director, had to go all the way to New York City to have such a seal made, but he was going there anyway to negotiate a first mortgage loan on the road. Dearing was back by May with the disappointing news that northern financiers were unwilling to loan money on an unsurveyed road with no definite route. He did, however, bring a finished seal with him, two concentric circles with the "Georgia Rail Road Company" embossed between them, the bottom of the inner circle inscribed Augusta, and in the center—a horse's head![4]

The seal question was easily resolved compared to the more important search for an engineer. Understandably, the board preferred to engage a member of the Army corps to do its location work because these professionals were experienced and, most significantly, their services were free. The corps provided this essential assistance to as many internal improvement projects as possible. By the mid-1830s, however, the military engineers were hard-pressed to meet the large volume of requests; the directors of the Georgia Railroad were particularly anxious to obtain the services of Colonel Stephen Long, a prominent and overworked member of the corps. After lengthy correspondence, however, Long could only promise to come to Georgia after he had located a Memphis road. In August the directors decided to send a representative north to examine railroads in that region "to avoid their mistakes" and to "look out [for] and employ if practicable a competent Chief Engineer."[5]

William Williams, the director who made the trip, presented to his board a written contract made with one "Mr. J. Edgar Thompson [*sic*]" on October 11. At first glance it would appear a stroke of sheer luck that a major improvement scheme located 1,000 miles south of Philadelphia would pluck a young man of only twenty-six from that city for the important position of chief engineer and lavish upon him responsibilities and emoluments that made him the envy of men twice his age. The element of chance was present, but Thomson also had numerous important professional contacts in Georgia and South Carolina. Watkins categorically stated that Major Wilson recommended his protege for the position, and although Wilson had been dead for nineteen months, there was some truth to the assertion. Wilson had maintained professional contacts in his native state and closely watched developments on the Charleston and Hamburg Railroad. He probably put in a good word for Thomson with that road's officials, who related it to Williams when he traveled to Charleston to take a coastal vessel north. Thomson was also personally acquainted with three men who went South to assume engineering positions on the Monroe Railroad, an ambitious undertaking chartered in 1833 to build from Macon to Forsyth. They corresponded regularly with him and may have been instrumental in bringing him to the attention of the Georgia Railroad directors. Certainly, the brevity of Williams' trip indicates that he had Thomson specifically in mind when he ventured north, and the contract he negotiated with young Thomson, which stipulated a salary of about $3,000 per year, indicated that he came highly recommended.[6]

Thomson arrived in Augusta on November 1, 1834, after traveling to New York, taking a side-wheel steamer to Charleston, and boarding the Charleston and Hamburg to his destination. Unfortunately, his surveying equipment, including a transit he had designed in collaboration with William Young, a Philadelphia instrument maker, which became the standard surveying instrument of the nineteenth century, was delayed for three weeks, slowing the survey. After Thomson secured a room at Mrs. Hall's celebrated boardinghouse on Broad Street opposite the post office, he immediately took to the field to reconnoiter the countryside. His incessant activity proved him to be just the type of Yankee Thackeray abhorred.

December was rainy and cold, but on January 5, Thomson presented Camak with his completed preliminary survey. In his letter, made public three days later, Thomson presented cost estimates for 112 miles, indicated a route out of the Savannah Valley that negated the need for an inclined plane earlier recommended, described his proposed superstructure, and even attempted to predict future earnings from the finished road. Camak promptly called for a $15 stock installment, and Thomson returned to the field with five assistant engineers to make a more precise location.[7]

The weather could not have been worse; on January 13 it started to snow, and before it stopped, eight inches blanketed the ground. On February 2, his Philadelphia friend, Richard Peters, joined the party ten miles west of Augusta in another snowstorm. Two days later the temperature fell to minus-ten degrees, finally driving Thomson to seek shelter; it was so cold that Albon Chase, editor of the *Southern Banner*, informed his readers that two black people froze to death in Athens. It snowed the entire week of March 5 and three days of the following week as well. By mid-March six to eight inches still covered the ground, but Thomson and his party slogged on. And the weather was not Thomson's only problem. His survey crew boarded at local homes along the route, but they soon found the inhabitants so hostile and insulting, fearing that the railroad threatened their profitable business of provisioning wagoners, that Thomson, the Quakers' son, was forced to arm the entire group and purchase camping equipage to live in the field.[8]

Despite the frustrations of that unforgettable winter, Thomson had the detailed profile maps completed by April 14th when the board authorized the letting of contracts for the first thirty miles of the "Union Road," the main line, to Greensboro. With better weather Thomson redoubled his efforts. That summer he sifted the bids for contracts, completed the surveys to Madison and Eatonton, and recommended that the Union Line be extended to the former town. The board on August 4, impressed with his location, authorized the letting of grading contracts for twenty-five additional miles. By September 1 Thomson announced that a total of fifty-four miles was under contract. The entire labor force that summer was composed of "Europeans," Thomson reported, working for $14 per month and board, with not a single reported case of sickness. The experiment, however, was to be short-lived.[9]

Thomson's flurry of activity left his directors hard-pressed to raise the necessary funds to keep up. On September 8 they called for another $15 stock installment and appointed a committee to draft a bill to introduce in the next legislature asking state credits for a loan. The following month the board decided to request banking privileges. Economy also became a company watchword, for back at the May 1835 annual meeting, some stockholders complained about the exorbitant salaries paid the engineers. After a rancorous debate, the convention approved a resolution stipulating that the engineers and their salaries were justified "for the present," a clear warning to Thomson that with a salary larger than the president's, he was a convenient target for the more fiscally conservative shareholders.[10]

The state legislature on December 18, 1835, granted the desired banking privileges and changed the company's name to the Georgia Rail Road and Banking Company. It located the principal bank at Athens and specified that the capital stock of the railroad was not to exceed $2 million, of which not more than 50 percent could be used for banking purposes until the road was completed. The shareholders quickly ratified the changes and authorized the issuance of an additional 7,500 shares of stock. The director's financial acuity and Thomson's unrelenting progress made the road's securities most attractive. When the new subscription books opened in Athens on February 15, that town quickly oversubscribed its allotment by 381 shares, and the stock averaged a 10 percent premium on only 50 percent paid in. Individuals resorted to advertising in the paper for shares.[11]

Buoyed by these successes the stockholders assembled on May 10, 1836, to hear paeans from their road's officers. Thomson took pains to recount the progress of the work and the inevitability of its rapid conclusion. With economy in mind he described the superstructure he planned to lay, built from heart-of-pine groundsills, crossties, and longitudinal sleepers, easily extractable from the local forests. The iron rails spiked to the sleepers were to be 2.4 inches wide and .8 inch thick. He promised the completed road would cost only $10,287 per mile, a reasonably accurate estimate as it turned out. To placate those who still believed the corporate seal represented advanced railway technology, Thomson carefully explained that the roadbed "will be formed so as to admit the use of horses, if an accession of business should take place beyond the capabilities of the Engine power provided." Actually, he had no intention of resorting to horsepower; he had already ordered from his Philadelphia friend, Baldwin, seven locomotives equipped with dual driving wheels and sporting the recently developed four-wheel leading truck. Since Thomson had to specify the distance between the drivers, he decided to make the road's gauge five feet to conform with that of the Charleston and Hamburg.[12]

Not only did Thomson go to Philadelphia for all his locomotives, but he also retained a firm in that city to acquire domestic and imported iron for him. Furthermore, it appears that at least several, and perhaps a majority, of the original contractors on the road were Philadelphia concerns. Rumors of the "foreign" invasion of contractors surfaced in the local newspaper as early as the first lettings, when it was reported that they "are principally from the Middle States," which may account for the experiment using white laborers. Provisions for their salary plus subsistence indicate the wage earners were imported from elsewhere.[13]

With few exceptions 1836 was a halcyon year for the Georgia Railroad and the entire nation. Ebullience and optimism were rampant in business circles, and Thomson, although not usually given to such overt manifestations, found himself caught up in the general euphoria. Unrealistically he predicted that his main line and the branch to Athens would return 14 percent on cost when completed, carrying upwards of 82,000 bales of cotton, 50 million pounds of backfreight, and an average of ninety passengers daily, plus the subsidized U.S. mail. Looking west of Madison, he enjoined the road to tap the growing fertile Tennessee Valley trade, to connect with planned railroads across Alabama, and to become an important link in the first connection between the Atlantic Ocean and the Mississippi River.[14]

Thomson spent almost as much time that summer trying to bring about these connections as he did in constructing his own road. During late June and early July, he and another engineer ran a quick location from Athens to Knoxville, Tennessee, for a potential linkup with the highly touted and promising Cincinnati and Charleston project. Later in July he went back into the field to run trial lines from Athens to the route of the proposed Hiwassee Railroad, a difficult undertaking that Thomson estimated would cost in excess of $3 million. He attended the Macon Railroad Convention in November to investigate a possible connection with the Montgomery & West Point Railroad (M&WP), then under construction. While at the convention he supported recommendations to the state requesting that it construct a public railway from Ross' Landing on the Tennessee River to some point on the Chattahoochee River and allow the Georgia Railroad to connect with the proposed road—ambitious dreams for a corporation that had yet to turn a wheel in revenue service.[15]

At home Thomson vigorously pushed the construction and extension of his own road above the village of Crawfordville, sixty-five miles west of Augusta. By the turn of the year, he had placed seventy-six miles to Union Point under contract and was prepared to start work on the Athens branch from the place. To ensure adequate funds for the work, the directors called for a $15 stock installment payable in September and marketed another 3,000 shares of the company's securities at the year's end. The new offering went quickly and at premiums in excess of 10 percent; in March 1837 shares with $65 paid in were auctioned in Augusta for $87 each. Moreover, the directors used the banking business as an important source of funds. Fully 80 percent of the board's time was devoted exclusively to banking operations. Thomson certainly did not mind, for it left him a relatively free hand to continue his work. The board was evidently impressed with his performance; it raised Thomson's salary in August to $4,000 per year, effective November 1.[16]

Despite the rapid progress of the project, its solid financial basis, and the dreams of a far-flung southern rail empire, by mid-1836 nagging problems had appeared. The biggest were chronic inflation and a severe shortage of labor. Thomson reported to the stockholders that white laborers had fled in "dread of a Southern Summer, [and] uniting with the high wages paid at the North, caused after the 1st of June an almost total suspension of our work." Not until late in the fall did the railroad attract enough whites back to the region to complete the graduation above Crawfordville, and then an exceptionally wet and cold winter further delayed progress into late spring of 1837.[17]

The inflationary wage spiral of 1836 and 1837 caused numerous construction companies to forfeit their contracts negotiated the previous year when commodity and salary levels were much lower.

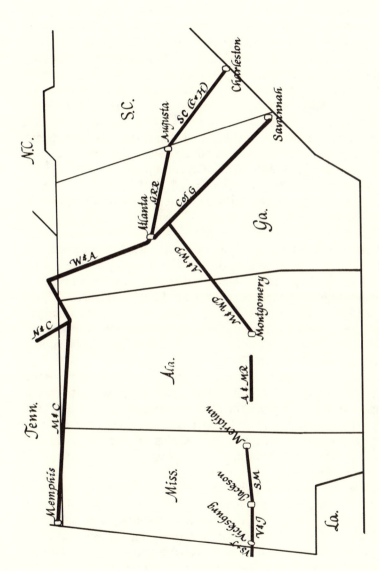

1. Thomson's Antebellum Southern Interests: The Georgia Railroad and the South.

Whenever possible Thomson awarded the defaulted work to local contractors who used slave labor easily procured in the off season. He also gained permission from his board in the fall to purchase seventy-two male slaves to take up the slack caused by the flight of northern laborers. After letting the work above Crawfordville to a local company that had a reputation for mistreatment of slaves, Thomson took advertisements in the newspapers to assure local planters that his contractor's relations with bonded laborers were "humane and such as should give satisfaction to their owners." His endorsement of their humanity had a salubrious effect for within thirty days the company hired 200 slaves for $15 per month plus subsistence.[18]

Labor was not the only commodity, however, to register a drastic price rise in 1836; the cost of iron soared, and Thomson could do nothing about it. But he did offset spiraling timber costs by negotiating a long-term contract with a local saw mill owner. And perhaps to create a "cost yardstick," as well as to insure an adequate supply, he induced his directors in January 1837 to purchase a sawmill. The same month he completed a car factory at Augusta to save money by constructing the road's rolling stock at home and built a small iron and brass foundry to facilitate locomotive repairs. Finally, Thomson delayed construction of the Athens branch until the end of 1837 "at which period," he explained to the stockholders, "we may reasonably expect from the fall in the value of labor, to effect much more advantageous contracts than at present."[19]

With all his troubles, however, Thomson arranged an impressive grand opening on May 2 of the first ten miles west of Augusta. A newspaper correspondent present at the festivities rhapsodized, "this locomotive, whose name is 'Georgia' started beautifully and majestically from the Depository, and following the impulse given, flew with surprising velocity on the road which hereafter is to be her natural element taking under her care and protecting, conveying and towing innumerable cars loaded with passengers, produce, and merchandize from other sections of our State." By the end of the year, Thomson had opened fifty miles of the road to a temporary terminal twelve miles west of the small village of Thomson, named in his honor. From there, private stage companies provided service to Athens, Greensboro, Gainesville, and Washington, Georgia.[20]

Thomson's progress in 1837 was made in the face of the economic panic that belatedly reached into Georgia. As early as February, the Georgia Railroad directors had noted the ominous financial signs and decided not to extend their obligations. On May 17, ten days after New York City banks initiated a wave of specie suspensions, the Georgia Railroad bank followed suit, and in a climate of fear the board asked Thomson to report whether "suspending the work on the Rail Road" was advisable. The chief engineer recommended the work be continued at the same pace; but the board's expansionary enthusiasm was distinctly on the wane. For the first time it appointed a committee to audit Thomson's accounts and called upon him to explain two errors. Moreover, the directors authorized William Dearing, who had succeeded Camak as president the year before, to purchase iron for the road, formerly Thomson's responsibility.[21]

As the 1837 panic became more severe, Thomson's dreams for northern and western connections began to evaporate. The Monroe Railroad failed in May, and throughout the summer rumors abounded that the hoped-for Cincinnati project was in trouble. In October the board sent an agent to that city with 2,527 shares of Georgia Railroad stock in a futile attempt to prop it up. The chief engineer of the Montgomery & West Point pleaded with the Georgia directors in February 1838 to assist his road; a request the hard-pressed board reluctantly denied. Although in relatively sound financial condition, the Georgia road was finding it difficult by the end of 1837 to raise the necessary working capital to continue construction. On the second day of the new year, the directors authorized Dearing to borrow $500,000 after Thomson warned that in the coming year he would need at least that amount to continue construction.[22]

Throughout 1838 Thomson pushed his contractors as hard as his resources would admit. He was successful enough to report to the stockholders in May 1839 that the road was in full operation for seventy-four miles and that iron was laid to within 200 yards of the Greensboro depot ten miles farther up the line. Disregarding the increasing financial difficulties, he called upon the shareholders to renew their efforts to connect with the Western & Atlantic Railway, the state road under construction. After all he pointed out, only sixty-five miles remained and the cost "will not exceed $1,200,000 an amount so trifling, compared with the immense benefits which will result to the Stockholders," that he simply could not "believe that there will be any difficulty in procuring it." He also retained hope for an eventual linkup with the moribund Montgomery road, which with the completion of the Middle Branch Rail Road would forge "a chain of communication between Augusta and Montgomery, the heads of Navigation of the Savannah and Alabama Rivers."[23]

Thomson's expansionary views ran counter to the road's worsening economic situation in 1839 and 1840. Retrenchment became the theme of numerous board meetings, and the pressure upon Thomson to economize led him for the first time into serious conflict with his employers. The board sought means to pay off the contractors already on the job and to raise long-term funds to finish the work, particularly the branch line to Athens and the westward extension. To help resolve these difficulties the directors ordered Thomson to suspend all employees "that can be done without detriment" and to sign new construction contracts only if the contractors agreed to accept 75 percent in the company's stock and 25 percent in cash, or, in the case of the Athens branch, if they would wait until 1841 for payment and consent to 7 percent on their withheld monies. Moreover, further iron orders were prohibited after the board discovered that the Tennessee state bonds used to pay for the iron were refused in London.[24]

At the end of July 1839, only six months after the directors had raised Thomson's salary to the princely sum of $5,000 per year, the board's committee on retrenchment reported salary reductions were a necessity. The directors' anxious mood was clearly mirrored in their refusal in September to honor Thomson's expense account of $145.50 for three trips north on company business. They tartly reminded him that with his salary now double that of the president, he should pay his own expenses, but admitted this should have been made plain prior to his incurring the outlay. Thomson suffered yet another rebuke on September 10 when the directors refused to consider any further westward expansion. The directors' decisions showed that they were quite confused about a proper course of action to weather what was now quite clearly a long-term financial catastrophe. At one incredible meeting in October, they refused to accept the report on retrenchment, resolved to cut all salaries 20 percent, rescinded the same, and finally voted to leave all questions up to the stockholders. Then they authorized Thomson to make the necessary surveys west from Madison for a meet with the state road and to let superstructure contracts between Greensboro and Madison. In January the directors inexplicably voted Thomson his $145.50 and declared a 4 percent dividend.[25]

To compound Thomson's problems an epidemic of "the fever" erupted in September in Augusta; by the time it had run its course a month later, it had taken 223 lives. At the same time cotton prices, which bore a direct correlation to rail investment in the antebellum South, began their inexorable fall to a point several cents per pound below the cost of production. While this price deflation in the fall of 1839 ought to have decreased labor costs as planters sought more profitable arrangements for their bondsmen, just the opposite occurred, especially in Augusta where workers demanded premiums during the epidemic. Other prices also remained high, as Thomson explained in his 1840 annual report. "For instance," he pointed out, "our iron in the shops, costs us, in consequence of the difference of Freight, about 25 per cent more than it would at the North, and our Engine men, and Machinists and Blacksmiths are paid 50 to 100 per cent higher wages."[26]

Even with the anomaly of cost inflation in the midst of depression, Thomson made slow but certain progress towards the completion of the road. An additional fourteen miles were completed moving the road's terminus to Greensboro, and travel on the three-and-a-half-mile Warrenton branch was inaugurated in 1839. A contract for the twenty-mile extension to Madison was let, and except for the inability to ship iron up the Savannah, due to inordinately low water and the ever-present labor problems, the road would have been completed in time for the 1840 annual meeting. Thomson confidently predicted to the stockholders that the segment would be in operation in time to bring the cotton crop down. Furthermore, he had finished the preliminary surveys to Stone Mountain. Despite an increase in transport costs, he was still able to report a 10 percent net profit on investment for the year, surprisingly within the magnitude of his visionary 1837 prediction.[27]

The 1840 annual meeting marked an important turning point in the affairs of the company. For the first time the Athens newspaper failed to include its usual notation that "harmony prevailed" in the meeting; the stockholders elected a new board of directors that included Thomson and was dominated for the first time by Augustians. Prior to that year only one director was a native of the river city while the rest represented Athens and the upcountry counties. This lopsided geographical representation made less and less sense as the work progressed, especially as the branch to Athens remained incomplete and as Augustians gained control of the road's stock. All this time Athenians, the progenitors of the project, apparently never brought pressure to speed up construction of their branch and sat complacently by, allowing the main line to bypass them. Even Albon Chase, the peppery local editor, an outspoken civic booster, never raised the questions editorially. The fruits of this lassitude matured in 1840 when Athenians lost their majority on the board. The confusion caused by the takeover, however, lasted several years. The board continued to meet in Athens until May 1841, usually attended only by the remaining four members from that town, and its influence declined commensurately. Thomson, for example, attended only three meetings in 1840. The company's principal bank remained at Athens for two more years while Augusta was still designated a branch. And not until October 1843 did the directors finally decide to move the annual meeting to Augusta.[28]

The 1840 corporate takeover was occasioned by the continuing precipitous decline in cotton prices, which in turn upset the precarious balance of Augusta's economy. The danger to Thomson and the railroad lay in the spread effects of these abnormally low prices, the most noticeable of which was the hoarding of specie and a drop in the value of securities and banknotes. To Augusta merchants whose sales depended upon the income generated by upcountry cotton sales and who were forced to remit currency to outsiders, particularly in Charleston and Savannah for inventory, the situation bordered on the intolerable. As their sales slumped so too did the value of their local banknotes and security holdings. Of special importance to the town's economy were the Georgia Rail Road and Banking Company notes, the mainstay of its circulating medium. Historically these banknotes had commanded confidence throughout north Georgia due to the bank's conservative issuance policies. But no matter how intrinsically sound the institution, the notes depreciated in the face of the catastrophic cotton market. By the end of February 1840, just prior to the fateful annual meeting, Augusta branch notes fell to a 5 to 7 percent discount in their hometown for the first time. As was true throughout the depression, the notes on the main bank at Athens carried an even heavier discount—at this date, 6 to 8 percent. Georgia Railroad stock fell to a low of $25 in 1840, and a block went in March 1842 for only $45 per share of $100 paid in. While two instances are insufficient to establish a price trend, the stock had fallen calamitously, enabling Augustians to buy control of the railway.[29]

The financial debacle that undermined the fragile foundations of Augusta's economic well-being led the merchants of that city, many of whom were stockholders in the Georgia Railroad, to exceed even their normal fiscal conservatism. They concluded when the Georgia Railroad banknotes began to decline early in 1840 that radical economy measures within the corporation could by themselves wrench their fluctuating values back to normal. In this they were joined by a significant minority of shareholders from the port city and upcountry who, in the heritage of "strict constructionism," interpreted the road's charter to read that only the stockholders could authorize construction west of Madison and considered any talk of further expansion as sheer folly. These two groups combined to wrest control of the road from the Athenians, whose more diversified agricultural and manufacturing economy was not as devastated by the drop in cotton prices, to force a general reordering of corporate priorities.[30]

The steps taken by the new officers to institute responsible managerial policies seriously exacerbated Thomson's already manifold problems and nearly forced him out of the company. The confusion of abbreviated board meetings in Athens and the general befuddlement over what policies to pursue, resulted in a two-pronged program: retrenchment and expansion, which caught Thomson in the middle. The Athenian directors, out of step with the new majority, authorized Thomson to secure the right-of-way from Madison to above Covington and let contracts from the former town to the terminus. They also sought funds to pay the contractors. At the same time the board committee on retrenchment was revived, and after careful consideration recommended no salary cuts; but it charged Thomson, at the very moment his engineering department was frantically pushing the work westward, to implement any economy measures he saw fit. In a very real austerity measure, however, the board voted to pass the October dividend.[31]

This dysfunctional corporate policy aroused the wrath of the Augustian stockholders at their 1841 yearly meeting. In addition, Thomson's annual report did little to improve their disposition. He chronicled only a series of misfortunes: the flight of white laborers to the Western and Atlantic (W&A) Railway for higher wages that stalled the work west of Madison; the May flood that swept away embankments and a temporary truss bridge; the low water in the Savannah River that prevented scheduled delivery of iron; the delay on the Athens branch caused by a lack of wood; and the decline in receipts due to the failure of the cotton crop. The shareholders' committee on the engineer's report thanked him for this "interesting & detailed information" and took special note of his exhortation to continue the work toward a connection with the state road. Then, in a rebuke, the committee admonished that "no prospect, however flattering, of distant gain or extraordinary profits can in the opinion of your committee, atone for the loss of character or credit, either to an individual or company," a statement Thomson wholeheartedly endorsed in principle, but which he must have thought absurd in this context.[32]

After the election of new directors, in which Thomson lost his seat, the selection of a new president, John King from Augusta, and the passage of a resolution to move the company's banking capital to the port city, the committee on retrenchment took the floor. The stockholders voted to retain Thomson but to reduce his salary to $3,000 per year, a clear indication that the committee had considered dispensing with his services. Without entering into specifics, the committee advised further retrenchment in the engineering department even as it admitted, Thomson "has done all on this subject, in his usual rigid economy, which the times & circumstances warranted." The committee's suggestions saved the company $5,200, almost two-fifths of which came directly from Thomson's pocket, and the mollified stockholders adjourned.[33]

Thomson, however, was furious and acted with unusual haste. He was doubly stung by the imputation that he was not worth his salary and that his policy of unrelenting expansion, designed to insure future earnings, was considered fallacious by the road's owners. When the new board sat for its first meeting on May 12, Thomson presented his resignation. After much debate, the directors selected a committee of three to treat with their chief engineer to see whether he could be persuaded to stay. During the following interval a compromise was effected whereby Thomson was allowed several months to travel north on unspecified "private business." On his return he agreed to continue as chief engineer at a salary of $3,000 until the road was completed, at which time he demanded an increased wage that would be "subject to negociation [sic]." The directors accepted the deal along with Thomson's resignation effective July 1, 1841. His name did not appear again in the board's minutes until December when both he and King were referred to as the chief engineer, a reference that was repeated in February 1842. Clearly, Thomson's authority and position within the company had been compromised.[34]

The affair was far from over. Thomson was not the type of personality to remain long in a clouded situation, nor was he one to freely allow public aspersions on his professional conduct. It is very likely that he demanded the question of his resignation and subsequent agreement with the board should be brought to a vote of the stockholders at the next annual meeting. Thomson's annual report of that year was certainly tailored towards that body's conservative outlook. He set the tone in his first paragraph when he pointed out, "the enterprise as originally contemplated . . . may now be considered as finished." A curious statement since the road's terminus was still Madison, and the board only two months earlier had resolved to continue construction westward if financial arrangements could be made. He also had some good news for the assemblage: receipts were up with a 6 percent net return, and traffic was increasing from north Alabama and east Tennessee, where he had sent agents during the summer of 1841 to advise local merchants of the wisdom of shipping via the Georgia Railroad route. To be certain there were still clouds on the horizon, especially the need to replace timbers in the road's superstructure. Thomson discovered the average life of the wood was only five years, and he warned that maintenance costs would rise sharply the following year. No predictions of the glowing promise of western and northern connections graced his report; it was a moderate, sober document in all respects that read more as a farewell statement than anything else.[35]

The committee on his report hoped that this would be the case. While it had no specific quarrel with his report, it did send a resolution to the floor "that in consideration of the necessity of rigid economy . . .

the services of the Chief Engineer be dispensed with, from & after his present year [sic] engagement." Committee members gratuitously added that their confidence remained "unimpaired in the capacity of & fidelity of the character of Mr. Thomson," and that if the company engaged in "future enterprise" it would seek to reengage him as its chief engineer. It was moved on the floor to strike out the sentence regarding Thomson's discontinuance, and the motion carried 12,653 to 5,295. Thomson had his vindication. The title of chief engineer was again indisputably his own, although he could do nothing about his salary reduction.[36]

On a more positive note, Thomson emerged with the firm friendship of president King, an influential state figure, whose political connections, acquired as a judge and U.S. senator from 1833 to 1837, were most useful. King supported Thomson's enthusiasm for the road's continued western expansion and was a southern industrial booster. He was engaged in cotton manufacturing in Augusta and conceived the grand design of diverting water from the Savannah through a canal to provide waterpower that he hoped would attract additional industries to Augusta. He wormed funds from his railroad for the improvement, and Thomson constructed the canal in 1845. The two men did much to further economic development in north Georgia and, at the same time, increased their personal fortunes.[37]

The three years subsequent to his ouster attempt were busy ones for Thomson. A month after the 1842 annual meeting, the board authorized contracts for the road from Madison to White Hall in DeKalb County. Reflecting the company's cash position, the contractors were required to accept payment one-quarter in cash, one-quarter in the railroad's 8 percent bonds, and the remainder in the stock of the company at par. That December the directors asked Thomson to let the work on the twenty-six-mile section between Madison and Covington. To meet the heavy cash outflow caused by this flurry of construction, the board empowered King to raise a $500,000 income loan at 6 percent and made the road's bonds convertible to stock, an increasingly attractive form of security.[38]

Thomson's more secure personal position was evident in his 1843 report. Fully one-half of the document was devoted to the westward extension, partially under contract, and to an exhortation designed to convince the shareholders that now was the propitious moment to finish the entire road. He pointed out that labor, materials, and land were cheaper than they would ever be again. If the tracks remained permanently abbreviated, he explained the company would be forced to rely upon local traffic in a region shackled "by a false system of agriculture" that exhausted the land, an obvious problem that newspaper editors had discussed as early as 1835 in articles such as one boldly entitled "Manure is Wealth." To assuage the anger of the conservative shareholders who demanded that the half-million-dollar loan be distributed as dividends, Thomson reported that despite heavy renewal and construction costs, the company still netted a full 6 percent profit. The meeting displayed little of the past rancor. The committee on retrenchment was disbanded; the formerly hostile committee on the engineer's report supported Thomson's demands for continued construction; and the stockholders easily defeated the conservative minority by agreeing to leave the disposition of the projected loan to the president's discretion.[39]

With stockholder and board support, Thomson redoubled his efforts to complete the connection with the state road. By July 1844 he had signed contracts for the entire road to within 15 miles of the Western and Atlantic and worried only that the possibility of an iron shortage might hinder the progress of the work. Thomson was now spending, exclusive of iron, about $30,000 per month for an average of almost $23,000 per mile. His strenuous exertions were applauded in the unusually placid 1844 annual meeting that set the precedent, widely emulated in later years, of referring all thorny questions to the president and the directors. The slow but steady rise in the value of the road's securities and the promise of a dividend were undoubtedly the most important determinants of stockholder passivity.[40]

The officers of the company were not reluctant to exercise the prerogatives passed to them. They vigorously pushed construction, and for the first time since the onset of the depression, they started protecting their immediate territory and revived their old expansionary dreams. On July 30, 1845 the directors loaned $100,000 to the bankrupt Monroe Railroad, virtually taking over that line to prevent it from being used against them by the rival Central of Georgia. Almost a year later, the board guaranteed, in conjunction with the South Carolina Railroad, the bonds of the perpetually undercapitalized and faltering Montgomery & West Point Railroad for a future feeder road

to the West. And a few months later the board persuasively demonstrated that the depression mentality had lifted by investing $50,000
in the stock of the Memphis Rail Road and Steamboat Company in
another attempt to tap the markets of the fertile Mississippi Valley.[41]

While his superiors adopted a broad view of the regional transport
situation that Thomson had urged upon them throughout the depression, he pushed the railroad to completion. By August 1845 the rails
were being spiked down outside Decatur, only six miles from the
junction, and the local newspaper heralded the event with over-
zealous enthusiasm. "Look out for *smoke* and a *great noise*," the
headlines blared, "Decatur will soon be a—'*sea port*'." The track
layers went right on by, and in early September reached the small village of Marthasville, the long-sought junction with the state road.
That metropolis boasted five houses and little else except pretension.
Even its name, honoring former governor Wilson Lumpkin's daughter, seemed inappropriate. One story relates that when Thomson was
asked to submit a new name, allegedly because Marthasville was too
long to write, he replied, "Eureka, Atlanta." One has difficulty con-
juring up an image of Thomson exclaiming "Eureka" about anything. More plausible was Richard Peters' version that when he asked
Thomson for suggestions, he replied Atlanta, "Atlantic, masculine;
Atlanta, feminine, a coined word but well adapted"—short, terse, and
logical in the authentic Thomson style. The broadsides went out in the
fall of 1845 announcing that the Georgia Railroad offered through
transportation from Augusta to Atlanta.[42]

The mandatory inaugural run took place on September 11. Its
scope, however, was somewhat more modest than the postwar transcontinental galas. The road's officers boarded a special train and
traveled the 173 miles in a leisurely twelve hours, arriving in Atlanta
after nightfall. As they made their way on foot to a house where they
looked forward to spending the night on the floor, King promptly fell
into an unfinished well about ten feet deep. He was so angry that he allegedly harbored a predisposition against the town for years. Thomson was not overly enthused about Atlanta's prospects either. "This
town appears to be looking up a little," he wrote his associate, Lemeul
P. Grant, "but unfortunately no person of Capital has located here to
commence business—and in consequence its progress to greatness
will be slow." The following morning the celebrants, their spirits

somewhat sobered from sleeping on bearskins, rode twenty miles up the state road to Marietta where, as Thomson related, they "set the town alive."[43]

The "festivities" were over—the completed road was opened for business on September 15. The daily operations and repair of the line for which Thomson was now responsible held no fascination for him. He made this clear in 1846 when he bid his stockholders farewell with "the last annual communication that I shall probably make to the Company—." In fact, however, he remained with the railway, albeit under altered circumstances, considerably longer. From Chattanooga he wrote King on July 22, 1846, apologizing for not having written earlier due to "a severe cold accompanied by considerable fever," with a plan for the road that "will enable me to participate in its management, and attend also, to some other engagements which I feel under obligation to look after." He suggested he assume charge of repairs, renewal of the road and its machinery, assist in freight arrangements, and make periodic operational recommendations to the board. "For the performance of these duties," he proposed, "I shall not ask more than $2,000 per annum." On December 8 the board finally passed a resolution explaining that Thomson "at all times be he where he may, . . . will be subject to the call of this company." For these responsibilities it voted him his desired salary of $2,000 and the title of chief engineer. In the face of his absence from Georgia, the directors appointed a permanent committee to oversee the engineering department. Probably at Thomson's urging, L. P. Grant was named resident engineer, and the last mention of Thomson by name in the board's minutes was entered on February 9, 1847 when he was ordered to start a survey for the Macon and Western.[44]

It appears certain that he retained his situation even after he accepted a job as chief engineer on the Pennsylvania Railroad in April 1847. He made at least two trips back to Georgia after moving to Pennsylvania, one in January 1848 and another in the spring of 1851, at a time when his duties on the northern road were particularly heavy. The Georgia Railroad continued to use the title of resident engineer until 1852, a clear implication that Thomson was still chief engineer. By then, however, he had sold 40 percent of his Georgia Railroad stock and bore enough responsibilities in Pennsylvania to keep him fully occupied.

Thomson's success in constructing and operating what was at the time the longest railway in the world under one management, in the face of the worst depression America had experienced, added to his already growing national reputation. His uncanny ability to keep overall strategic objectives in mind, even while performing mundane professional tasks, lifted him above the ranks of ordinary engineers. As his stand demanding continued expansion during the heart of the depression indicated, he was not afraid to forcefully present his views when he thought he was right. And in the case of the Georgia Railroad, he was. The road was one of the most prosperous and well-managed companies in the nation when he left to go north. And Thomson was wealthy enough by that date that he no longer needed full-time employment. During his thirteen years in the South, he had invested his considerable earnings in a large number of projects and schemes, providing the region with some badly needed venture capital. To his delight, many of his investments were "proffitable."[45]

3

THE ENTREPRENEURIAL URGE

Early in his career on the Georgia Railroad, Thomson became involved in numerous financial speculations scattered throughout Georgia, Alabama, and Tennessee. By any standards of the period, he was a moderately wealthy man and was in an enviable position because his wealth was more liquid than that of his friends who owned slaves and plantations. Over the thirteen years that he was with the Georgia road, his total income from salary alone exceeded $44,000, while his wants and needs were minimal. With no family to support, his only regular personal expenses were the maintenance of a room in Augusta and his keep while out on the road. He invested his considerable surplus in stocks, bonds, land, and commodities, looking in most cases for short-term quick profits.

His investment habits, developed in the depression-wracked South, changed little over his lifetime. The majority of his financial ventures were always rail-related—in the securities of railways themselves; in nearby land; in minerals or mineral fabricating companies such as coal, iron, oil, and steel; and in municipal securities, particularly those of towns and cities about to become rail centers. While in the South, he also developed a tendency to spread his financial risks as widely as possible among trusted personal friends, usually co-workers. Often the membership of these speculative groups overlapped, but normally Thomson's counsel prevailed within the various tight, little circles.

He liked to invest in promising projects at their inception rather than trade in the securities of well-established concerns. The risks inherent in his approach were much greater, and over his career Thomson suffered some egregious losses, but he minimized this danger by not committing his money until he had inside information on the project; usually he knew at least one person in the business who would feed him the needed intelligence. Thomson also took the larger view of any concern's prospects. Since his profession did not tie him permanently to any region, as was the case with most merchant-capitalists, he was in a better position than most to grasp the overall business situation, particularly in the railway industry. A fledgling road that might become a link in an emerging north-south or east-west rail artery had good remunerative prospects, no matter how short or small the local population. The same held for end-to-end rail combinations, a particular favorite of his, and for bridge companies that would connect portions of a through route. Over the years his interests migrated farther west to take advantage of the developing opportunities there. Throughout his lifetime Thomson was both a conservative, cautious entrepreneur and something of a plunger, but even when he entered a risky speculation, it was only after much aforethought and with reliable inside information.

Thomson's first sizeable southern investment was in the stock of a railway about which he possessed a wealth of information—his own. By the 1837 annual meeting, he owned fifty shares and held proxies on another ninety. From 1842 to 1848 he was not listed as a voting stockholder, but it was most improbable that he sold his holdings in that disastrous market. More likely his stock was voted by a close friend; Benjamin P. Warren, for example, president of the Georgia Railroad Bank-Augusta, handled Thomson's eighty shares in 1847. The chief engineer continued to buy his road's securities and four years later he had a $14,000 investment in the company. He slowly liquidated his holdings after going North, until by 1854, the last year his name appeared as a stockholder, he held only forty-one shares.[1]

A major reason Thomson did not invest more heavily in the Georgia Railroad was his constant involvement in various other schemes. Unfortunately, few complete records of his financial dealings survive; the best information is in his letters to L. P. Grant. While Grant was frequently Thomson's financial ally, he also had arrangements that excluded Grant. Thomson mentioned some of these in passing, but others are simply lost. Correspondence between the two men covered the period of 1840 through 1851, with the bulk of the letters written between 1843 and 1848. Unfortunately, the papers suffered heavy water damage leaving about 20 percent of them unintelligible. What remains, however, is a fascinating portrait of a man and his friends seizing opportunities to expand their wealth, to further the fortunes of the Georgia Railroad, and to develop the region. If the period covered by the surviving correspondence is indicative of Thomson's activities for the seven earlier years, then he was an incredibly busy man indeed.

The letters show that Thomson speculated in the commodities market with some regularity and began much earlier than his January 1846 note in which he told Grant that he had just sent Charles T. Pollard, president of the Montgomery & West Point Railroad, $2,500 to buy cotton for him "if the market is favorable." He seemed to be an old hand at playing that volatile game. If conditions there did not look good, he indicated he would instead purchase drafts on Philadelphia and New York banks to take advantage of a discount for his trip north that summer. He sold his cotton at 8 1/2 at four months in April, a price perhaps a cent above the prevailing Augusta level, but he complained to Grant, "the proffits are no great shakes." Another scrap of evidence indicates that the normally cautious Thomson could move quickly when he saw a chance to exploit a temporary commodity price spread. In December 1846 he mentioned that salt was selling in Charleston and Savannah for $1.40 a sack, while at Mobile it was quoted at less than 70 cents. Within a week he joined with Pollard, who had an intimate knowledge of Alabama transport costs, to exploit the differential. Thomson did not tell Grant how the speculation fared, but the rather offhanded manner in which he mentioned it indicated his familiarity with the southern markets.[2]

Thomson entered numerous small speculations that illustrated his widespread interests and knowledge. Some of them he merely mentioned tantalizingly in his letters. For example, in January 1841 he tried to have a Monroe Railroad bill discounted; the fact that several of his friends were officers on the road meant that he had probably invested in the company prior to its 1837 bankruptcy and held his paper in the hope that reorganization and an anticipated state subscription would eventually give it some value. He had largely despaired of the project by 1842, however, concluding rather graphically that "the Monroe Rail Road can never be made to clean its teeth if finished—unless ours should never reach the terminus."[3]

By then he was seriously considering investing in the bonds of the rival Central of Georgia. He finally bought them after writing Grant, an engineer on the road, several times asking for detailed information on the Central's situation. The curious fact was that the securities promised no windfall profits; in fact, Thomson admitted, "I have no idea they will be met at maturity," and, "I have no expectation that the Bonds will advance in price." He cleared up the mystery of why he bought them at all when he explained to Grant on April 10, 1842, that "the continuation of our Road depends in a great measure on the progress of yours. Our people appear to think that operations will cease on the C.R. Road in a very short time all together and hence do not feel that anxiety to push forward this work." In other words, Thomson was subsidizing a rival's construction to convince his own timid stockholders that a real competitive threat existed. At best he hoped to at least recoup his investment. Thomson was so impressed with Grant's knowledge of railway affairs, however, that he hired him away from the Central.[4]

The Georgia's chief engineer also liked the profit potential of state and municipal bonds in Georgia and Alabama. In November 1846, he wrote Grant, by then an engineer on Pollard's road, to ask his president "whether the [Montgomery] City-Bonds he referred to can be had for 85 for their face—." If so, Thomson wanted to sell his Georgia state bonds and reinvest, which he did sometime during the next six months. As Thomson shifted his funds into Pennsylvania speculations, however, he became anxious to get rid of his Montgomery bonds. In a note to Grant almost a year later, he queried, "what is [sic] Montgomery City Bonds worth? I would sell at par and throw in the interest due." Apparently he did, for he never referred to them again. If he bought at a 15 percent discount, he netted a nice profit in less than a year; but then he was reasonably certain all the time that the bonds would reach par.[5]

Ever the farmer's son, Thomson always kept his eyes open for profitable real estate opportunities, and not all of them were along his road. One of his earliest was something of a puzzle. On May 20, 1842, just after Thomson survived his ouster motion, he wrote Grant intriguingly, "if we do not make arrangements to proceed with our own work in June—I intend going West to look after My Iowa Speculation about the 1st of July;" his only mention of this investment. The territory was flooded with new settlers and the passage of the 1841 Preemption Act made it possible for homesteaders to claim 160 acres before they were offered at public auction and to pay for them later at $1.25 per acre. Thomson perhaps purchased a parcel of land under this act, or even back in the land boom of the mid-1830s, to hold for appreciation.

Another explanation also exists, based wholly upon circumstantial evidence. When Thomson was ordered to fire all unnecessary engineering personnel in 1839, one of the first to go was a "L.P. Thomson, Ass't. Engr., $1,200," very probably his older brother, Levis P., whose employment may have raised questions of nepotism among the directors who were on public record as determined to hire local engineering talent whenever possible. Thomson may have helped to establish Levis on an Iowa farm, for he did not return to work the family homestead when Thomson repurchased it. Moreover, Levis' only son, Edgar Levis, may have been so named to show his appreciation.[6]

Iowa, however, may have been something other than simply an investment. Moodily, Thomson reflected in October 1845, "now that the excitement attending the construction and completion of our Road is passed, I feel desolate, the monotony and vexations of a finished Road are anything but agreeable and present no object to accomplish which can enlist ones [sic] feelings like the expectation of some great enterprise." He always enjoyed the chase more than the kill, and in this state of mind, he turned philosophical, revealing a bleaker, more depressing side of his personality, which was rarely apparent.

I have been a Slave so long to Rail Road Companies that I feel some inklings after freedom and had made up my mind to spend next summer in examining into the resources & Beauties of the West & North West--with a view of determining where I shall set myself down to eke out the remainder of my days. Like most poor devils who have spent the best of their days in the pursuit of Phantoms—I am now . . .

and sadly the rest of the letter was obliterated by water stains. Clearly, with the advent of "Manifest Destiny," western lands lured him with the promise of a chance to unwind and renew his spirits. Note the ever practical Thomson was also determined to look over the resources of the country.[7]

At the very moment he was pining for the pristine solitude of the

wilderness, he was deeply engaged in more traditional land speculation much closer to home. Unfortunately, his real estate investments are difficult to separate from property acquisitions he made for
the railroad. It was common practice on the line for company officers
to purchase right-of-way on their personal accounts and then transfer
the titles to the company in order to obscure the real direction of the
line and keep land values depressed. As the road's general agent,
Thomson was responsible for all land purchases, a task he found most
distasteful. "I could never hear the word Right of Way again unless
the 'of' could be stricken out," he once exclaimed in frustration. He
frequently was obligated to attend long, drawn-out court proceedings,
and they plainly taxed his patience. They also left him with a lifelong
aversion to lawyers, men he viewed as little more than licensed
thieves. His correspondence was peppered with derogatory remarks
about them: "the Judge must be getting hungry for a fee," "your Decatur lawyers must be more fond of creating difficulties than healing
them," "I could hardly think they are such Num Skulls," and in reference to a case before a mediating commission, he dourly predicted it
would "probably choke the thing to death--the committee being all,
save one, lawyers." Later, in a damage claim against the Pennsylvania Railroad, he wrote the plaintiff, "Capt. Tyler informs me that
you are by profession a lawyer and hence will only look on one side of
the question." And yet for all his antipathy toward the legal intricacies
involved in land acquisition, he did not allow them to stand in the way
of a little property trading on his own account.[8]

Three months before the Georgia Railroad was completed, Thomson and Grant jointly purchased some land in Atlanta. By September,
Thomson advised selling off one-half of the property at public auction,
perhaps to increase the value of the remaining portion. A month and a
half later he offered to swap his interest in a house and lot in Covington, jointly owned by both men, for one of Grant's Atlanta plots, a
clear indication that he had speculated earlier along the route of his
road and was now more optimistic about Atlanta's prospects. Thomson could also be shrewd, even with his partners. He dickered with
Grant, complaining in December 1846 "the price of your Atlanta lots
are [sic] too high for me—your temperament is too sanguine—,"
waited, and then finally struck a bargain. Thomson was out to turn a
quick dollar from land transactions. Less than a year later he had

liquidated Atlanta speculations. He asked Grant to send "a statement of our agreement about the Atlanta lot trade, I believe that there were [sic] no writing passed between us on the Subject." Undoubtedly, the Atlanta speculation was characteristic of many other deals; with his knowledge of his road's route, he could not lose.[9]

All Thomson's sundry speculations paled, however, in comparison to his involvements in three southern railways, the Montgomery & West Point, the Nashville & Chattanooga (N&C), and the Southern Railroad of Mississippi. His speculative interests in western roads were first aroused in 1845 by the prospects of the M&WP, a shaky venture the Georgia Railroad officers had bailed out of difficulties several times because they feared it might fall under the sway of the Central of Georgia. The panic of 1837 and the ensuing depression hit the little company hard, and in 1839, after three years of intermittent work, it still had only twenty-five miles of rail laid. Four years later, desperate for capital to upgrade its plant to qualify for a mail contract, the company negotiated a joint guarantee by the Georgia and the South Carolina Railway for $25,000 of its bonds. The presidents of the guarantors, however, were named trustees of the M&WP with power to sell the road on ninety days notice, which left the property in vassalage to the two eastern giants.[10]

After the consummation of this deal, Thomson became interested in the property. He recognized that its location, if a connecting road were finished, would link it with the Western and Atlantic, the Georgia Railroad, and the Central of Georgia, via a tributary road at Atlanta. In this eventuality both the Georgia Railroad and the Central would pay a high price to control the little eighty-eight-mile road. Thomson began his takeover in June 1845 with characteristic caution. He wrote Grant, whom he had planted in the M&WP transportation department, "our Stock [Georgia Railroad] has now run up so high that I don't feel disposed to invest in it and may if the thing will do speculate in your Road if there is any offering." Over the next six weeks Thomson carefully examined the matter and questioned Grant extensively on the road's prospects. He made up his mind to act, convinced that the road would "make Montgomery the greatest inland town in the South—." "I would still if it come in your way," he advised Grant in September, "be glad to take what you can purchase at 20 cents—say 100 or 200 shares, or go your [sic] halves in the Speculation & hold on joint account for the time being." After some additional thought, he added, "I am satisfied the work will be carried through in a very short time—and when completed it will pay handsomely on 20 cents—there can be no question on this point."[11]

The day after the Georgia Railroad's inaugural run Thomson bought into the road. "You will find below a check for the $1200," he told Grant, "you desire to pay for the Montgomery Rail Road Stock. You can also draw upon me for the other $1200 payable at the Geo. Rail Road Bank at sight—." Thomson had formed an investment group that included Pollard, Grant, John King, Benjamin Warren, and other Augusta "parties" to buy up all the stock they could lay their hands on. But he warned Grant, "you must keep entirely dark on this matter—and more so as not to excite suspicions—." Uncharacteristically, Thomson concluded his letter with an admonition to "Destroy This."[12]

In late September Grant proposed a plan for the complete takeover of the road. Complicating the situation, however, was a prior lease of the line; Thomson rightly feared that buying out the lessees would consume the "Lions share" of any potential profits. He sent Grant some judicious advice, the same counsel he followed, "in any step you may feel constrained to take let it be done with the utmost deliberation—don't act under feelings of excitement, but wait for cooler moments—." Grant began negotiations to buy up the lease and the 1700 shares of stock the lessees had received in lieu of cash for construction work. Since the Augusta group controlled only 1700 shares, and another 1923 remained in "outside" hands, the lessees' shares were pivotal for the road's control. The lessees, however, demanded a premium of $25,000 for their shares, which would raise the Augustians' investment to 43 1/2 per share, certainly more than they had anticipated. Then there was the minor matter of the $850,000 that Thomson estimated was necessary to complete the road and bring it up to standards. Thomson, by this time, was emerging as the spokesman for the Augusta group. "If this matter can be explained so as to enable me to represent the thing fairly to our folks," he promised Grant, "there will be no difficulty in closing the trade." Thomson wanted, of course, to dissuade the lessees from demanding a premium, pay the 28 1/2 per share, and put the majority and minority stockholders on an equal footing. He was unable to strike such a bargain, but he did convince the outside shareholders to agree to sell their stock only to persons approved by the new board, on which Thomson held a seat. The deals with the lessees and the minority faction were completed by November 2, 1845, and Thomson with characteristic engineering gusto promised to hurry out to advise Grant.[13]

The Augusta group had no trouble raising the money to renovate and begin expansion of the road. In mid-April 1846, the Georgia Railroad directors approved, in conjunction with the South Carolina Railroad, an endorsement for $125,000 of the M&WP's first mortgage bonds. In return that company had to operate its line in close conjunction with the Georgia road, finish its construction to West Point, and offer the Georgia Railroad first option on any future stock issues. A month later Thomson admonished Grant to send regular detailed reports every six months as "these fellows here [Augusta] want information and I wish to be prepared to give them what is necessary or desirable." Thomson obviously could be a bit devious when he thought it necessary.[14]

The first contracts were quickly let by June, and Thomson bombarded Grant with advice on contract prices, specifications, superstructure, and even asked Grant to draw up and submit a construction bid for one of Thomson's friends. To save money, Thomson did not recommend that the road's gauge be widened to five feet to make it compatible with connecting roads and ordered Grant to build the cheapest line possible. Thomson helped Grant out by providing springs, castings, and wheels at cost from the Georgia Railroad's Augusta shop to enable him to cope with the increased traffic caused by the demands imposed by the Mexican War. Bond sales were going well, and Thomson was certain he could dispose of the entire issue if only the interest was payable at Augusta. With cash flowing into the treasury, he urged Grant to "adopt the more energetic means to finish to Auburn in season—."[15]

Thomson's continued absence from the South in 1847 prompted him to resign his seat on the M&WP board, but did not immediately dampen his interest in the project—he was too heavily committed. He continued to correspond with Grant, offering him advice on general strategy; in his spare time he undertook to raise monies for the line in Philadelphia and New York. Thomson also indicated in his letters that he fully understood the complex relationship between finance, strategy, personalities, and outside circumstances. He warned Grant in September, "I have no idea of continuing our road to West Point unless the Georgia Rail Roads tend that way." Quite out of his usual expansionary character, he suggested the road stop construction at Opelika and depend upon local traffic rather than risk funds only to find no Georgia connections at West Point. Two months later he reiterated his conservative policy more strongly, arguing that expansion past Opelika would almost certainly cause "irretrievable bankruptcy—The whole concern would then pass with certainty into the hands of the Georgia & S. C. Rail Road companies under the mortgages they hold—." All the Georgia Railroad had to do was to postpone its plans west of Atlanta, allow the M&WP to overextend itself, foreclose, and then connect with the line. The M&WP security holders, many of whom were connected with the Georgia Railroad, would lose nothing, and the Central of Georgia would be thwarted. Thomson obviously sensed something like this was afoot. He counseled "firmness & Prudence" to hold Pollard in check: "we are too small potatoes to control the policy of other lines and must be controlled by them." The stalemate lasted until 1849 when the M&WP completed the last twenty-four miles to West Point. The Georgia Railroad finally committed itself to aid in the completion of the Atlanta to West Point route; with such a connection guaranteed, the Montgomery road had no more reason for hesitation.[16]

By then, however, Thomson had apparently withdrawn from the enterprise. Grant, Thomson's eyes and ears on the road, left in 1849 to take a job as engineer on the Atlanta & LaGrange Railroad although he still drew a salary from the Georgia Railroad. Thomson probably sold out in 1847 or 1848 when he unloaded his Montgomery city bonds, selling his stock to other members of the investment group or to the Georgia Railroad as stipulated in the April 14, 1846 agreement. He had never been able to oversee the work personally to protect his investment, and by 1847 he was geographically far removed from the scene. Moreover, the road was probably "too small potatoes" to hold his attention for long; he had entered it as a speculative venture under the impression that if completed rapidly, he could sell out at a handsome profit. And undoubtedly he did make some money; it was a pretty safe "inside" deal. But he was now outside the inner council of the Georgia Railroad and was no longer directly privy to its thinking, and by 1847 he was busy locating the Pennsylvania Railroad and promoting the proposed 150-mile Nashville & Chattanooga Railway.[17]

Thomson's association with the Tennessee road began on April 17, 1846, when a Colonel Martin of that company visited him and offhandedly remarked, "I suppose you are the man we shall have to get to make us a survey." Thomson at the time was only half employed by the Georgia Railroad, bored with his routine, and seeking "some great enterprise" to occupy his energies. The N&C appeared to be just that. Projected to connect the cities in its name and with its estimated cost of $1.5 million it promised to be an undertaking of the Georgia Railroad's scope. Furthermore, the road got off to a promising start, acquired a Tennessee charter late in 1845, and laid plans for raising subscriptions. Thomson accepted Martin's offer, made the preliminary location for the road in June and July 1846, and published his findings in a twelve-page pamphlet the following year.[18]

The company appealed for stock subscriptions to the towns along its projected route and to distant cities expected to benefit; its efforts were well rewarded. A total of $1 million was subscribed by Nashville, Murfreesboro, and Charleston. Thomson helped raise a contribution from the latter city through Senator John C. Calhoun, whom he had approached early in 1846. N&C officials also asked the Central of Georgia and the Georgia Railroad for help. Rebuffed by the former company, they had better luck with the Georgia Railroad where Thomson, who was now referring to "our Nashville project," paved the way for a respectful hearing by his former colleagues. On April 11, 1848, the Georgia Railroad directors, after a personal request from N&C president Victor K. Stevenson, agreed to subsidize a $250,000 stock subscription. The new line's promising prospects induced individuals to subscribe another three-quarters of a million dollars to the company.[19]

Thomson invested early, as was his wont once he made up his mind to enter a project. At his death he still held 120 shares, a $12,000 investment, but he probably initially purchased many more shares at a sharp discount, sold most upon completion of the road, and held the rest for dividend income and use as collateral. Certainly Thomson exercised the prerogatives of a large influential stockholder. He secured a position early in 1848 for Grant's brother, James, on the

N&C engineering staff to act as his inside informant. James corresponded regularly with Thomson for a year, and in March 1849 he gleefully wrote his brother, "I have just received a letter from Mr. Thomson, giving me the title of Chief Engr...N&CRR, care of V.K. Stevenson, President." Thomson also made it clear why he bestowed this position upon James Grant, "I must advise with him freely on all matters," Grant reported, "whether the Co. pay him anything or not." Thomson also expected Grant to see that the line's final location adhered to Thomson's survey with no costly detours. As late as 1851, Thomson still exerted considerable force within the company. Grant was involved in an altercation that year with Stevenson, whom Thomson persisted in calling Stevens, and with Thomson's backing, Grant "made him succumb," an unusual circumstance indicating that powerful outside pressure was involved.[20]

The extent of that power may be seen in a subsidiary enterprise Thomson entered. On November 27, 1847, the Tennessee legislature incorporated the Chattanooga Iron Manufacturing Company, obviously a spin-off from the N&C, an attempt to exploit the iron ore and wood available in the area before the completion of the rail junction drove land values higher. The investment combine included a galaxy of important southern entrepreneurs, but they were all unable to oversee their property. Thomson was in Pennsylvania even as it was chartered; King remained in Augusta; George W. Crawford joined Zachary Taylor's cabinet as secretary of war in 1849; Ker Boyce, a wealthy cotton merchant, stayed in Charleston; and Farish Carter was preoccupied with managing his vast landholdings in Georgia and Alabama. In 1852 the company's charter was amended to allow stock issuances up to $1 million, and the iron works was put into operation the following year. It apparently never reached its backers' expectations, was leased in 1856, and subsequently sold. The investment's initial glowing promise, however, certainly whetted Thomson's continued interest in the N&C, and the project indicated just how widespread his business contacts were throughout the region. He would call on them all to promote his most ambitious southern scheme, a transcontinental.[21]

The idea dated back to the 1830s, but Thomson embraced the concept late and only after he became president of a major northern line. The individuals allied with him in supporting the project, however, underscored the fact that nineteenth-century America was often an incredibly close, intimate society revolving around overlapping personal and professional contacts crossing state, regional, and sectional boundaries. Moreover, as the antebellum period neared its bloody climax, the dividing line between politics and the business world narrowed and sometimes disappeared. Thomson helped shrink that gap; a combination of personal contacts and political necessity prodded him into becoming an active proponent for the southern route to the Pacific.

His involvement in transcontinental affairs began with a letter from a perfect stranger, Thomas A. Marshall, president of the Southern Railroad of Mississippi, all of fourteen miles long between Jackson and Brandon. Marshall was seeking funds in 1852 to complete his line another eighty-two miles to the Alabama border. He had met with the Georgia Railroad directors to ask for a guarantee of his bonds and a competent engineer to locate his road. The board denied his first request and suggested he contact Thomson in Philadelphia for an engineer. On August 26 Marshall wrote Thomson and gave him a contractual carte blanche to hire an engineer for the Southern. Thomson engaged Haupt, and by November he was in the field. On Thomson's advice, Haupt toured the South Carolina, the Georgia, the Montgomery, and the Alabama and Tennessee River Railways, all lines destined to form the nucleus of any future southern transcontinental. Haupt imbibed of the southern dreams, finished his location, and published his findings in which he strongly implied that a southern transcontinental was merely a matter of time because its advanced progress gave it a superior claim to federal consideration for aid. Thomson may have instilled such an idea in Haupt's mind before he left or Haupt's assessment might have sparked Thomson's interest, but he kept a watchful eye on the progress of southern lines that might be included in any future Pacific road.[22]

Actually, Thomson could not have ignored the slave-state claims if he had wanted to, for the leading proponents of the southern route became active in Pennsylvania politics. As the president of a large corporation seeking legislative cooperation and locked in battle with the politically sensitive Pennsylvania State Works, he could not remain an innocent bystander, especially after one of the state's leading political figures, Simon Cameron, became involved with the Southern

Railroad of Mississippi. Cameron was probably the co-contractor for the Southern's extension who was enigmatically referred to in an 1854 issue of the *American Railroad Journal* as the "responsible and energetic Company in the North." The identity of one of his partners may be discerned in a note Haupt wrote to Cameron reporting, "I have another letter from Marshall which I wish to show you when we meet." The lure was land. Congress that year was debating a federal land grant to the Southern and Marshall reminded Cameron bluntly, "when we agreed to make you jointly interested with us in the land our belief was that you could bring to the support of the bill a large majority, if not all of the members from Pennsylvania and with such support we had no doubt of its passage." The odds are great that Thomson was also an interested party, for he tried without success to persuade his former comrades on the Georgia Railroad to purchase almost $50,000 of the Southern's bonds. The Pennsylvania combination successfully wheedled a grant of 270,000 acres out of Congress for the Southern, which had already received 2 percent of all federal land sales in the state. The Cameron co-partners, however, never constructed a mile of road.[23]

Several of Thomson's southern friends were also involved in the construction of railroads between Charleston and Texas that were destined to be included in a transcontinental line. The Georgia Western, chartered in 1856 to connect Atlanta with Jacksonville, Alabama, counted Richard Peters its president and L.P. Grant its chief engineer. Two years later Grant, a partner in the construction firm of Fannin, Grant and Company, had the contract to build the Vicksburg, Shreveport and Texas Railway across northern Louisiana to connect with the Southern Pacific at Jonesville, Texas, on which Grant was also the contractor. Moreover, a short forty-five-mile road, the Vicksburg and Jackson, connected the projected VS&T with the Southern; and Marshall, who was certainly in a position to know, told Cameron in 1854 that he thought the V&J was owned in Philadelphia.[24]

Thomson then had ample reasons by 1856 to take up the cudgels for a congressionally chartered southern transcontinental; his own interests were inextricably involved. In a lengthy letter, undated but probably of that year, he appealed to Congressman Alexander H. Stephens, a Whig advocate of Pacific schemes, to support a route located between the thirty-second and thirty-fifth parallels. Stephens, later the Confederate vice-president, began his legal practice in the early 1830s in Crawfordville, located on the Georgia Railroad, and served in the state legislature from 1836 to 1842. In both capacities Thomson could not have failed to know him and was therefore appealing to an old friend. In his letter Thomson naively swept away a quarter century of disruptive sectional tensions that had stymied federal aid contending that the arguments arose "from the personal want of correct information." The northern route, he continued, was objectionable due to topography, climate, and the simple fact its terminus would be 500 miles north of San Francisco. The "middle routes" north of the thirty-fifth parallel were "in a financial and engineering sense impractical and not worthy of further examination for a Rail-Road." Thomson left Stephens with only two alternatives, a route from St. Louis or one from Shreveport, and he obviously favored the latter. He asked Stephens to call for a competent survey, a request he made with the full knowledge that the secretary of war, Jefferson Davis, had reported to Congress in 1855 that the thirty-second parallel was the most superior route. Thomson's recommendation of that route may have militated the charges of sectional prejudice hurled against Davis, but it was certainly not the observation of a completely disinterested party.[25]

Thomson's support for a southern transcontinental became even less objective in 1859 after he met with the president of the Southern Pacific, Jeptha Fowlkes, a physician from Tennessee, who offered him the presidency of the road at the considerable salary of $25,000 per year. Fowlkes desperately needed Thomson's good name, national reputation, and financial contacts to rescue the faltering company. Thomson was tempted, if the railroad first retired all its debts, some of which were owed to his friend, Grant, settled its legal quarrels with the state of Texas, and raised at least a quarter of a million dollars in cash. The sheer magnitude of the project attracted him; he found transcontinentals irresistible. On January 23, 1860 he wrote Samuel Barlow, president of the Ohio and Mississippi Railroad that he had given in, "I have accepted the presidency of the Southern," he declared without qualification "and as soon as we get fully underway will have to give up the Penna. R. Road—." He cautioned, "this, however, is between ourselves." Thomson apparently verbally agreed to accept the job and set about reorganizing the company's board, packing it with old friends such as King, Pollard, Stevenson, William Sneed from Mississippi, and Barlow, hoping that their influence would help the railway win a government subsidy.[26]

In mid-February he went "to consult with our friends" at the capital, where he must have been rudely awakened by the depth of sectional antagonism he found; he was soon arguing with Pennsylvania Congressman John Covode, a staunch supporter of the Pennsylvania Railroad, that "any Bill to accommodate the whole country must embrace both a Northern & Southern line—," despite his earlier assertion to Stephens that the nation could not afford two roads. He now rationalized that "the increase of wealth and population of the country will make both pay." He concluded with a telling appeal to Covode's sense of political reality: "the large amount of Iron required for these Roads must induce the certain cooperation of all the Penna. members." Covode understood; both he and Thomson had large personal investments in the Pennsylvania coal and iron industry served by Thomson's railroad. The timing of Thomson's last congressional appeal, however, was miserable. Stephen A. Douglas' railroad-political strategy that resulted in the Kansas-Nebraska Act, and later warfare in the Kansas Territory, killed any chance for a federally aided transcontinental over any route. Yet Thomson steadfastly remained firm in his conviction that a Pacific road was necessary, practical, and potentially profitable.[27]

His advocacy of a southern transcontinental and his other financial and personal interests in the South after 1847 showed that Thomson took a bit of the South with him when he left that region. His experiences there had a tremendous impact on his private and professional attitudes; he went north with a great deal more than mere satisfaction for having engineered, constructed, and managed a great railway, more than an interlocking web of regional investments, more than profits from those ventures, and more than an intimate personal association with that region's emerging entrepreneurial class. His thirteen years in the South had convinced him that the region's peculiarities were overstated and not fundamentally incompatible with the national norms, as he identified them. He believed they would become even less so as the new transport systems knit the young nation more closely together, creating interregional economic dependencies. It was men like him who would help mend the rent in the national fabric, rational men who pursued concrete goals for the good of all concerned, or so Thomson would argue early in the Civil War. His southern experiences had made him one of those men; he took home valuable experience in all phases of railway management that instilled in him a larger view of business affairs.

On the Georgia Railroad, Thomson for the first time had been responsible for a line's operation and maintenance. He found such tasks restrictive, but he took his charge seriously, and the Georgia Railroad was a well-run operation. Thomson established an enviable safety record with primitive equipment; only nine accidents marred the road's first decade, and its first deaths were not recorded until June 1841 when a broken rail toppled a locomotive into a drainage ditch on top of the engineer and a company-owned slave, killing both. Accidents came in bunches, with four in 1841 and three over a three-month period in 1846–1847, coinciding with the need to replace the line's superstructure. Drunks were Thomson's greatest safety hazard—they seemed to have a compelling urge to sleep on railway tracks. In a four-day period in August 1841, two were run over in separate incidents. Again in April 1845, a sleeping intoxicant "was horribly mangled." The only accident caused by carelessness during Thomson's tenure took place in December 1845 when two freight trains collided head-on. Without telegraphic communications, this type of mishap was difficult to prevent.[28]

This otherwise excellent safety record was due in part to Thomson's careful maintenance of the road's machinery and roadbed. He insisted that exquisite care be given to the locomotives on which he kept exacting records of expenses per mile. His high standards of maintenance were possible because the seasonal business of the road, concentrated in the fall and winter, allowed the slack season for thorough repairs. He replaced the rotting superstructure even as he pushed new construction forward, and at the completion of the entire road, he was already replacing the old strap iron with the new, safer T rails.

Thomson's most confounding and irritating responsibility, aside from dealing with lawyers, was setting rates. He wrestled with the problem every year; and no matter what he decided, he was always maligned. Publicly, Thomson garnered a reputation for favoring in principle high rates even if they discouraged traffic, and he constantly advised his shareholders to seek legislative sanction for them. He justified his position by pointing out the intimate relationship between rates and stock dividends. The true interest of any road, he thought, should be its net profit, not the gross tonnage it carried; rates therefore should be adjusted to bring in "a reasonable percentage on the cost of the work." He was not unmindful of the fact that lower rates might attract more traffic with a commensurate rise in net profits, but he was leery of the proposition. He bluntly communicated his suspicions to his stockholders in 1843: "while too high rates will in a short time lessen the amount of the receipts of the road; on the other hand, a very reduced scale, may add greatly to its business, without a corresponding increase in the nett [sic] profits. A just medium is to be observed," requiring exact knowledge of the cost of transport, an idea of what price the freight could reasonably bear, based on an accurate prognostication of future commodity prices, and an awareness of rates charged on competing lines.[29]

In an agricultural region raising a few staple crops, Thomson understood lowered rates would not necessarily call forth a significant increase in tonnage because the planters' production was limited by land and labor. With a high fixed overhead, they planted and harvested all they could regardless of the market and transport situations. Only when planters shifted crops, as happened around Athens in the 1840s when soil exhaustion and low cotton prices forced the planters into grain cultivation, did Thomson realize financial advantage from lowering rates. In this case, he reduced charges for corn and induced the planters to increase their exports of the crop.

After eight years of raising rates only to draw intense criticism from his shippers, some of whom were stockholders, and then lowering them only to see profits fall, he capitulated in 1845 and asked the board to appoint an executive committee to take charge of the entire rate-making apparatus. Thomson, however, carried his rate predilections to the Pennsylvania Railroad where it was only with difficulty that his subordinates convinced him to retreat from his firm belief in the efficacy of moderate rates and to try a tariff structure on bulk commodities pegged at or below the cost of transport to call forth additional business. The idea worked in Pennsylvania where it would not have in Georgia due to regional economic differences. Moreover,

Thomson's rate experiences in the South helped to convince him later that the only sensible rate policy was one of collusion between competing lines.[30]

Thomson also left the Georgia Railroad with firm convictions regarding the true principles of railroad organization. His confidence derived from trial and error, since the only real precedent for organizing 250 or more employees strung out over 200 miles was on the South Carolina Railroad. Initially, as portions of the road were opened, he placed the entire transportation department under Richard Peters, who was responsible for operations, repairs, car construction, accounts, and road maintenance. Thomson soon found that Peters was badly overworked, and he reorganized his first four responsibilities into separate departments, each entrusted to a superintendent. For maintenance of the road, three supervisors were appointed, each responsible for a division averaging fifty miles. The flow of authority went directly from Thomson to Peters to the other superintendents and supervisors. This simple organization was well suited for the line in the 1840s, with its lack of bureaucracy, minimum of paper work, and heavy dependence upon mutually compatible personalities for smooth functioning. Furthermore, it was an organizational scheme whereby superiors could quickly recognize and reward a talented individual, an ideal that appealed to Thomson, who always had an uncanny eye for spotting persons of unusual ability. He later applied a modification of this same organizational structure to the Pennsylvania Railroad.[31]

Managerial responsibilities gave Thomson valuable insights into the importance of personalities in a large corporation. He saw that the stockholders remained complacent so long as the dividends continued regularly, and the road evidenced no signs of obvious mismanagement. When these conditions were met, the directors had little to fear in the way of outside interference. This was obvious in the annual meetings after 1843, which were more social affairs than exercises in corporate democracy. Thomson also learned how to deal with labyrinthine board politics. He came to realize that an officer on any road had to do more than just perform his duties satisfactorily; he had to have firm support from at least some directors. Opposition from within the board could break even the best railroad men as Thomson found out in 1841–1842, but a close personal rapport with directors could insure against this possibility. By 1847 he was financially allied in the M&WP speculation with at least three of his board members: Bowdre, Warren, and King, who helped him obtain his $2,000 yearly stipend after the road's completion and in return for only the lightest responsibilities. Later, on the PRR, Thomson carried the art of board manipulation to its highest form in which his directors became little more than sycophants.

The Georgia's chief engineer learned that an understanding of personalities and reliable sources of traffic were the keys to running a profitable operation. The fact that his railroad was an extension of the South Carolina line made Thomson acutely aware that the prosperity of the more settled East depended upon the natural resources of the West. This belief led him to vociferously advocate, even when the notion was unpopular, the absolute necessity for his company to connect with western railways. He learned to always look beyond his own termini and above the minutiae of the daily business to view the larger picture, to understand that his line's future depended upon the vagaries of other roads, to appreciate the commercial importance of through routes, and to grasp the intricacies of railway tactics and strategies. Thomson's habitual broad outlook on railway affairs helped raise him above the growing swell of railroad managers to a position of national importance.

In a multitude of important ways, Thomson, the Pennsylvania Quakers' son, fit well into prewar southern society. Politically, he shared many of the old South's values and verities. He left the region in 1847 as, what could best be described as a Henry Clay Whig, a man for whom he once ran a special train so that up-country folks could hear the perennial presidential aspirant discourse. Thomson's Whiggery, however, was closely circumscribed by his professional and class interests; he was most sympathetic with the viewpoints of the Whig planters and merchants in the section. In the best tradition of Adam Smith, Thomson always viewed politics and politicians as only necessary evils to maintain domestic order, and his outlook certainly placed him in the mainstream of nineteenth-century political thought. Although he held no philosophical brief for the emerging southern fascination with the theory of states' rights, so ably enunciated by John C. Calhoun and others, neither did he appear to oppose it. While on the Georgia Railroad Thomson discovered that the state legislature was more responsive to business interests than was the federal government, and from a practical point of view, he did not find Calhoun's outlook abhorrent.[32]

Thomson's success in dealing with state legislatures contrasted with the frustrations he suffered in Washington, D.C. Tariffs on iron, for instance, fluctuated widely, and as a purchaser of the commodity and in harmony with the South's low-tariff stand, he suffered as rates rose relentlessly. Later, when in the coal and iron business himself and favoring high protective tariffs, rates went down no matter how much lobbying he did. The federal post office caused him nothing but grief, and he died convinced that department owed his railways a fortune for carrying the mails at a loss for thirty-six years. He had only slightly better luck securing federal land grants, even with great expenditures of money and effort. Thomson never fathomed federal banking policy. As an inveterate traveler and user of banking facilities, he was in sympathy with the idea that some kind of central banking system was necessary to facilitate trade and travel. When the government finally created a national banking system and issued a common medium of exchange during the Civil War, Thomson spent the remainder of his life trying to have the paper greenbacks recalled.

On two important points Thomson found himself in complete political harmony with his southern friends. He firmly believed that governments had the authority to aid private internal improvement projects everywhere, but not the power to interfere with domestic social relations anywhere. That the South depended more than other areas upon federal and state monies for transportation development has been ably documented. Whether the region was inherently incapable of financing its internal improvements through private investment is less certain. All four of Thomson's antebellum southern railroad projects appealed, however, to either state or federal governments for direct financial aid with varying degrees of success. He was supported in every instance by his southern associates who considered the petitions a way of equalizing the tariff imbalance in which southerners paid a large proportion of the hated duties only to see the funds spent in the North. Thomson apparently concurred with this line of reasoning, or else he was pragmatic enough to take advantage of his associates' sectional proclivities.[33]

Even with the demise of the Whig party in 1852 and the emergence two years later of the Republican party, which claimed his allegiance, Thomson did not wander far politically from his southern compatriots. His Republicanism eschewed the antislavery impulse that initially brought the party together and instead embraced the Old Whig economic tenets, such as high tariff, aid to internal improvements, and the homestead act that found an uneasy home in the new party. While Thomson became an apostate on the protection issue in the 1850s when his financial interests changed, he remained in league with his southern friends on internal improvements and free land. Although southerners blocked passage of a homestead bill before the war because they feared the political consequences of nonslaveholders taking up western land in large numbers, Thomson looked at the proposal strictly from the perspective of enticing people into the West as rapidly as possible to develop its natural resources. Opposing a fundamental Republican doctrine, he was perfectly willing to allow homesteaders to bring their slaves into territories.

Thomson viewed the South's peculiar institution, in contradistinction to his Quaker upbringing, entirely in economic rather than in moral or humanitarian terms. He was always wary of moral causes and emotional crusades such as abolition; an eminently practical and empirical man, he considered slaves as simply property and efficient labor. Soon after coming south, he indicated that he had no objection to the institution. He casually included in his 1836 annual report his need for machinery, slaves, and eight overseers. He used hired slaves whenever possible on the Georgia Railroad's construction gangs, and he continued the practice on his M&WP project. He even attended to the details of working the bondsmen. He once warned Grant that his overseer "will have all your Negroes in the woods," for "his temper is not sufficiently equitable for a Negro driver." Thomson advised, however, that as bad as the driver was, he might "do" to direct hired slaves instead of the company's bondsmen—an interesting distinction.[34] In light of the region's scarcity of skilled labor, he recognized the immense value of the system in stabilizing the supply of well-trained workers. And Thomson evinced the same admiration for a skilled slave as he did for any talented man. On one occasion he told Grant that if a white man could not handle the tricky job of attaching locomotive drivers to axles, "send up for Negroes at the Steam Mill who understand the business—."

Nevertheless, he imbibed the regional viewpoint that slaves were first and foremost property. His earliest forthright statement to this effect was in 1846 when he bemoaned to Grant, "we shall fail in our plan of Purchasing Negroes as the funds will not probably be forthcoming in season, and moreover, that kind of *property* has advanced prodigiously!" Despite rising slave prices, their indispensability to his projects was obvious when four months later Thomson implored Grant to have his subordinate "make an arrangement with some of the Negro traders to increase his force." He made explicit his assumption that the peculiar institution was a benign part of the national fabric sanctioned by 200 years of precedent in a letter he wrote to Peters after the first battle of Bull Run. In his lengthy recital of the reasons for the bloodletting, Thomson did not even mention slavery, although he catalogued every other possible cause from stupidity to greed. He accepted and exploited the institution as he found it, without reflection; but it implicitly colored his political and social outlook and reinforced his inherent Whiggish commercial conservatism.[35]

Thomson left the South only reluctantly in 1847; he had developed a strong affinity for the region, its people, and its culture. But the Georgia Railroad was completed, and its officers evinced no desires to expand it further. He was plainly bored by routine operations, and the Nashville & Chattanooga was the only nearby project grand enough to spark his interest. He might have accepted the job as chief engineer on that line had the project not remained in the doldrums in 1847, as its sponsors strained to raise needed funds. Thomson was also watching the progress of those who dreamed of connecting Philadelphia with Pittsburgh by rail. Backers of the Pennsylvania Railroad organized, raised enough money to start construction, and offered him a position as chief engineer of that vast enterprise before the Tennessee road was ready to come off the drawing board. He hesitated, seriously considered waiting for the N&C to get underway, then changed his mind, and accepted the offer. His decision marked an important turning point in his career. In a decade he would become one of the most important, albeit one of the least visible, railway executives in the nation, something he could never have done had he remained with a southern railway. He reached the pinnacle of his profession, however, by applying the lessons he had learned so well during his southern sojourn. The man who traveled north early in 1847 carried with him a mountain of baggage from that region.

4

THIS GREAT UNDERTAKING

Thomson had a good idea of what lay before him that spring. The Pennsylvania Railroad promised to be the largest project of his career, linking Harrisburg with Pittsburgh, across some of the most inhospitable country in the Middle Atlantic region. The prospects at once excited and depressed him. It was the kind of enterprise that fired his imagination; it was big and it was bold, a work that would require every bit of technical expertise he could muster, an improvement of national importance involving the expenditure of millions of dollars that would bring him into close contact with leading eastern businessmen. On the other hand, he was almost forty years old and starting to feel his age. He faced the same responsibilities, hard work, and physical discomforts as when he arrived in Augusta years earlier. It would be the same process all over again, tramping across the countryside in all seasons, sleeping outdoors, and enduring the unending procession of lawyers, contractors, suppliers, and the like through his office. It also promised to be a task of considerable duration. And with his southern engagements and the possibility of taking hold of the Nashville & Chattanooga, he was not certain he wanted to tie himself down that long. Since the fall of 1845 he had been free to pursue ventures wherever he chose, and he liked it. He had an assured income from the Georgia Railroad that was at least five times above the national average and funds enough so that he need not worry about money. He had an ideal situation and he was reluctant to give it up, no matter how enticing the offer. In fact, when the Pennsylvania's board offered him the position of chief engineer, he turned it down. As usual he went straight to the heart of the matter, explaining to Grant in a rather abrupt manner, "I must decline and save myself some hard work for the next 5 years."

He reconsidered though, possibly because he saw the opportunity to do for his native city and state what he had done for Augusta and Georgia; his Pennsylvania had fallen far behind in the race to tap the burgeoning western trade. Although earlier the state had stretched its financial resources to their limit, attempting to overcome New York's supremacy, its efforts were futile. "Clinton's Folly," had opened western markets for the Empire State in 1825, and all the Keystone State's exertions over the next twenty-two years had failed to alter western shippers' preference for the more northerly route. Loss of this vital trade affected Philadelphia severely. That port, once a serious contender for honors as the young nation's premier city, had by mid-century suffered a serious relative decline. Whereas in 1820 the Quaker City had only 9 percent fewer people than New York City, by mid-century the gap had widened to a full 34 percent. Philadelphians wondered why, despite all their efforts, they remained an ever-distant second to New York City, and worse, were even threatened by their exuberant upstart rival to the south, Baltimore.[1]

When it became apparent in the 1820s that the more daring New Yorkers had stolen a successful march upon them, Pennsylvania notables began a noisy campaign for improved transportation between Philadelphia and Pittsburgh. New York, however, had been able to skirt the Allegheny Mountain barrier, while Pennsylvania unfortunately was not blessed with a natural valley route through the mountains; they simply had to be scaled. That reality cast serious doubt on the proposition that a canal, at least one with water in it, could be built across the state. Technical opinion was passionately divided on the subject.

The same heated disputes were taking place in Boston and Baltimore, cities similarly affected by New York's internal improvement. Spokesmen in all three urban areas doubted the feasibility of merely imitating the Empire State; but the most attractive alternative, railroads, were in the 1820s strictly experimental, their dependability and capacity to cope with long grades as yet unproven. Ultimately, each metropolis chose a different alternative. Bostonians delayed until railroads had proved their worth and in the 1830s reached out to Troy, New York, with the Western Railroad to tap the trade at the eastern end of the Erie Canal. Leading merchants in Baltimore were much more adventuresome. They invested heavily in the Baltimore & Ohio Railroad, gambling on an untried technology for their financial salvation and pioneered many of the rail industry's advances.[2]

Philadelphia opted for a middle course and chose to imitate New York's canal where possible, but to connect Philadelphia with the Susquehanna River and to cross the mountains with railroads. When finally completed in 1834 at a cost of over $12 million, the ungainly improvement meandered 394.5 miles across the state. The Pennsylvania Main Line never seriously threatened the Erie Canal. It was thirty-two miles longer, had over twice as many locks, and struggled over elevations almost four times higher than its northern counterpart's. The work never even earned enough to cover its construction costs, and the drain on the state's treasury drove Pennsylvania to the very verge of bankruptcy during the 1839 depression. The improvement, however, was not without its benefits. The long-isolated central portion of the state gained a reliable, if slow, means of transport and shipped large quantities of iron ore and coal out to Pittsburgh, giving impetus to the growing iron industry around the city. Although the Main Line aided industrialization and commercial agriculture on the state level, it did little to improve Pennsylvania's competitive position vis-a-vis its neighbor to the north.[3]

State leaders recognized their plight, but there was little they could do about it; furthermore, they had no idea of what to do until the state legislature in 1845 resolved to allow the Baltimore & Ohio Railroad to build a line from Cumberland, Maryland to Pittsburgh. That act galvanized Philadelphians to action. If Baltimore captured the Ohio Valley trade, Philadelphia would be cut off from its hinterland and gradually would be reduced to simply another provincial Atlantic city. In response to the threat, Quaker City leaders decided to support construction of a railroad to Pittsburgh to beat the B&O to the Ohio River. A few weeks later, city representatives presented the legislature with a petition to charter the Pennsylvania Railroad. B&O supporters were also in force arguing for a renewal of that company's franchise to build to Pittsburgh. After two and one-half months of heated debate, the legislature did the obvious; it passed both bills. The Pennsylvania Railroad was incorporated on April 13, 1846, and eight days later the governor extended the B&O's franchise. The B&O act, however, stipulated that it would become void if the PRR raised $3 million in stock subscriptions with 10 percent paid in and placed at least thirty miles of road under contract by July 30, 1847, a mere fifteen months away.[4]

Thanks to the Philadelphia councils' $1.5 million subscription and an equal amount pledged by individuals, the company was able to formally organize early in 1847. The thirteen directors who took their seats for the first time on March 31, represented a cross section of Philadelphia's elite: two financiers, six merchants, four manufacturers, and one merchant-manufacturer; none were experienced railroad men. At the meeting they elected Samuel V. Merrick president with a salary of $5,000 a year. A native downeaster who owned a fire engine factory and iron foundry, he had been a charter member of the prestigious Franklin Institute and was a compulsive joiner. Merrick held seats on the boards of practically every civic organization worthy of the name and still found time to dabble in city politics. In their next three meetings, the directors discussed engineering problems. Director John A. Wright, who owned the Freedom Iron Works near Lewistown, Pennsylvania, had been Thomson's assistant engineer on the Georgia Railroad and recommended his old boss to head up the engineering corps. Admitting to Grant that "I am sorely tempted to accept," Thomson vacillated, weighing the proposition carefully, and finally decided not to take it. His refusal must have signaled his hesitation, because Wright persisted. The road's directors went ahead on April 9 and selected Thomson as chief engineer anyway. Painfully, he made the decision to cast his lot with his native state, but by now practiced in ways of corporate politics, he withheld his acceptance until the board delegated more authority to him. Specifically, he demanded the sole right to hire and fire all personnel in his department; the directors agreed, and a week later Thomson formally accepted the position.[5]

He was under inordinate pressure; he had only three and one-half months to locate and let contracts for the first thirty miles of road to beat the B&O. Characteristically, once he had made up his mind to accept the job, he plunged into it with determination. To save time, he procured the old Main Line survey maps from the state's Board of Canal Commissioners and frequently took to the woods with his survey crews to check prospective routes. In the midst of all the bustle of finding the best line west of Harrisburg, the road's eastern terminus, and east of Pittsburgh, he was also advising Grant on the M&WP project. Thomson was plainly awed by the task that loomed before him, and he attempted to impart some of its flavor to Grant. "This Pennsylvania Road will be a stupendous undertaking—," he wrote proudly, "deep cuts, high Bridges, & tunnels here loose [*sic*] their terror—one of our lines has six tunnels in as many miles."[6]

But Thomson had the project well under control. By early June he recommended to the board that it authorize contracts for the first fifteen miles at each end of the road, and a week later it complied. Actually, Thomson was not quite ready. He had gone out and walked the entire eastern survey and decided that it was all wrong and would have to be relocated. Haupt was hired for the rush job and finished the first 17 1/2 miles toward Lewistown in time for Thomson to let the contract on July 16; a week later he completed arrangements to construct the first fifteen miles on the western end. He had just barely nipped the B&O; to meet the paid–in requirements of the legislature, the PRR's board had to ask some wealthy shareholders to pay their installments early. On August 2 the governor declared the B&O's charter null and void.[7]

A month later Thomson was out in the field overseeing construction at the eastern end, complaining to Grant that "it is disagreeable to be journeying about the country so much." At the same time future prospects rather excited him, "there will be some bold work on these lettings—tunnels of 1/2 a mile long are not considered bug bears—... Our Bridge across the Susquehanna will be an extensive affair—1200 yards long and 46 feet high—." Thomson's lot had eased somewhat because the board decided not to push the construction on the western division until Pittsburgh subscribed $500,000 to the road's stock. Nevertheless, Thomson had survey crews in the field all across the state seeking the best route. He concentrated his efforts, however, on preparing to let the contracts by November to build to Lewistown. To speed up the process he asked Merrick to vest him with the power to negotiate for the company while modestly assuring his president "I am naturally indisposed to seek authority." The board acceded to his request, and Thomson let the last forty miles of work to that town on schedule. By the end of the year, he had located the entire eastern

President Thomson at midcentury. Courtesy of the Division of
Archives and Manuscripts, Pennsylvania Historical and Museum
Commission, Harrisburg, Pennsylvania.

division, all 134 miles from Harrisburg to the Allegheny Mountains, and he had its construction underway in earnest.[8]

His work on the Pennsylvania left Thomson with a sense of *deja vu*. As on the Georgia Railroad the bulk of his time was consumed in dealing with contractual details. He oversaw everything from ordering ties, spikes, iron, and even locks, to mediating disputes between contractors, subcontractors, and the company, as well as negotiating for a right of way. All of this could make Thomson irritable, and his letters manifested a strain of peevishness that kept surfacing in many of his dealings. But such mundane tasks could also bring him influence and important contacts. A case in point was Thomson's authority to specify locomotive dimensions. While seemingly a minor prerogative, it enabled him to pass the bulk of his road's business to his friend, Matthias Baldwin, the Philadelphia jeweler turned locomotive manufacturer, whose mechanical abilities were the equal of Thomson's. Simply by specifying exactly what he wanted in terms of previous Baldwin products, William Norris, Baldwin's competitor in the Quaker City, could not get the contracts; of the PRR's first twenty-six engines, twenty-three were built by Baldwin. Thomson and the rotund, deeply religious locomotive manufacturer became fast friends. In the process, their dealings became increasingly informal. In the summer of 1850, for example, they met at the seashore where Thomson gave him a verbal commitment to purchase ten steam engines. Nine months later the chief engineer finally informed his board of his promise, and without debate it ratified the order. That kind of business rapport made the two men close financial allies, and for a quarter of a century they invested their private means together in various speculations across the nation. The Jersey shore episode also illustrated the degree to which Thomson's board deferred to his technical expertise. His directors also showed their confidence in his abilities and judgment after he had been with the company only nine months by raising his salary to $5,000 per year.[9]

Their trust was not misplaced. In his first annual report in June 1848, Thomson proudly informed the stockholders that he had 100 miles of road, the Susquehanna bridge, and several tunnels under contract. But in a sense he was too efficient, for as in Georgia his construction outlays were outrunning the company's ability to raise funds. The board had vowed to build the road, estimated by Thomson to cost $7.8 million, exclusive of the expense of crossing the mountains, without resorting to debts. The Georgia Railroad had used the same methods a decade earlier, and Thomson had supported the policy and earnestly recommended it in glowing terms to Grant for use on their southern projects. Pennsylvania, he explained, proposed to build "this great undertaking...without borrowing a dollar—The plan adopted is to pay interest at once on all subscriptions and continue it until a sufficient extent of Road is built to command a considerable travel and trade." A great advantage Thomson foresaw was that "by this plan the Stock will become a favorite investment for small capitalists who live on their income."[10] In theory the idea was attractive, but in practice the income was insufficient to finance construction across rough terrain. Moreover, small investors simply did not possess enough capital to feed the PRR's insatiable maws during its first five years. Had not the city of Philadelphia subscribed heavily to the first stock subscription, the corporation would have had great difficulty just meeting the financial requirements of its charter.

By August 1848, Thomson was feeling the severe financial pinch. When the directors wrote him that the shortage of funds might slow the work, he cheerfully advised Merrick that disbursements for the following month were expected to be 50 percent higher. Even a midsummer pledge by Allegheny County to purchase 20,000 shares of the road's stock did not alleviate the situation. He was forced to curtail letting the more expensive sections on the route by mid-August. Under heavy pressure from his board to proceed even more slowly, Thomson, ever the expansionist, was still optimistic. "I feel quite confident that we can, even without a departure from this cautious policy—," he predicted, "secure the completion of the Road to Lewistown in all next March."[11]

Finances continued to be tight for the remainder of the year and became critical the following April when no buyers in London could be found for the Philadelphia bonds used to pay for the city's stock. The board increased its exertions; members made public appeals for subscriptions, sold shares to the Spring Garden and Northern Liberties districts, and sent delegations to all the towns along the route to drum up local public support. Thomson trimmed his expenditures to the minimum and tried to persuade his contractors to take a healthy slice of their payments in the road's stock. Norris even received a contract for a new locomotive by accepting $1,200 of his own past due notes and $1,500 in the road's stock. Conditions deteriorated so badly that contractors complained to the board that funds paid them were found to be under protest.[12]

Money markets eased by mid-summer, however, and as Thomson approached the opening of the first section to Lewistown, enthusiasm for the project mounted. In July he was brave enough to report his mountain surveys to the board. Conditions improved so rapidly that the directors authorized reletting work west of Lewistown and even considered starting construction on the western end. Thomson indicated that he would like to let five of the heaviest sections out there; for these he needed about $180,000. To ease the company's cash shortage, he even offered to "be one of 20 at 95 cents or one of 10 at 90 cents to take the amount of [Allegheny County] bonds necessary to pay for the graduations of [these] sections . . . the money to be furnished as fast as required for the work." Thomson was as much motivated by his firm belief that "the idea of a total suspension of operations upon the Western Division should not be entertained for a moment," as he was by his quest for profit. His old expansionary enthusiasm was bubbling to the surface again, and he pushed work on the western sections hard.[13]

The financial stringencies worsened the already strained personal relations between Thomson and president Merrick. As early as December 1847, Thomson had threatened to quit and was dissuaded only when the board raised his salary. The basic issue appeared to be a matter of who was going to run the company. Thomas Cope, a Quaker on the PRR's board, noted in his diary that Merrick had invited him to his office on January 8, 1848 to read Thomson's "private correspondence" to him. Cope quickly realized "that jealousies exist as to their relative prerogatives, powers & rights . . . He charges Thomson with disrespecting his orders & . . . of entering into contracts of his own mere notion, without consulting him or the Board." The problem was still unresolved three months later when the chief engineer again considering leaving because, as he explained to Grant, "the old President and me cannot get along cordially." Thomson was more specific in his letter to brother James Grant, "I have not been pleased with my position here at all," because of Merrick who was "at all times at the seat of the power of the Company," and who Thomson thought, "manages to be continually throwing obstacles in my path—."[14]

Thomson's formidable foe, Samuel Merrick, the first president of the Pennsylvania Railroad. Courtesy of the Division of Archives and Manuscripts, Pennsylvania Historical and Museum Commission, Harrisburg, Pennsylvania.

The informal corporate structure and personality differences exacerbated the conflict between the two most important men on the railroad. The board had never clarified lines of authority within the company, and in the absence of a well-defined chain of command, Thomson refused to consider Merrick his superior. He did, however, reeognize the president's authority as a member of the board. The chief engineer pointed out that both he and the president were elected by the board and hence accountable only to that body. Merrick viewed the situation in a very different light. As president he was charged with administering the daily affairs of the company. The board made the long-range decisions; the president was responsible for their overall implementation, and the chief engineer executed those plans pertaining to his department. Each man, fearing he would lose, avoided bringing the question before the board for resolution. They preferred to leave their working relationship dependent upon their ability to persuade each other. Such an arrangement between two strong-willed men was fraught with possibilities for conflict.

The likelihood of disputes was enhanced by the fact that the two men were responsible to different constituencies. Thomson simply had to build the best road possible at least cost to the stockholders. His job was dealing with immediate physical realities. Merrick was no engineer and never pretended to be, but he had to represent Thomson's technical point of view and actions to potential and actual shareholders, particularly those in Philadelphia. As a representative of that city's merchant elite, he was beholden to their financial welfare. And he was not hesitant to admit it. In his second annual report he was most candid. "The road," he grandly proclaimed, "is being built by the business community for the benefit of trade," a rather narrow view when contrasted with Thomson's vision of a "great national enterprise" connecting the Ohio River with the Atlantic Ocean.[15]

The two men clashed repeatedly over everything. Thomson frequently complained that Merrick intervened for Philadelphia friends who held contracts with the road. For example, in May 1849, Merrick met with a dissatisfied contractor and pledged to increase payments for excavation work, but he failed to inform Thomson, who insisted on paying the prices previously agreed upon. When the contractor appealed to the board to honor Merrick's promise,

Thomson was caught in the middle. The chief engineer was also rankled by Merrick's demands for long, detailed reports. When the board required monthly reports in 1847, Thomson sent in an exceedingly long one and petulantly suggested that any further reports would "require more of the time of the officers . . . than will be consistent with the true interests of the Company." The board backed down, and Merrick instead irritated him with frequent requests for special reports.[16]

When the completion date for the first section neared, Thomson became anxious because no plans had been made for operating the road. Finally, on December 19, 1848, he bluntly urged the directors to get busy; and he wanted some questions answered. "From the number of persons that have applied to me for situations," he wrote director Colonel William Patterson, "and at the instance of the President and other members of the Board, I am led to believe that I am expected to participate in its management." The board finally informed him that it was true; in addition to all his other duties he was to create and staff the transportation department.[17]

Three months later Thomson submitted a complete plan of organization that met no opposition. His choice of Haupt to be general superintendent, however, immediately started a board fight. At least four directors, led by Merrick and William Patterson, had long sought to restrict Thomson's authority whenever possible. When the chief engineer nominated his own candidate for a position that would control the patronage of the whole road, they tried to discredit Haupt as a tactic to diminish Thomson's influence. Merrick led the attack, charging that Haupt was unfit for the job; he was too young, only thirty-two years old, and inexperienced. Knowing that he had a majority of the board behind him, Thomson allowed his opponents to bluster throughout the spring of 1849. Finally, in an attempt to calm the opposition, Haupt was named superintendent of transportation, and Thomson agreed to assume personal responsibility for his performance and to accept without additional pay, the position of general superintendent. The directors accepted Thomson's compromise but delayed Haupt's ratification until less than two weeks before the road was opened. The board was badly polarized.[18]

Two days later, Merrick, smarting over the board's support for a man he considered his subordinate, presented his resignation as president at a special meeting. The directors quickly accepted it and on August 25 unanimously selected Patterson, Merrick's ally, as the company's new president. Patterson, a wealthy banker and financier, was chosen because he represented the same influential Philadelphia constituency as Merrick. Patterson had handled the incredibly complex affairs of Biddle's Pennsylvania Bank when it had gone bankrupt in 1841, had organized the Union Trust Company of Philadelphia, and like his predecessor, was active in city politics. He was also a judicious choice because he kept the growing tensions on the board from the public's view. Merrick retained his seat on the board and chaired its road committee, a position of authority that boded ill for the chief engineer and Haupt.[19]

Thomson was guardedly optimistic about the change. He admitted to his business associate, James M. Bell, "my intercourse with Col. Patterson has thus far been very pleasant—his manner is very off handed but not coarse like his predecessor—." By now well versed in the art of corporate diplomacy, Thomson was seeking the right tack to use on Patterson. "It is possible as you state," he agreed with Bell, "that a firm footing may alter his tone—But not being exceedingly anxious to retain my post I don't think I would suffer long any change for the worse."[20]

The eagerly awaited opening of the first sixty miles to Lewistown took place on September 1, 1849. The inaugural run was an unpretentious affair with two trains scheduled to carry officers, directors, and a few notables from cities and towns served by the line, to inspect the fruits of Thomson's labors. Despite the restrained nature of the celebration, residents all along the road were caught up in the excitement of the occasion. A. K. McClure, a venerable state politician, later vividly remembered that day when the first train puffed into the little town of Mifflin:

The country people were out by thousands to see the railway train to which nearly all of them were entire strangers. A dense mass was packed in the little level close to the road, and the high hills close by the western side were literally covered with intensely anxious and wildly enthusiastic people. The shriek of the locomotive announced its coming, when within a mile or two of the station, and the whole audience moved as if electrified, and when the train came into the station with its majestic sweep, deafening shouts responded to the weird cry of the engine.

When the westbound train, pulled by the little 4-2-0 locomotive, *Mifflin*, reached Harrisburg, it made an unscheduled stop to allow the passengers refreshments. Haupt found the delay had been ordered by Patterson, but it assured a head-on collision between the only two trains operating that day. Haupt rushed to dispatch another locomotive up the road to arrange a meet, thereby averting the disaster. For years he cited this instance as an example of what happened when inexperienced rail managers interfered with the operations of a road.[21]

The opening spurred Thomson to redouble his efforts to finish the eastern division. After working almost two and one-half years without running a single revenue train, he opened 137 miles for business in twelve months. By Christmas 1849 the road was finished seventy-two miles to McVeytown; in June 1850, Huntingdon residents thrilled to the sound of their first steam whistle, and on September 16, Bell's Hollidaysburg friends gathered at the depot to celebrate the arrival of the first train in that locality. Early the following year, Thomson's construction crews finished the line to the new town of Altoona. The company had purchased land in the area for shops, and a village grew up around the job opportunities. Thomson named the area Allatoona after the pass in northern Georgia, but when the town lots were platted and sold, the name was shortened to Altoona. Once again, however, he left his mark in his nation's atlases.[22]

The PRR connected at Hollidaysburg in October 1850 with the state's Portage railroad. Unable to go around Allegheny Mountain, the commonwealth built ten inclined planes, powered by steam winches, to lift cars up the 2,570 feet and to ease them down to Johnstown. The thirty-six mile Portage, bracketed on either end by canals, was both inconvenient and slow; it had always been a bottleneck in the state works. Thomson and his board, however, were well aware of how much it was going to cost them and how much time it was going to take to push their railway over, around, or through the mountain. To save time they decided to construct the western division first and use the Portage temporarily to connect the two divisions until they could assault the mountain.

Use of the Portage immediately dumped a whole new set of problems into Thomson's already crowded lap. The PRR promised to be anything but a friendly adjunct to the state system; it threatened the jobs of everyone connected with the Main Line. Yet from the start Thomson needed the cooperation of the board of canal commissioners because his road depended upon the state's Philadelphia and Columbia Railroad for its connection with the state's port city and therefore had to jointly make schedules and set rates. Until the PRR reached the Portage, the commissioners were quite cooperative, loaning Thomson maps, delivering construction material, and allowing the PRR to construct its roadbed along and across the canal, sometimes destroying state buildings and other appurtenances. When Thomson began negotiating schedules for the Portage, however, he ran into trouble; the canal commissioners refused to operate the inclined planes at night, which meant passengers had to leave Philadelphia either at 4:00 A.M. or at 11:00 P.M. to avoid a wait at the base of the incline. When canal officials closed the Portage for the winter just a month after the PRR made its connection, Thomson protested privately. Publicly, however, he put the best face possible on the situation. He informed his stockholders that the closing was to make repairs and renewals that would allow the Portage to operate during subsequent winters.[23]

To placate the canal board, Thomson went to great lengths in his annual reports to argue that his company and the state system were allied in Pennsylvania's interest against outside improvements. The biggest difficulty as Thomson saw it, was that the canal commissioners would not lower their rates. Haupt went farther; he candidly informed his board that the PRR's high rates, caused by its dependence upon the state works, made it uncompetitive. Yet when the canal board finally agreed in 1851 to keep the Portage open during the winter, it blithely raised its tolls over the inclined planes 33 percent. Thomson also noted that delivery times on the canal system averaged seven days while the B&O touted two-day service over the same distance, making him one of the earliest observers to recognize that the element of time was becoming critical in the competition for western trade. As the clash between the PRR and canal commissioners ground endlessly on, he became even more anxious to push his construction over the mountains and across the western division.[24]

Work had proceeded fitfully on the other side of the mountains. Only after the road was opened to Lewistown, did Thomson put the entire western division under contract, and even then he was far from certain that the company could pay for it. A spate of labor troubles compounded his problems. All construction came to a violent halt in

February 1850 when Irish laborers, recruited for the back-breaking heavy work, struck after repeated clashes with native American workers. Anti-Irish sentiment was rife throughout the nation as crop failures in Ireland drove millions of Irish to the United States, where in many instances they displaced local workers, especially in unskilled jobs. On February 27 Edward Miller, in charge of the western division, reported to the board that the Irish were rioting all along the road. Although they were soon persuaded to return to their jobs, they struck again before the end of May. This time Miller secured a bench warrant empowering the Greensburg sheriff to clear the strikers from company property. Rampant violence and property damage continued until mid-June when, as Patterson delicately informed the stockholders, "admirable police arrangements made under the sanction of the Board [but not recorded in its minutes] by Edward Miller, Esq.," led to the eviction of the striking Irish and the employment of a new force; undoubtedly Thomson, who viewed labor as simply another commodity to be purchased at the lowest possible price in the open market, concurred with his action. Patterson warned that if there were any repetition of such problems, "a firm local judiciary and a reliable military force are ready to assert the supremacy of the law promptly and effectively."[25]

At the height of the strike, Thomson was trying to find the money to bridge the troublesome mountain gap. The chronic treasury shortage that played havoc with his construction schedules, forcing him at times to even cease work in mid-contract, finally caused him to change his mind about the proper way to finance railroads. He reversed his former position and suggested to his directors that if they did not resort to debt financing, he could only let the lightest contracts in the mountains. Since he knew that his advice was not likely to be followed, he also proposed that the board petition the Philadelphia councils for a further subscription of $1 million. The directors, however, preferred to rely upon a blue-ribbon committee of 100 citizens they had formed to drum up new subscriptions. By July it had raised slightly over $1 million, but almost all of that was pledged to finish the work on the western division; Thomson was allotted only $86,000 for lettings on the mountain division.

It was not enough. He wrote director David Brown in October, "you will perceive that our engagements are considerably in advance of our means." At year's end the board, still not convinced that floating a bond issue was prudent, asked the legislature to subscribe to 40,000 shares of PRR stock to be paid for with 5 percent state bonds. The directors pointed out the rapid progress of rival companies; the entire route of the B&O was under contract, financed in large part by a $4 million Baltimore subscription, and the Erie Railroad was rushing under a deadline to reach Lake Erie in 1851 before it lost $3.75 million in subscriptions. Since Pennsylvania had been forced to default on its obligation in 1842 after overextending itself to pay for the state works, the politicians predictably did not risk repeating the experience. The board had passed the resolution mainly to impress upon its stockholders the serious need for funds.[26]

Always the bearer of bad financial news, Thomson wished his directors a happy new year in 1851 with the information that the work was slowed on the western division due to a labor shortage, and construction costs were higher than expected, thanks to the 3,700-foot tunnel at the summit of Allegheny Mountain that he had put under contract. Digging in the bore was hard, as water continually poured in, and the rock proved to be unstable and in need of heavy shoring. But Thomson had to start the work to make certain that it would be ready when the rest of the road was finished over the mountains.[27]

Forced to postpone contract lettings on the mountain division, Thomson also slowed the work elsewhere to stretch available monies. He was obviously chafing at the treasury's restraints just when he could see an end to the major construction. His board was questioning closely his every estimate, which irritated him, especially since the cost of the whole eastern division was only $10,000 more than his preliminary estimate. When Patterson raised his eyebrows at one projected outlay, Thomson grew testy: "I believe that my estimates in aggregate have not led the Board astray—," he asserted, "and I trust that in their present form they will be deemed satisfactory." By late spring 1851 he was tired and ill-humored when he left to spend a month in Georgia. Upon his return he stayed out on the road for most of the summer; in September he spent all but one week along the line inspecting the construction. On the way back to his office in Harrisburg on October 1, the weary Thomson was again thinking of resigning. "I felt strongly disposed to say to James [Grant] that I would go to his road [N&C]—;" he wrote Grant, "but the inducement offered was not sufficient to make me pull up stakes." Besides, he was making progress. At the end of the year he had opened fifty-seven miles on the western division, leaving only a twenty-eight-mile gap to connect Harrisburg and Pittsburgh via the Portage. A finished railroad was tantalizingly close.[28]

While Thomson maintained his furious pace that fall, the board was becoming desperate. Although it reported to its stockholders that year that it had a $125,000 surplus in the till, the treasurer informed the directors privately at their first meeting in 1852 that the road actually had a deficit of about $150,000.[29] Patterson and the board blamed "the instability of money markets" for their lack of funds, but by 1852 the board plainly was no longer able to efficiently conduct the business of the company. Its part-time directors could neither afford the lengthening amounts of time required nor master the intricacies of the increasingly complex railway business. The steadily growing pressures were clearly evident in the large turnover among board members; by January 1, 1853, eleven of the original thirteen members had left. With such instability, the board was unable to maintain its continuity, preserve its ostensible powers, or execute them effectively.[30]

Aggravating matters was a complicated behind-the-scenes struggle for control of the road. Its outcome catapulted Thomson into the presidency and initiated a managerial trend that profoundly affected the governance of the corporation for more than a century. The struggle was caused by the serious personality conflicts, the ill-defined chain of command, the financing disputes, and the difficulties of a Philadelphia board trying to operate by mail a railroad headquartered in Harrisburg. As long as the line remained in its formative stages, the organization could and did remain rather informal, dependent upon personalities rather than rigid regulations. When sections of the road were opened in 1849, however, requiring delicate cooperation with the state commissioners, the operation of a transportation department, and the continuance of westward construction, the directors discovered that they had some new and very complex problems on their hands. These difficulties acted as a catalyst that ultimately forced a public confrontation between the badly divided board and the executive officers of the company.

Prior to the opening of the first segment of line, Thomson was undoubtedly the most important official on the road, as the board recognized by the authority it granted to him. But from the first, Thomson had clashed repeatedly with Merrick. His right to attend board meetings, even without a vote, enabled him to argue personally for his policies and often to win the support of the road committee, whose functions were ill-defined and whose authority overlapped both Merrick's and Thomson's. Moreover, Thomson's frequent access to board members, both officially and privately, led to the development of factions within the board that eventually hardened into two antagonistic groups revolving around the president and chief engineer.

The denouement began in February 1849 when Haupt indicated that he expected to be accorded the right to attend the board's sessions. In this he was rudely jolted when he was unceremoniously asked to leave his first meeting. Further complicating the organizational structure was the fact that Haupt also refused to recognize the authority of the president, but unlike Thomson, Haupt directly challenged Patterson. When the latter gave him a direct order, Haupt denied in writing that the president had the "right to *command*." The board cleared this matter up with unaccustomed rapidity by passing a resolution ordering "the General Superintendent be informed that the Board expect from him a compliance with the instructions of the President." While this clarified Haupt's accountability to the president, it pointedly excluded the chief engineer from the same "compliance," and Thomson continued to sit with the board whenever he was in town.[31]

In the fall of 1851, the severe personality conflicts brought many of the road's underlying organizational problems into sharp focus. A special board committee chaired by Merrick, who was still determined to oust Haupt and thereby embarrass Thomson, laid a report before the directors charging Haupt with insubordination. In sixteen meetings over the next three and one-half months, the board demonstrated its inability to deal with both the personnel questions it confronted and the more important underlying problem of internal accountability. In rapid succession the directors allowed Haupt to present his defense, heard Merrick's rebuttal, voted six to five to sustain Haupt, refused to accept the resignations of Merrick, Patterson, and their two permanent allies on the board, and in a turnabout, voted Haupt's ouster by eight to three, then finally by a tally of six to five, asked Haupt to continue! All this feverish activity divided the board into three factions—the four members of the Merrick-Patterson clique; three members staunchly allied with Thomson and Haupt; and four formally uncommitted members, one of whom usually sided with the former group and three of whom tended toward the Thomson camp. By December 1851, the board was paralyzed by internal dissension. Moreover, someone leaked the whole imbroglio to the press, and the January 3, 1852 edition of the Philadelphia *Evening Bulletin* carried copies of the committee's charges against Haupt, his defense, and an acrimonious exchange of letters between Haupt and Merrick.[32]

The publicity accompanying the board fight tended to explain the altercation solely in terms of personalities, which masked the more serious implications of the quarrel for the future of the road. Ironically, in light of Thomson's later career, he and Haupt championed the prerogatives of the board. Haupt had succinctly stated their position in his defense before the board when he pointed out that they "derived their powers not from the President immediately but from the Board." Only after the general superintendent was forced to acknowledge the authority of the president (and Thomson could not have been unmindful of the implications this held for his own position) was a clear separation forced between the stockholders' elected representatives and the professional managers operating the property. Patterson, who did not know a boiler flue from a fishplate, was thereby placed in the unenviable position of having to rely on experts who were personally antagonistic to him to operate the road and on the support of a badly divided board to sustain his own position. The instability and vulnerability of the entire corporate organization was starkly apparent to all by January 1852.[33]

With the board torn by internal altercations and the company's financial situation precarious, supporters of Thomson and Haupt began to hold regular meetings at director George Howell's store at Ninth and Chestnut Streets. Christian Spangler, Washington Butcher, and occasionally other board members met with important PRR stockholders to plot strategy. They finally determined to run an opposition slate of directors at the next annual meeting, headed by

Thomson, their choice for the road's presidency. Thomson did not attend any of the gatherings, but he undoubtedly knew of them, for Haupt was conspicuously active in their deliberations. The "conspirators" selected Spangler and Haupt to meet with the chief engineer to convince him to make the race.

They located Thomson late in 1851 out on the western division and brought him back to John Wright's house at Freedom Forges near Lewistown. Haupt later related that Thomson was extremely reluctant to challenge Patterson at the annual election, fearing that if he lost he would have to resign as chief engineer, which would "seriously effect [sic] his position and prospects." After badgering Thomson all night and carefully explaining to him that Patterson and Merrick commanded only the support of Philadelphia's silk-stocking aristocracy, and arguing that Thomson would appeal "to the workers, the solid business men, and the commissioners of the districts," Thomson finally gave his "reluctant consent." Undoubtedly, Thomson did hesitate—that was his manner. He rarely jumped boldly into anything without first considering the full ramifications of his actions. That he was afraid of losing his job if he lost seems doubtful. For almost five years he had considered leaving the company; just three months earlier he had again entertained the idea. A position for him as chief engineer on the N&C was still available. What probably made Thomson wary of the proposition was his fear of losing. To resign to take another position was one thing; to quit after failing to oust incumbent directors was quite another.[34]

He was ambitious enough, however, to see that standing for the road's presidency would be a major turning point in his career. His tenure on the Georgia Railroad had taught him that once a railroad was constructed, the chief engineer ceased to be its most important corporate officer; he became simply a technical overseer. With the PRR on the brink of completion, Thomson undoubtedly realized that his value to the board would soon plummet. In all probability he would leave for employment on another road, once again repeating the endless cycle of bickering with contractors, wooing board members, and bustling up and down the line prodding the workers, a routine he was beginning to find distasteful. While the presidency would also involve him in routine, at least it would be new routine and would offer him an opportunity to widen his professional horizons into broad areas of finance, strategy, and the law. The job's contacts and prestige would also expand and enhance his personal speculations. Furthermore, he would be at least one level removed from the tiresome daily management of the line. Haupt's comment, however, that only after he and Spangler convinced Thomson that he had a good chance to win would he "reluctantly consent" to make the race, was the most revealing.

"The City of Philadelphia," Haupt remembered, "could not have been more exercised by a National Election."[35] The campaign waged in the newspapers throughout January 1852, turned primarily upon which side was responsible for the dissension on the board. The only other issues to creep in were a charge by Merrick that Haupt, and by implication, Thomson, had personally profited from his affiliation with the railroad and the question of whether the company should issue bonds. Specifically, Merrick accused Haupt of seeking preferential rates for hauling lumber from his timberlands located near the road at Clearfield. In a letter to the newspapers, Haupt, undoubtedly speaking for Thomson as well, firmly upheld his right to speculate in whatever property he wished, but he drew a strong distinction between his private affairs and professional position. "If while holding office on the road, I should sell timber from my own lands to the company, even at lower rates than it could be procured elsewhere," Haupt explained to the shareholders, "I would commit an act which, although often done under similar circumstances, and considered proper, my own convictions of duty and self-respect would not allow me to approve." When their Clearfield Company began operations, Haupt ordered the road's employees not to purchase any timber from the concern. Neither was its lumber accorded preferential rates on the PRR; Thomson's personal ethics would not permit it.[36]

Many stockholders who followed the exchange in the newspapers between Merrick and Haupt suspected that there must be some truth to the allegations. These widespread suspicions partially obscured a fundamental policy decision that had to be made quickly—how to raise enough funds to keep the construction going. Thomson advocated floating a bond issue to finance construction on the mountain division. In a lengthy newspaper advertisement the morning of the election, he suggested the question be brought before the stockholders for resolution, indicating that the board's present course would eventually make a bond issue mandatory anyway. Privately, he was telling his supporters that the road's treasury, instead of having $125,000 on hand, had at least a $500,000 deficit, a subtle way of accusing Patterson of juggling the books to put the best face possible on his policy of relying upon stock subscriptions. The public debate was so emotionally charged and the problem of the bonds so dull by comparison, that the issue did not figure prominently in the election's final outcome.[37]

The labyrinthine behind-the-scenes politics were more important. The night before the election, a group of prominent supporters met with Thomson and convinced him that Haupt was endangering the ticket. Behind the move was James Magee, a former member of the board, a large shareholder, and a fellow investor with Thomson in his new lumber and coal schemes. Magee wanted a relative of his to have Haupt's job. Thomson called Haupt in and explained the situation. Haupt agreed that Thomson could publish his resignation if Thomson saw fit. The next morning Thomson craftily published a note that Haupt would not be a candidate for "reelection." Since Haupt was not elected in the first place, the notice was misleading, but it compromised Haupt's future with the company. That same evening in Spring Garden where the commissioners were instructed to vote for Thomson, the Merrick-Patterson forces sought a meeting with them to change their minds. Thomson's supporters rounded up all the commissioners they could find, locked them in an empty apartment, and provided them "with creature comforts" until morning.[38]

On February 2, 1852, PRR stockholders met and balloted. The returns gave the Thomson slate control of the new board. Patterson and Merrick both lost their seats, drawing only 22,000 votes to Thomson's 30,000. Interestingly, Brown and Thomas Lea, fervent Patterson and Merrick supporters, led all returning members with 46,000 votes. Both men, however, seeing that their influence on the new board would be nil, resigned two days later.

As was the board's custom when the directors met for the first time, the candidate for president remained outside the room. On February 3, with Thomson standing in the hall, the new board unanimously selected him as the Pennsylvania Railroad's third president. They bade him enter and offered congratulations all around. Thomson took his chair at the head of the table and called the meeting to order. A new era was about to begin.[39]

5

TRUNK LINE MASTERY

Thomson's assumption of the post he was to hold for the remainder of his life marked an important turning point in the Pennsylvania Railroad's fortunes. Over the next twenty-two years he came to personify the company; Thomson created a personal fiefdom, a business empire he ruled with paternalistic devotion. The measure of corporate democracy, so carefully delineated in the company's 1846 charter, whereby fundamental powers flowed from the stockholders through their directors to the road's managers, was reversed. By the Civil War, Thomson held the reins of power, and authority flowed downward from his office to the owners. The thousands of stockholders acquiesced because Thomson gave them exactly what they wanted—high stock values and an almost uninterrupted flow of healthy dividends.

The stockholders unwittingly abetted their own demise in the board election of 1852. When they chose Thomson and his slate of directors, they departed from earlier precedent and voted in a man who was primarily beholden not to the well-being of the Philadelphia mercantile community, but to the welfare of the railroad. They selected a professional manager, not a spokesman; the means had become the ends. In his search for more business, Thomson often made policy decisions inimical to the interests of the city that had given birth to his corporation. He never felt it necessary to apologize, because he assumed that his road's prosperity always redounded to the advantage of the port city. It was basically a matter of priorities.

The new president did not set out in 1852 to usurp the prerogatives of the stockholders and directors; their decline proceeded slowly. Possessed of consummate self-confidence bolstered by long experience,

Master of the Pennsylvania Railroad on the eve of the Civil War. Courtesy of the Division of Archives and Manuscripts, Pennsylvania Historical and Museum Commission, Harrisburg, Pennsylvania.

Thomson knew what he wanted to do—complete the road to Pittsburgh to rid himself of the canal commissioners' constant interference. Moreover, fifteen years earlier he had recognized the West as the source of future profits, and he wanted the Pennsylvania Railroad to be the first to tap that bonanza. To do that he was willing to stretch the company's resources to their limits and oppose the parochialism of stockholders, board members, state politicians, and Philadelphia businessmen.

In his untiring efforts to strengthen his road, Thomson increasingly relied on his own judgment. Although never independent of the board or stockholders, he increasingly bypassed both in the 1850s, as indicated by the progressive infrequency of board meetings. In his first year as president, when he needed the board's sanction for floating large loans to finish construction, the directors convened a record seventy-one times. Each year thereafter the board had fewer meetings except in the panic year of 1857. By the end of the decade the board was assembling only thirty times a year; when Thomson was at the height of his power in 1872, it met only sixteen times and he missed six.[1]

The minutes of those meetings are also revealing. After Thomson's first year in office, full and open board discussions gradually diminished, fewer formal votes were taken, and the importance of the standing board committees declined. The directors achieved unanimity on policy questions more often and the minutes reflected this agreement with their increasing terseness. His gathering of the reins of power was barely perceptible to the directors and all but unnoticed by the road's stockholders, who learned of their company's affairs only through Thomson's annual reports. In the mid-1850s it became standard practice for the board to refer questions to Thomson for action. Not surprisingly, this trend started with small matters, much of it the irritating detail that inevitably found its way to the board, but by the eve of the Civil War, even strategic policy matters were often left to Thomson's discretion. While he decided the important issues, the directors handled the inconsequential details. The minutes reveal an "Alice-in-Wonderland" situation in which the board regularly approved expenditures of millions of dollars without a formal vote, while the august directors heatedly debated a $100 donation to the Altoona YMCA, the gift of a lot to a Baptist church, and an endless number of other "gratuities." With the board immersed in trivialities, Thomson exercised his responsibilities as he saw fit.[2]

Loyalty to the president became a key to success in the managerial ranks and quelled possible dissatisfaction from that quarter. More-over, Thomson was in an unique position to promote such allegiance from the first; empowered to staff the engineering and transportation departments, he gathered a group of talented and ambitious men about him, many of whom spent their entire careers with the company. While president he established the policy, which survived long into the twentieth century, of promoting from within; but he was not looking for lackeys. The men he groomed for the front office were an uncommonly strong-willed lot. Except for Henry Foster, all of Thomson's possible corporate heirs were at least a decade younger than he. Scott was the only important officer on the road over fifty years old when Thomson died. A whole executive generation was missing, and its absence was not the accident of war or premature deaths. It simply was never there. Thomson, in more than one respect was the "old man" of the company, but his knack for spotting and pro-moting young talent was more than repaid by their unswerving fidel-ity to him and his policies.

With loyal subordinates, an agreeable directorate, and quiescent stockholders, Thomson by the late 1850s was free to manage the Pennsylvania much as he wished. As long as he did not grievously miscalculate and threaten the company's financial stability, his position was secure. And Thomson was not the type of man to make such errors. His quiet deliberate style inspired confidence and helped him to avoid potentially fatal, rash mistakes. His manner overlaid his obsession with work and his attention to detail, which encouraged the board to delegate to him the more important problems. Moreover, he had the unmistakable advantage of experience; where his predeces-sors had had to rely upon him for advice, particularly on technical and contractual matters, Thomson could draw upon his own resources. Surveying, construction, purchasing, equipment design, transporting, rates, finance, labor, and corporate politics had all been his lifeblood since 1836. He was familiar with practices on other roads and kept the monthly tonnage and income figures for the B&O, the Erie, and the New York Central (NYC) at his fingertips for comparison with his road's performance.

Thomson was not without his liabilities, however. He was a poor presidential choice for a company that required numerous legislative and political favors. He simply was not a political man and knew it;

fundamentally, he had no respect for politicians. He once sent a revealing telegram to John W. Garrett, president of the B&O, that read in its entirety, "the position referred to within will never be admitted, and is too ridiculous for a Rail Road Man to advocate—It may do for a politician to maintain—." At first, Thomson, like Merrick and Patterson before him, personally handled the lobbying chores at Harrisburg, but finding that he despised the constant beseeching and resenting the inordinate drain on his time, he soon delegated political responsibilities to his vice president. Henry Foster and later Scott, enjoyed the give and take of the political arena where they achieved great successes. Scott raised legislative manipulation to the status of an art, and for over two decades the Pennsylvania Railroad reigned supreme in state politics, further securing Thomson's position in the company.[3]

Merrick's and Patterson's public opposition to Thomson served to make him unpopular with Philadelphia's leading mercantile figures. Thomson could do little to ingratiate himself with such influential men, for both former presidents remained popular figures in city politics. Instead, Thomson cultivated the city's industrial leaders, many of whom sold their products to the Pennsylvania Railroad; they were Philadelphia's *nouveau riche* on the verge of supplanting the established mercantile order. Furthermore, thanks to the wealth and power of his corporation by the late 1850s, Thomson was a leading state and regional figure. As Pennsylvania's largest employer, with almost 5,000 employees scattered across the state on the eve of the war, and with millions of dollars flowing annually into the company's coffers, he could not be easily ignored. He never openly challenged the Quaker City's merchant denizens; he overshadowed them.

The new president's rather grim public visage and lack of spontaneity, gregariousness, charm, and humor, were not obvious assets either. If the road's highest office had been a popularity contest, Thomson would have remained chief engineer forever; but he managed to turn his sober demeanor to his advantage. The press portrayed him as the thoughtful man with a steady hand on the corporate helm. The Pennsylvania Railroad became the stolid corporate maiden of the Northeast largely through its identification with his personal qualities. Thomson used Scott for the necessary glad-handing and back-slapping. Quick-witted, dapper, handsome, and well-met, he was perfect as Thomson's *alter ego*. Each provided what the other lacked, and the combination of reserve and brashness, caution and daring, practicality and imagination, proved a potent management team.[4]

Thomson's prewar mastery of the Pennsylvania Railroad was unique. The legendary railroad "barons," such as the Vanderbilts, Goulds, Huntington, and Harriman, dominated the heady postwar years. They obtained their licenses to rule through ownership, while Thomson consolidated his position without a significant holding in his own road; at his death he owned only 1,400 shares. He foreshadowed a later trend in which railway operation was divorced from ownership. He rose to power on the Pennsylvania by reason of his professional skills and wide experience, which combined to serve his company well. Because the Pennsylvania underwent the managerial revolution earlier than other major roads, the company avoided the unsettling postwar financial manipulations that plagued eastern lines. Although Thomson ruled at the expense of the stockholders' prerogatives, he used his power to create what later became "the Standard Railroad of the World," paying substantial regular dividends, pioneering technological improvements, and providing the public with standards of comfort and dependability that ranked with those offered anywhere on the globe.

His railway was not even finished, however, in 1852, and Thomson's election as president did not magically conjure up the badly needed funds to complete the mountain division. With an empty treasury, he confronted a pile of unpaid bills almost as high as the Allegheny Mountain he was trying to tunnel. Thomson moved quickly; he was a veritable whirlwind during his first three months in office, dashing off to Harrisburg to oversee the legislative campaign to allow the company to increase its stock offerings, chairing public meetings to drum up support for raising over $200,000 he needed to collect Philadelphia's and Northern Liberties' conditional subscriptions, and making arrangements to offer a bond issue. He qualified for the conditional subscriptions by strong arming acquaintances to buy stock; Thomson signed Bell up for $10,000 of the road's securities, reminding the Huntingdon banker that the Pennsylvania passed a lot of business his way. Thomson bought over $26,000 worth on his own account, and as he tactfully phrased it, "have got friends since to relieve me of most of it." By the end of his first month in office he had promoted over $200,000 in stock sales and confidently wrote Bell, "we begin to look out of the woods now."[5]

The legislature finally allowed the Pennsylvania Railroad to issue an additional 80,000 shares of stock, but Thomson was under no illusion that the new offering would sell well enough to meet the company's heavy needs. Accordingly, he called a stockholders' meeting on April 5 at which they voted to authorize the sale of bonds. To enhance their attractiveness, particularly in England, the bonds were convertible to capital stock any time before December 1, 1860. Three million dollars worth were marketed on September 16, 1852, and they sold very fast at slightly above 103.[6] In fact the bonds were selling so well that by October the board was debating how to collect interest on the money pouring into the treasury. That happy state of affairs, however, was short-lived. Eight months later high construction expenses and the cost of aiding midwestern feeder roads had seriously depleted the surplus. Worse, the Crimean War unsettled American money markets, and domestic bond sales fell to almost nothing.[7]

Undaunted, Thomson sailed September 7, 1853 with $1 million in securities for England where he found that English investors, worried over the crop situation and the bullion drain from the Bank of England, were contracting American investments. Thomson went to the Barings and Rothschilds, who offered to sell his bonds for a 1 percent commision and a brokerage fee, but he refused, and instead placed as many bonds as he could with smaller brokerage houses in London and Paris. When he returned in late October, he had sold less than one-third of the bonds with only $36,000 paid in; a few went for as low as 90 in London.[8]

The Pennsylvania's business was booming by 1853, and the road desperately needed additional equipment and a double track to handle the heavy traffic. Improvements were prohibitively expensive, and as the remainder of the company's first mortgage bonds moved fitfully on domestic and foreign markets, Thomson secured legislative authorization for a new $5 million second mortgage. The bond markets were so bad by the time the issue was prepared for sale on June 1, 1854, however, that Thomson withheld it and resorted to short-term borrowing to meet the road's bills payable. Finally, in August he ordered the new chief engineer, Haupt, to make no more contracts and to curtail those already underway.[9]

The pace took its toll, and by 1855 Thomson was clearly tired. He had wrestled with the road's interminable financial problems, pushed the construction, carried the company's political responsibilities, dispatched a mass of daily minutiae all without a rest. Moreover, he had just married. True to form, Thomson married within the Pennsylvania Railroad's family. His bride, Lavinia Francis Smith, at twenty-nine, was a full twenty-one years his junior. Descended from old Connecticut stock but raised in Fishkill-On-The-Hudson, her older sister, Elizabeth, was Henry Foster's wife. Vice-president Foster introduced Thomson to his young sister-in-law in the late 1840s, and their friendship undoubtedly blossomed slowly. Deliberate as always, Thomson postponed going up to Fishkill to marry her until 1854. From all outward signs, however, it was a happy union. As one of five children, she brought Thomson for the first time in two decades a close family. Interestingly, like Thomson's own, it was predominantly female: Lavinia's mother, who lived to be eighty-eight years old, her three sisters, and a lone brother. Thomson's brother, Levis, had died earlier, so he had only two unmarried sisters remaining in his own family. Moreover, in a tragic series of circumstances, the entire Foster family save one, died within four years, and Foster's orphaned daughter, Charlotte Francis, came to live with the Thomsons in 1860. Thomson treated her as his own child, loved her dearly, adopted her on his deathbed, and provided for her future financial needs.

For the first time since he was nineteen, Thomson enjoyed the protracted companionship of his own family by combining business with pleasure in an 1855 European sojourn. He sailed on June 15 with Lavinia, her sister Christina, and his sister Adeline, and remained abroad for almost four and one-half months, a sharp contrast to his earlier flying seven-week voyage. They landed in Liverpool and went directly to London where Thomson tried to place his bonds. The party then leisurely toured England and Scotland until September when they crossed the channel to Paris. Thomson brought an official commission from Pennsylvania's Governor Pollard appointing him that state's representative to the Paris Exposition, but he also took the occasion to make the rounds of the city's financial institutions. After a hasty look at continental life, Thomson returned home, renewed in body and spirit, to resume the daily challenge of managing one of the largest corporations in the world. His European bond sales were so poor that he did not even bother to draw up a written report of his activities for his board.[10]

Luckily, Thomson was not as desperate for capital as he had been; the road was completed from Harrisburg to Pittsburgh. The troublesome Allegheny Mountain tunnel shafts had been joined in 1853, and the bore was opened for regular business the next February, at once rendering the Portage unnecessary. Thomson had located and built a 245-mile main line with 136 miles of double track that cost, exclusive of equipment and interest charges, $10,801,917. That sum was $2 million over his 1848 estimate due largely to unforeseen difficulties in digging the tunnel and the heavier-than-expected excavations on the western division. Nevertheless, the road was substantially constructed and located with such skill that more than 125 years later, trains still rumble over Thomson's roadbed.

The most famous and picturesque attraction of the finished road was Thomson's Horseshoe Curve west of Altoona, an engineering feat of no mean proportions. The sweeping, almost two-mile-long curve, really a switchback to enable locomotives to pull heavier loads up the Alleghenies, remains a monument to Thomson's engineering genius and stubborn determination to achieve quality at almost any effort. Always a believer that the best road was one with the easiest grades, he spent scarce construction funds in order to save money later. Almost fifty years after, Haupt clearly remembered that "more than a dozen lines were required to be run at the Horseshoe Curve to equalize gradients before the final location was decided upon." It is an engineering feat that boggles the imagination; Thomson ran his rails into a valley and then back out again to gain distance to achieve higher elevations with acceptable grades. In the process his crews hacked out ledges along two mountains and dug and transported millions of cubic feet of fill dirt to build up the roadbed across two valleys. The result was not only an engineering triumph that saved the road millions of dollars in transport costs over the years, but a vista of awesome beauty visited by thousands of people every year. The man had an imagination, one that operated on a grand scale to conceive the idea of the curve; it may be the only accomplishment for which he is remembered by most people, but it certainly is a worthy one.[11]

Such technical sophistication helped the Pennsylvania to show a profit from its opening that eased Thomson's consolidation of power within the corporation. The road's net profits increased rapidly from only $167,208 in 1850 to almost $2.3 million ten years later. The preponderance of traffic on the road flowed west to east resulting in inefficient equipment utilization, but the higher eastbound rates more than compensated for the cheap "backhauls" from Philadelphia. The road's operating ratio, the expenses of running the line as a proportion of gross income, remained in the 50 percent range, average for a well-run railway in the mid-nineteenth century. Thomson had no trouble keeping his stockholders happy with regular dividends although they remained modest, in the 6 to 8 percent range, until 1862 when the glut of wartime profits left Thomson's treasury awash in undistributed cash. Had he been willing to defer maintenance, he could have increased them earlier, but Thomson, the engineer, would have skipped dividends until the shareholders threw him out before he would have operated a property of which he could not be proud.[12]

More than most railway presidents, Thomson took a consuming interest in the physical condition of his line that made it one of the best maintained railroads in the world. He was also always on the lookout for new ideas and improvements. He was one of the first railway executives in the nation to investigate substituting coal for wood in his locomotives. He was amazed that his road consumed 60,000 cords of wood a year, and as supplies of standing timber along the line were rapidly depleted he sought alternatives. While in England in 1855 he met William Palmer, who was there reporting on coke manufacturing processes for an American trade journal. Thomson immediately saw the possibility of using coke in his locomotives and hinted to Palmer that there might be a job for him on the Pennsylvania when he returned home. Thomson already had his engineers testing bituminous coal and coke on two locomotives, and by 1857 he was convinced that they were more efficient and strewed the countryside and passengers with far fewer sparks and cinders than the woodburning variety. Later that year Thomson hired Palmer as his private secretary, paying his $900 yearly salary from his own pocket. He also gave him the responsibility for supervising the coal tests.[13]

Within twelve months Palmer had developed a coal firebox with a five-year life expectancy and was experimenting with a "smoke consuming" contraption. It worked to his satisfaction and claiming fuel savings of 50 percent for the coalburners, he invited his president to view the results. Thomson made a holiday out of the excursion, riding out with his family in a special car to cross Allegheny Mountain behind a coal-burning engine. They went up to cool Cresson in mid-July where, as Palmer described, they "partook of an excellent dinner, rolled a couple of games of tenpins, drank from a spring of mountain water as pure and cold as I have ever tasted," and then rode to the tunnel. Thomson was in an expansive mood, for he allowed "the ladies" to ride on the locomotive through the tunnel and down the other side for a better view. He was also suitably impressed; he ordered all passenger locomotives equipped with the new coal fireboxes and "smoke consuming" devices. By 1860 freight engines were being equipped as well for coal, each saving the company six cents per mile. Thomson's Pennsylvania was well on its way to becoming the first American railway to abandon wood as a fuel; by 1865 all of the company's locomotives had been converted to coal.[14]

Thomson was also quick to adopt, often at great expense, promising inventions developed elsewhere. A prime example was the Loughridge braking system. Prior to its introduction, brakemen stopped trains on signal from the engineer by running along the tops of cars and manually turning down the brakes on each. Although improvements were made during the decade of the 1850s, the inability to stop a train easily restricted both its length and speed. Loughridge invented a mechanical braking system that enabled the engineer from his locomotive to set the brakes on all cars at the same time. Although stopping was not as instantaneous as it became after Westinghouse's air brake was proven on Thomson's road, it was far faster than any other system then devised. Thomson was so satisfied with the system's performance that he had all his road's passenger cars equipped with it by the end of 1859, allowing faster express trains while providing travelers with a greater margin of safety.[15]

The superb physical facilities and strong financial position of Thomson's Pennsylvania strengthened his road's competitive position in the East. When he assumed the presidency his major rivals, the NYC, Erie, and B&O stood on the verge of completing their lines to the Great Lakes and Ohio Valley. From there the race was on for the prized western connections, Chicago to the north, and Cincinnati and St. Louis to the south. The road that secured links to these cities first stood to control the trade of the rapidly developing upper midwestern states of Indiana, Illinois, Michigan, Wisconsin, and Iowa and of the Mississippi River; the potential value of these strategic prizes was enormous.

In the early 1850s, Thomson's road suffered geographical disadvantages. Wedged between competitors to the north and south, the New York roads anticipated easier routes across northern Ohio and Indiana into Chicago, while the B&O, finished to Wheeling, Virginia, was in a better position to cross southern Ohio, Indiana, and Illinois to the river cities. If Thomson's competitors pressed their advantages, the Pennsylvania would be left with only the central routes reaching out to the less important inland cities such as Columbus, Indianapolis, and Springfield. Complicating the Ohio railroad situation was the fact that it was exceedingly fluid; no local lines dominated the state's transportation network. But none of the eastern trunk lines could afford delay; they had to invest in speculative Ohio railways if only to keep them out of competitors' hands.

By 1852, Thomson was convinced that he could hesitate no longer. Several important Ohio roads were in financial difficulties, and, if he could raise the funds to bail them out, he stood to gain their good will and, more importantly, a voice in their councils. As was his wont, once Thomson made up his mind, he moved. With an unfinished road and facing huge expenditures for double tracking, he invested well over $1 million in western railways. His impetuosity irritated some conservative stockholders who believed that when the Pennsylvania reached Pittsburgh it was finished, but they failed to realize that their corporation was assuming a life of its own. Thomson wanted the Ohio rail map to conform as closely as possible to his own strategic desires. He knew that the Ohio roads were simply a means to greater ends— the control of the Mississippi Valley trade and ultimately that of the Pacific coast. Thomson, however, was caught in the web of his own reasoning. Believing that no road could long remain profitable depending upon local trade, he was forced constantly to expand; his terminus always had to be on the cutting edge of the commercial frontier as it relentlessly moved west. As he never tired of telling Lavinia, "we cannot stand still for that means slipping back, we must constantly go forward." Had he lived long enough he undoubtedly would have shared Edward H. Harriman's dream at the turn of the twentieth century of girdling the globe with his own rails.[16]

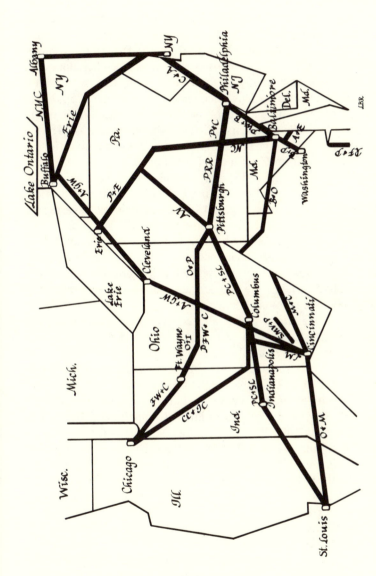

2. Thomson's East: The Pennsylvania and Ohio Railroads (the Midwest Roads).

Thomson's initial efforts in 1852 were more modest, however. Strategically, he envisioned the possibility of acquiring connections to Chicago and Cincinnati. Of the two routes, he found the Chicago line potentially the most important, and he pushed hard for its completion. The connection was composed of three independent lines, and Thomson invested in all of them for his PRR. Only four months after taking office he persuaded his stockholders to subscribe $150,000 to the stock of the Ohio and Pennsylvania to run from Pittsburgh to Crestline, Ohio. Having taken the first step, he pushed hard and by the end of the year had wrung a subscription of double that amount for the Ohio & Indiana from Crestline to Fort Wayne.

Money was tight in 1853, and late that year, the O&I was in trouble. When that road's officers appealed to Thomson for more help, he sent Haupt out to inspect it. The chief engineer suggested the Pennsylvania invest $737,000 to complete the O&I and to aid the Ft. Wayne and Chicago Railroad, its extension to the "Windy City." Haupt's report, however, could not have come at a worse moment. The Pennsylvania's second mortgage bonds were not selling, and Thomson had curtailed the double tracking; the directors refused to support Haupt's recommendations.[17]

The board's failure to act jeopardized its existing investments. The NYC had gained access to Cleveland by 1856 and was pushing west just when the Pennsylvania's three Ohio allies collapsed. Thomson pressured them to consolidate into a single company by threatening to deny further help unless they complied. He voted the Pennsylvania's stock in the June elections for consolidation and when the new Pittsburgh, Ft. Wayne & Chicago Railroad Company (PFW&C) was incorporated on July 28, 1856, he was elected a director. He advanced it another $100,000 from the Pennsylvania's treasury; and the Fort Wayne, by extending its own indebtedness, pushed its tracks to Plymouth, Indiana, but staggering under a huge load of financial obligations, the enterprise was driven to the very edge of bankruptcy by the 1857 panic.[18]

Thomson saw that if his road wanted to keep its vital western connection, he would have to take hold of the work personally. On January 5, 1858, he had himself elected the Fort Wayne's chief engineer, promising to complete the remaining eighty-two miles to Chicago if the company turned over to him all its assets for his use to further the work. The formal agreement was signed on April 13 and amounted to a takeover of the midwestern line. Thomson then hastened to arrange new real estate and construction bond issues to raise badly needed cash. The road's securities were not very attractive, so he eased out the road's president, George Washington Cass, and assumed the added responsibilities of the job himself. Thomson's name and the gradual easing of money markets led to the slow appreciation of the company's securities. In addition, Thomson could not resist a little speculation on his own account. When contractors who had accepted the Fort Wayne's bonds in partial payment needed working capital, Thomson began buying them at a 50 percent discount. He also purchased some bonds to carry the work and the extent of his liability was illustrated in 1862 when his board awarded him $47,000 as compensation for pledging his personal credit to the road. He provided contractors with working capital, and the news that he was buying for his own account probably enticed other investors to do likewise. On Christmas day, 1858, the inaugural run was made between Philadelphia and Chicago. Having discharged his obligations and sold his bonds at a profit, Thomson appointed a Pennsylvania Railroad engineer, T. Haskins DuPuy, as "acting president" of the Fort Wayne.[19]

At Thomson's moment of victory, however, the midwestern road was near collapse. With a debt too large to be maintained from declining revenues caused by eastern rate wars, the company entered receivership on December 7, 1859. A protracted fight for control ensued between its principal creditors; only the intervention of New York corporate lawyer and later Democratic presidential nominee, Samuel Tilden, brought about a settlement. Five men, appointed by the road's bondholders, purchased the railroad at a foreclosure sale in October 1861. Thomson had resigned the Fort Wayne's presidency in March 1860, and Cass, elected a director of the Pennsylvania in 1859, reassumed his former position. Since the PRR held less than 20 percent of the midwestern company's stock, Cass was important for maintaining friendly relations with the feeder road. The crush of Civil War traffic brought undreamed of profits into the Fort Wayne's starved till, and Cass wisely plowed much of the money back into the property and reduced its debt load. The railway emerged from the war much strengthened and the PRR's most valuable ally.[20]

Thomson was less successful in his attempts to influence lines in central and southern Ohio. He had staked his hopes early on the Marietta & Cincinnati Railroad, a bright prospect he thought in an emerging series of lines that would connect Pittsburgh to the Ohio River City. In September 1852 Thomson had pushed his board hard for a $750,000 subscription to the M&C; and it was one of the few times in his presidential career that he lost. The best he could get was a $100,000 subscription to the stock of the Springfield, Mt. Vernon & Pittsburgh Railroad, a more circuitous proposed route to Cincinnati. Thomson hated to lose; at the next stockholders' meeting, he succeeded in having that body vote the $750,000 investment in the M&C.[21]

The Pennsylvania's president lived to regret his move. The board hedged the subscription with so many restrictions that the M&C did not receive its money for six months. Moreover, the road was so poorly managed that its officers used the funds to retire old debts instead of completing their route. When in 1856 the company went bankrupt, much to Thomson's chagrin, he tried to merge it with another line to form the Ohio Valley Railroad, the same technique he had used with the PFW&C. This consolidation failed, however, and he wrote the entire investment off to profit and loss in 1858. His opportunity for a rail connection with Cincinnati via the Ohio Valley evaporated with the demise of the M&C.[22]

Thomson's investment in the Springfield road fared little better. Never a financially healthy company, its officers were soon back, hat-in-hand, asking Thomson to double his subscription. He refused, and three years later, having given up on the road's prospects, he exchanged its stock for securities of the Steubenville and Indiana, a much shorter central route toward Cincinnati. Thomson had high hopes for the S&I because he was already involved in constructing a connecting road to it, the Pittsburgh and Steubenville. When finished, the Pennsylvania would own a line into the Midwest with great potential for acquiring further connections.[23]

In the decade of the 1850s Thomson laid the groundwork for the great system of midwestern railways he later acquired. He enabled his road to offer through-service on the PFW&C to Chicago, and across central Ohio on allied lines to Cincinnati. In Cincinnati, it competed with its rival, B&O, for influence over the Ohio and Mississippi

Railroad for an entrance into St. Louis. Strategically, he had placed the Pennsylvania in an excellent position to connect with any future transcontinental line that might be built south of Chicago.

At the same time that the Pennsylvania's president was plotting corporate strategy to bolster his road's western receipts, he was involved intimately in overseeing daily operations, technical details, finances, construction, renewals, political relations, and his own personal affairs. The pace he maintained was physically debilitating. Moreover, the panic that began in the fall of 1857 and quickly deepened into a full-fledged depression further compounded his problems. Competition among the eastern trunk lines became increasingly ferocious as they fought for the dwindling traffic by lowering rates while always seeking to maintain their profit margins.

The financial crisis was the catalyst that finally prompted Thomson to overhaul his company's organization. The old departmental operating structure that dated from 1852, when the road was still incomplete and traffic levels were much lower, had provided for staff officers centrally located to direct the company's operations, finances, construction, repair, freight and passenger business, and maintenance and motive power. Since then, the road's gross revenues had more than doubled, and, in the year of the crisis, Thomson had thousands of employees strung out over 400 miles, handling almost $5 million annually. He desperately needed more accurate and up-to-date information on his costs in order to set competitive rates that could still make a profit. At a personal level, he had to lift some of the burdens from his own shoulders.

Thomson's new organizational structure, completed by December 1857, was eventually copied all across the country. Thomson's thought processes lent themselves to creating organizational solutions to complex problems; his engineering background trained him to think logically, to recognize cause and effect relationships, and to create mechanisms that operated with a minimum of friction. Furthermore, his appreciation of others' talents and his belief in allowing young subordinates the greatest measure of freedom whenever possible, naturally led him toward a more decentralized structure. His starting point, however, was the work of another engineer, the Erie's general superintendent, Daniel C. McCallum, who had outlined a new organization for his road just two years earlier. McCallum had experimented with breaking his line down into operating divisions. Thomson took this idea and merged it with his and rival B&O departmental structures to create the first line and staff managerial organization in American corporate history. Thomson's scheme allowed men at the lower levels enough authority to demonstrate their talents, although always under the oversight of higher line officers. To accomplish this, the road between Philadelphia and Pittsburgh was divided into sections, each with a divisional superintendent responsible for everything in his baliwick. A general superintendent was placed over all divisional officers to coordinate operations. Thomson's plan clearly delineated the lines of authority from employees at the lowest divisional levels through the general superintendent. Motive power, maintenance of way, and accounting officers were carefully included in the chain of command at all levels. Forms were standardized, and information flowed smoothly through prescribed channels. Responsibility was widely spread, and many of the road's future leaders gained their first taste of authority at the lower levels of the company's line organization. A divisional superintendency quickly became a springboard to the front offices; Scott, Carnegie, James McCrea, and Robert Pitcairn, all gained valuable experience and notice in that job.

At the staff level, the president, vice presidents, assistants, general superintendent, controller, auditor, and treasurer, made general policy and, as Alfred Chandler noted in his study of early corporate management, dealt with "things." By contrast the line organization handled people. Thomson's old engineering corps was the only department that did not fit into the new scheme. Its loyalties were divided. Resident engineers in staff positions were responsible for the planning and upkeep of the whole road, an arrangement consistent with Thomson's earlier views on the importance of the profession, while the divisional superintendents directed the work of engineers assigned to them at the line level. Once again Thomson's personal predilections influenced every facet of the road's operations.[24]

The new corporate structure, which took effect in early 1858, freed Thomson from the necessity of overseeing his road's daily operations for the first time in six years. He welcomed the relief, for he was deeply involved in strengthening the Pennsylvania's position in his native state, creating the corporate colossus that would come to dominate Pennsylvania's political scene. His problems at home were critical to his success in the short term, yet Thomson understood corporate business strategy far better than he comprehended the vagaries of public opinion and the political process. Furthermore, he had to consolidate his internal position in the company while dealing with the external forces that threatened his ability to compete. That he mastered both attests to his abilities to succeed even in areas that he knew were not his forte.

6

THE POLITICS
OF PROFIT

Thomson's Pennsylvania was the last eastern trunk line to suffer from debilitating physical and political restrictions. As long as his native state remained unwilling to write off its investment in the Main Line and relinquish the patronage the works provided, Thomson's position remained uncomfortable. He had freed himself from dependence upon the Portage road when he had finished the Allegheny tunnel in 1854, but he still had to work closely with the state canal commissioners because they operated his connection with Philadelphia. The more profitable the Pennsylvania became and the larger the deficits on the state works, however, the less cooperative the canal board was. Increasingly, Thomson had to resort to the state legislature to force that body to be more tractable or to evade the commissioners' authority altogether. His involvement in state politics required of Thomson a degree of subtlety and tact difficult for him to maintain, especially as the debate over the future of the state works aroused passions across the state. Moreover, large public corporations were none too popular in Pennsylvania, and he found he had to tread warily. He did not enjoy the political give and take, but early in his presidential tenure he discovered that political matters and corporate diplomacy consumed an ever greater proportion of his energies.

Only the fact that the state's policies endangered the very prosperity of his road was enough to prompt Thomson to take up the political cudgels. The chief peril was a tonnage tax the legislature had embedded in the company's charter to protect its investment in the state works. The tax was initially five mills on each ton carried over twenty miles when the canals were open, and then it was lowered to three mills but collected at all seasons. In addition, the Pennsylvania had to pay tolls for its use of the connecting segments of the state works and faced the dismal prospect of paying them forever on the state-controlled Philadelphia and Columbia Railroad. Rate-making and scheduling were nightmares, and of course the Pennsylvania's charges had to reflect the tolls and tonnage tax it paid. Thomson rightly feared that his high rates would drive through trade to other states, leaving him only local traffic.[1]

Even that trade, however, was hindered by state restrictions. Bulk cargoes like coal were potentially a most profitable local tonnage for the PRR, a business Thomson had to discourage, explaining to Seth Clover, the canal board president, "we did not wish to carry it while burthened by a prohibitory State tax." Thomson particularly wanted to haul coal in what he liked to call the "dull season" and would have done so on a large scale had he been able to persuade the canal board to lower its tolls on the P&C. Its rates were so high, however, that English coal sold more cheaply in Philadelphia than the native product. Seeking relief, Thomson went to the state legislature asking that the tonnage tax on coal and lumber be removed. On May 7, 1855, that body agreed to a trial if the Pennsylvania cut its rates to reflect the lower carrying costs. The experiment proved a huge success, and the Pennsylvania rapidly captured a large proportion of the trade in those commodities.[2]

The Pennsylvania's president was particularly vexed by the canal board's control of the P&C. The state road was not well maintained, its passenger tolls were high, and the tracks were so close together that Thomson had to build special narrow cars. At times the canal board's policy defied rationalization. Early in 1852 the board leased its P&C passenger business to a private company and refused to allow Thomson to operate his cars over the line. On advice of counsel Thomson went to the legislature for redress. Finding none, he prepared to sue the canal commissioners, and dropping his inhibitions about fighting the board in public, he unleashed a barrage of newspaper advertisements attacking the stupidity of its policy. Privately, Thomson admitted to Bell "I have kept my cool under this move of the Board," but, "if we have to go to the Canal Board, Cap in hand, for all favors or common justice, or Bribe our way through, I shall soon determine to quit my post, and a State, where such outrages are permitted with impunity." Conspiratorially, he added "I have had my suspicions that Col. Patterson has been at work with them, aided & abetted by others—in our company."[3]

In early 1853 Thomson convinced Pennsylvania Governor William Bigler to adjudicate the impasse. After two meetings the governor worked out an agreement in which Thomson purchased one-half of the private contractor's passenger cars in return for permission to operate PRR equipment over the line. The contractor continued to receive one-half the profits from the passenger and mail business just for selling tickets over the P&C.

The highly political nature of the state's transportation business made Thomson's job considerably more difficult. Pennsylvania's legislature, like those in many other states, was not renowned for its probity or altruism, and coupled with the voters' distrust of corporations and Thomson's own inclinations against bribing public officials, his political relationships were often strained. Also, Thomson at first was less amenable to political maneuverings than his predecessors. Thomas Cope remembered that in 1848 during a meeting of PRR officials to consider a stalled piece of legislation it was "hinted that a majority could easily be obtained, by the rise of a little money among the members, which several present said was not unusual." A few years earlier, a B&O investor had run into Cope on the street and talk turned to the Maryland road buying a right-of-way in Pennsylvania. When Cope questioned whether that could be done, his friend "slapt his hand on his breeches pocket, exclaiming, 'Mr. Cope, we can do anything with your Legislature.' " Patterson had paid about $2,500 annually to hire "legislative services," but when Thomson prepared to go to Harrisburg in March 1852, he called a special meeting of the board to discuss the propriety of such expenses. Thomson argued that the expenditures were wrong, and the board upheld him. The following year, however, he found that he did not have time to handle the political chores and hired lobbyists to represent the company's views. Beginning in 1854 he annually sent Foster in his stead to the legislative sessions.[4]

As Thomson became further removed from the political action, he became less squeamish about political morality. Always a pragmatic soul, he realized that he had to accept and work with the political system as constituted if he was to be successful. For example, he quickly discovered that free passes were potent weapons and used them for all they were worth. In 1858 his company allotted annual tickets to the governor, state department heads, canal commissioners, railway managers, and newspaper editors; everyone else, including members of the state legislature, had to petition for a pass. That same year Foster was given company funds to use in the legislature and the road paid retainers for political services. Yet when Thomson was advised that he might have a chance to repeal the detested tonnage tax, he showed he still had a strong notion of what was correct and what was not. "I am satisfied," he wrote back, "that this company cannot procure the necessary legislation without resorting to means that all proper minded persons must condemn." Two years later, however, he countenanced Scott's questionable tactics in Harrisburg on behalf of repeal, but then he was only indirectly involved in the details. Late in the decade he was also much freer to discuss such political machinations, for all corporate strategy sessions were off the record; no legislative matters were entered in the board minutes after 1858.[5]

The state legislature kept Thomson politically off-balance by periodically dangling before him the chance for removal of the tax—if he would come up with enough money. Faced with the annual drain on the state's treasury, political leaders sought to restore the state work's profitability or to get rid of it and salvage some portion of the commonwealth's huge investment. As early as 1852, the legislature moved to lease the whole system to a private company. Thomson knew what private company the solons had in mind and succeeded in defeating the measure. Two years later the state offered to sell the works for $10 million. Thomson nibbled at the bait; if he could acquire the P&C and the legislature would rescind the tonnage tax, he indicated that he might be interested. The legislature refused to consider the deal.[6]

But once the legislature sensed that Thomson could be persuaded to buy, the only question was how much he was willing to pay. The state lowered its asking price to $7.5 million in 1855 and, as a sweetener, offered to lift the tonnage tax for another million. After lengthy consultations with his board, Thomson turned the proposition down. It could not have come at a worse moment, for retrenchment was the order of the day on the road. But the legislators definitely had Thomson's attention. Throughout 1856 he filled the newspapers with articles designed to stir up public opinion for a sale on his terms. He attended several of the 1857 sessions and lobbied hard for a favorable deal; he succeeded only too well. The bill as passed, provided that if Thomson purchased the state works for $9 million, the state would rescind the tax, exempt the PRR from all other state taxes, and relinquish its right to purchase the railroad. The canal board immediately brought suit in the state supreme court to block the sale. That body upheld the constitutionality of the sale and the tonnage tax relief, but decreed that the legislature had no right to exempt the corporation from state taxes forever. Since the tonnage tax provision was part of the clause that was declared invalid, it meant that Thomson would have to continue to pay the tonnage tax even if he bought the Main Line.[7]

Thomson and his board had only a week to decide whether they still wanted to go through with the deal. Afterward, Thomson indicated that "if my vote had determined the matter the Company would not now have been troubled with them." He argued to await the next session to repair the objectionable clause, or to go ahead and build a new road to Philadelphia. He was not, however, unmindful of the political consequences of such actions; he wrote Bell, "I knew where we would have stood if we had refused to purchase—." Thomson was finally swayed by the argument "that the interest of Philadelphia required that the work should be bought at some considerable sacrifice—." So on the evening of June 25, 1857, he walked down to the Merchants' Exchange where a great crowd of curious onlookers had gathered. When the auctioneer asked for bids, he offered $7.5 million. As the auctioneer went through the motions of entertaining higher tenders, silence fell over the throng. The gavel banged down and Thomson slipped out of the crowd, the rather discouraged owner of what he later called "the Elephant."[8]

The purchase almost doubled the Pennsylvania's funded debt, but Thomson had gained possession of a route from Philadelphia to Pittsburgh and was at last free to set his own rates and schedules to make his road more competitive, even with the remaining three-mills tonnage tax. That levy loomed ever more ominously after the 1857 panic caused business on the road to level off, necessitated across-the-board salary reductions, and forced Thomson to skip his November dividend. The almost $200,000 his road paid in tonnage tax that year hurt. But the ridiculousness of the situation most irritated Thomson; he had to pay a tax to protect a line of inefficient works that he had just purchased. He thought that an absurdity only a politician could defend with a straight face.[9]

Thomson assaulted the legislature in 1858 in full force to have the tax removed. He handed out free passes liberally in the right quarters, formed a special board committee to oversee the campaign, hired counsel to advise on legal technicalities, and attended some legislative sessions with Foster. Thomson even had both Philadelphia city councils publish their strong endorsements of his appeal; it was all to no avail. Politicians outside Philadelphia were afraid to touch the issue because their constituents firmly believed that the state would make up for the lost revenue by raising their property taxes. Rebuffed, Thomson sued the state to test the constitutionality of the levy on the basis that Section 10, Article 1 of the United States Constitution forbade a state from taxing interstate commerce. And to force the issue he stopped paying the tonnage tax; at the end of the year his company owed the commonwealth $319,000.[10]

An adverse opinion on the suit and Scott's election as vice-president of the Pennsylvania in March 1860 after Foster's untimely death, roused the company's officers to action again. They had done nothing in the 1859-60 session because the state's political leaders were embroiled in presidential and gubernatorial politics. After the court decreed the tax was really a fee for the privilege of doing business in the state, that Thomson had to pay over the monies he had collected, and that only shippers had the right to sue since they paid the tax, the irrepressible Scott charged into the fray in the spring of 1860. A clever political creature, he laid his groundwork carefully, buying advertisements in newspapers all over the state, influencing editorial opinions with promises of liberal advertising by his railroad, and personally wooing members of the legislature. To divide the opposition coalition of rural representatives and delegations from the Pittsburgh area, he boldly approached the Pittsburgh Board of Trade, long antagonistic toward the Pennsylvania because of what it considered rate discrimination, and promised the PRR would aid several local railroads and make the rate adjustments the area's businessmen desired. It worked; the repeal passed both houses in 1861, and the governor was induced to sign the measure.[11]

The tonnage tax repeal was decidedly unpopular. All but one of its supporters in the house from outside Philadelphia were defeated in their reelection bids. Scott succeeded in his efforts only because the breakup of the union and the formation of the Confederacy that spring diverted public attention from his attack on the tax. Opponents of repeal returned to the next session, however, determined to undo Scott's handiwork. They formed an investigating committee, to which Scott won the right to name five members, that uncovered a mass of fraud and deceit practiced in the name of Thomson's Pennsylvania Railroad. The committee subpoenaed Scott, who had been called to Washington as assistant secretary of war, to testify, but a friendly sergeant-at-arms failed to locate the Pennsylvania's elusive vice-president. When Democratic committee leaders sought to corner Scott, President Lincoln posted him to the Southwest to investigate military transportation problems. The wide publicity given to his political chicanery added to the already existing popular sentiment against the Pennsylvania. Moreover, the inability or unwillingness of Thomson, who supplied a medical certificate indicating that his health was precarious, to testify before the committee blackened his and Scott's reputations.

The rabidly antirepeal legislature of 1862 failed in its mission only because Scott's bill was a marvel. The act was framed as a contract between the state and the Pennsylvania that could be altered only by consent of both parties. The legislation also cleverly expanded the road's influence within the state. The bill stipulated that Thomson invest the $850,000 in unpaid tonnage taxes in the first mortgage bonds of a dozen unfinished Pennsylvania railways that promised to become feeder lines for the PRR. In one stroke that clause enabled Scott to attract votes from new districts and extended the Pennsylvania's economic and political sway.[12]

Public fears that Thomson's company was growing to gargantuan proportions that enabled it to exact tribute from the state were given a fillip during the tonnage tax debate when Thomson gained control of the Northern Central Railroad (NC) connecting Harrisburg with Baltimore. Throughout the decade he had looked east and south for potential connections even as he stretched his resources to expand into the West. His link with New York City over the Camden and Amboy Railroad was not a satisfactory arrangement since he had little leverage over the New Jersey company and his competitive position would be immensely improved by a Baltimore connection that could steal traffic from his rival headquartered in that city. The key to Thomson's southern expansion was the NC, jointly controlled by the B&O and the Reading Railroad, that tapped a rich coal region in Pennsylvania, drawing that trade away from the PRR. Furthermore, Thomson was threatened by the NC's ambition to build a line from Harrisburg to New York City, which would give the B&O control of a route to the nation's biggest port.[13]

Simon Cameron, a man who always stood ready to combine his personal business with the public's, was the moving force behind Thomson's takeover of the NC. In June 1860 he approached Thomson and Scott, who desperately needed Cameron's political help in the tonnage tax fight, with a proposal to join him in capturing the NC. Thomson was intrigued, but since the Pennsylvania had no legal right to purchase stock in other corporations, he would have to buy it on his own account. He was sobered by the size of such an investment, and he wanted more information before staking his own funds in the venture. Scott reported to Cameron on June 28, "I had some talk with the Old Chief on the subject of your letter—how much have you under your control now and how much more will be required—?" Cameron owned enough NC stock to entice Thomson to begin quietly buying the road's shares.[14]

The PRR's capture of the NC succeeded through a lucky turn of events. Lincoln's election in November drove stock prices sharply down and Garrett and the Reading, caught in a financial pinch, threw their NC holdings on the market where Thomson and Cameron quickly purchased them. When the NC shareholders gathered at their annual meeting in March 1861, Thomson voted almost 13,000 shares which, along with Cameron's 8,000, gave them close to 50 percent of the outstanding stock, enough to control the company. The Pennsylvania legislature cooperated with a special act in 1861, quickly approved by the shareholders, enabling the Pennsylvania to buy Thomson's stock. The following month the board compensated him for almost a quarter of a million dollars. Thomson gained direct access to Baltimore, strengthening his competitive position and an entrance into the South from which the Pennsylvania would launch its postwar southern empire.[15]

Thomson's control of a line to Baltimore worsened an already straitened competitive situation in the East. Railway officers everywhere were beginning to realize that the eastern railroad network was overbuilt; there simply was not enough trade to keep the railways, steamboats, and the Erie Canal operating to capacity. Moreover, a series of short crops and the panic of 1857 shrunk available traffic. With large capital investments in fixed plants, the railroads' failure to work them at near capacity levels spelled disaster because whether used or not, the interest charges had to be paid.

Each road faced different competitive conditions. The northern lines, the Canadian Grand Trunk, the NYC and the heavily indebted Erie, fought the Great Lakes' boats and the Erie Canal for their shares of the trade and were forced to reduce their charges in the summer to stay competitive. To the south, the PRR and the B&O vied with Ohio River steamboats, the Pennsylvania state works, and with each other. In addition, the B&O owned a steamship line plying between New York City, Philadelphia, and Baltimore that forced the Pennsylvania to lower its rail rates to those cities. Generally, however, the Pennsylvania and the B&O, even though fiercely antagonistic toward each other, aligned against the combined New York roads, although these coalitions often broke down over the struggle for influence with the still relatively autonomous railroads in the Midwest.[16]

Officers on all four roads recognized very early that free competition harmed everybody in the business. Instead, they sought arrangements that would allow each a satisfactory profit and stabilize the competitive situation. The presidents attempted to create artificial conditions in which such crucial differences as geography, connections, physical plant, efficiency, and capitalization, would be rendered irrelevant. Like most businessmen they preferred the security of the known to the possibilities of the unknown. In their anticipated perfect world, all roads would charge predetermined rates, high enough for healthy profits but low enough to encourage yearly traffic increases to keep their trains fully loaded. The agreements, if adhered to, would also secure the midwestern rail situation since the roads in that region had to rely upon the good will of their eastern neighbors for through traffic interchange.

Such collusion was extralegal; the arrangements could not be enforced at the bar, but efforts to rationalize the railroad business were not considered immoral or conspiratorial. The inviolable laws of competition later espoused by Herbert Spencer and William Graham Sumner, and legally enshrined in the nation's laws by Justice Stephen Field, lay in the future. The older concept of community interest still reigned supreme. In the 1850s the managers of public thoroughfares were entrusted with the responsibility for acting in the higher name of the common good. Stockholders, employees, suppliers, contractors, and others, who earned their livelihoods from the railroads and were dependent upon the corporations' fiscal health, were still by definition an integral part of the community with equal considerations to its largess. The distinction between people and *the* people had yet to be made. Rate setting did not draw down moral thunderbolts upon the railway managers' heads. Newspapers calmly reported the St. Nicholas meetings and the actions taken in them. The commentators assumed that the participants acted for the public's benefit as well as for their own. They made no distinction between the two objectives.

When railroad officials attempted to operate in a spirit of cooperation, however, they discovered the eastern railway world was real and imperfect. Starting in 1857 the scenario was almost unvarying; the presidents met in the winter or spring when waterways were choked with ice, usually at New York City's St. Nicholas Hotel, to set rates, train speeds, and schedules for the coming busy season. Just as regularly, by July 4 at least, one of the presidents had secretly cut rates and allowed rebates and drawbacks to attract more traffic; a general rate war erupted often dropping fares to below the cost of carriage, threatening the financial health of the weaker midwestern roads. Nasty letters flew among the presidents, hurried meetings were held in August, and by September new arrangements were hammered out to handle the fall crops. The season would end, and the whole rigamarole would begin anew. In the four years before the war, at least fifteen conferences were held to renegotiate defaulted agreements.

The only element of compulsion to obey them was self-interest, but it was also in self-interest that all of the presidents violated the pacts they had so solemnly signed. At one point in 1858, a particularly bad year for St. Nicholas agreements, Thomson proposed after yet another compact, "we will put up a forfeit of $100,000 dollars if the rest will do the same, that it will not be violated." His fellow presidents refused, for at times it was not in their interest to maintain the *status quo* and often they were not responsible for violations. All major roads hired commission agents to solicit and make arrangements for through traffic. It was in these agents' interest to corner all the trade they could get at whatever they had to charge, often allowing secret rebates and drawbacks to their preferred customers. Railway presidents had little control over them; if they fired the agents, they simply took their customers to a competitor's road. While the system theoretically saved the companies money, it made maintaining the St. Nicholas agreements a nightmare; Thomson and Scott spent thousands of hours checking out alleged violations by their own agents.[17]

The four trunk line presidents started making St. Nicholas pacts early, and after the 1857 panic, often. The first meeting, called by Thomson to "consider plans for maintaining rates," took place sometime before 1852. Haupt remembered that the session was "like a Quaker meeting, no one taking the initiative in the way of business." He finally sidled over to Thomson to ask who called the gathering. When Thomson told him, his subordinate suggested, "why do you not rise and state the object of the meeting and nominate a chairman and secretary?" Thomson simply replied, "you do it." As the decade progressed, the PRR's president became less reluctant to speak up.[18]

When Thomson did speak out he was usually the voice of moderation. He rarely strayed from his notion that railway officers should charge a reasonable rate for transport that would bring in profits and call forth additional traffic. As president of a major truck line in a fiercely competitive territory, he amended his original ideas to include a firm belief that cooperation was better than competition. Moreover, his perspective on the whole situation radiated outward from his office; he assumed that whatever was good for the Pennsylvania was also beneficial for his native state and the nation. As he explained to his shareholders in 1859, he expected reasonable railway men would have no trouble "agreeing upon remunerative rates, abolishing injudicious practices, and effecting a harmony of purpose conductive to mutual advantage of the railway interest and the public."[19]

Whenever possible Thomson advocated negotiating formal pacts between competing lines; he once wrote Garrett during an 1859 rate war: "it seems to me to be the duty of those entrusted with the management of the immense capital invested in the four lines to meet in the proper spirit." Thomson assumed that his fellow presidents were also imbued with the same sense of duty and responsibility and that reasonable men could work out reasonable solutions to their problems. He expected agreements to last. Just before the presidents met to negotiate such a pact, he wrote Samuel Barlow, president of the Ohio and Mississippi (O&M), he hoped "the treaty to be formed therein, may prove as lasting as the Constitution of the Union, made after a similar trial of the inefficiency of the Confederation without concessions to the general good." When it did not, Thomson lectured Garrett on what fidelity to trade arrangements meant, "We neither stoop to get trade by unfair means, or poach upon our neighbors [sic] grounds—."[20]

Thomson was far from naive, however, and after a succession of treaties broke down, he sought some method to enforce them. When he could not convince other presidents to put up bond to insure their performance, he sought outside mediation. When all semblance of rate agreements broke down in 1859, Thomson and Garrett hired poor Barlow, whose O&M was a battered victim of the PRR—B&O squabbles, to act as a mediator in the East. Barlow succeeded in bringing representatives of the eastern trunks to the negotiating table, but try as he might, he could not wring an agreement from them. In part his failure was due to serious personality differences. Erastus Corning of the NYC hated Charles Moran of the Erie, and it took heroic efforts just to get the two men into the same room. Thomson and Garrett, with similar personalities, although Garrett was a bit more outgoing, had their own personal differences as well. When Garrett refused to attend a president's meeting, Thomson for one of the few times in his life lost his temper. "The truth is," he snarled, "that you are quite as much blinded to what is fair and right when it conflicts with your propensities to monopolize traffic as either of your Presidential colaborers [sic] and the sooner you thrust off the assumption of 'injured dignity' and meet for free and frank discussion without excitement, the better." Garrett remained unmoved and later in the summer Thomson, still in the white heat of indignation, charged, "I have but little faith in your high sounding expressions and promises."[21]

On at least one point, Thomson himself was unyielding. He would never allow rates on the New York City traffic to equal those to Philadelphia and Baltimore; he consistently maintained lower tariffs to those cities to take into account the shorter distances. It was a policy Pennsylvania presidents pursued to the end of the century and a perennial cause for rate wars. Thomson hated the disruptions caused by such disputes but would not shrink from entering one to preserve his rate differentials. And he could be brutal. During an 1858 melee he pressured his connections to make common cause. He demanded of the O&M's superintendent, "Does your company make a proportionate reduction with us in fares . . . or not?" The superintendent lamented to Barlow, "I do not like to agree to it but do not see how we can escape." As rates continued to plummet, he predicted to Barlow that if the war was not ended "rail road securities will sink to a depth so profound that the light of resurrection morning will not reach them."[22]

Conditions never reached that state of affairs; by 1860 the depression was lifting and traffic volume increased on all roads. Rate-making machinery worked much better in prosperous times; with enough traffic for everyone it made sense to enter into what Thomson described as "full and cordial cooperation in a fair division of all trade to and from competing points at remunerative prices." Railway leaders continued to accuse each other of cheating, but the tone of their letters indicated that they were not spoiling for a fight. In fact, at the year's end, Thomson was even happy, "we have as much as we can handle from the West," he crowed. Efforts to control eastern competitive conditions ended with the outbreak of war. The problem then became not the fair allocation of minimal traffic, but rather how to handle the mass of wartime material thrown over all roads. It was just the kind of challenge Thomson relished.[23]

7

THE MIXED
BLESSINGS
OF WAR

Railway managers everywhere greeted the outbreak of the Civil War with abject gloom. The hostilities injected another major element of confusion into the world they were struggling to rationalize. For those roads unfortunate enough to run north-south or lie near war zones, such as the Illinois Central, Louisville and Nashville, Northern Central, and the Baltimore & Ohio, the fighting brought disruption and destruction. Even for those lines far removed from the bloodletting, secession threatened their security values, cut off overseas credit, destroyed long-established political relationships, and threatened increased federal regulation.

By the summer of 1861, however, earlier apprehensions had dissipated. Railroad officials clearly realized the war brought in its wake great opportunities as well as serious problems. The conflict finally spirited the northern economy completely out of the doldrums, and after the Confederates closed the Mississippi River, midwestern agricultural produce that usually floated downstream to market crowded the eastern trunk lines. Furthermore, the farmers brought in bumper crops during the war while European harvests throughout this period were uniformly poor, creating a huge export market for American products. Traffic loads on northern roads increased exponentially, and with the B&O often closed, three lines carried the bulk of the passengers and freight. In six months the situation had shifted from inadequate trade to support four roads to an excess of business for three. The necessity for cooperative arrangements disappeared; everywhere rates climbed, debts fell, profits soared, and equipment wore out.

Thomson's reaction to the nation's plight was entirely in keeping with his empirical proclivities and moderate disposition; he recoiled in horror at the very idea of the breakup and war. Like the majority of people on both sides of the Mason-Dixon Line, he did not think the sectional differences were serious enough to warrant a civil blood-bath. Undoubtedly, Thomson's thinking was colored by his Quaker background and his long experience in the South, but as a commercial man Thomson could not see why anybody would want to disrupt centuries-old sectional trade patterns that were profitable for all concerned; and as a native of a city with close southern commercial ties, he was further dismayed. Lacking strong moral qualms about the institution of slavery and wary of extremism in any guise, he had nothing but contempt for the abolitionists of his own party and supported attempts to find some solution to the sectional divisions, short of war. That was why he gladly accepted an appointment in January 1861, after five states had already seceded, to a special committee to draft a statement publicizing railroad managers' attitudes toward the crisis. The group produced a paper that strongly supported the efforts of Senator John J. Crittenden of Kentucky to avert war. The so-called "Crittenden Compromise" proposed prohibiting slavery north of the 36°30′ Missouri Compromise line, but giving the institution guaranteed federal protection south of there. Thomson wholeheartedly supported the committee's position because it appeared to him to be entirely sound while the alternative, war, was the height of irrationality.[1]

When the war broke out in April, Thomson, like most Americans on both sides, expected it to last less than ninety days. But as it dragged on through the long summer, and especially after Union troops were routed at the First Battle of Bull Run, he began to wonder if the conflict would ever end. He poured out his thoughts on the problem in a long letter to Richard Peters, who had stayed in Georgia and was supporting the Confederate cause. Not surprisingly, Thomson blamed the war on the politicians and the more he thought about it the angrier he became. The origins of this rebellion, he fumed, "have no other foundations than those usually manufactured by that disease of the Brain, which in all countries and ages has caused politicians to sacrifice their country to promote their own personal ambition—." He defended the Republican administration, denying that it had any intention "to coerce your people to do anything inconsistent to their honor, duty, and best interests—;" it only wanted to insure that the nation was "not reduced to the level of the Spanish Republics of South America to be kept in continual alarm by political aspirants or dissatisfied statesmen—." Thomson believed the war would have been justifiable only if "the government committed some flagrant act of injustice" under the Constitution. In that case, Thomson promised, "you would have here a party that would insist upon and insure the removal of your grievances."[2]

Thomson ignored forty years of sectional strife and its underlying moral problem of slavery; in fact, he never even mentioned the region's peculiar institution. Instead, he took a popular, narrowly political, and economic view of the war, one in which the conflict could only be considered as the ultimate absurdity. Deceived by their political leaders, southerners, in his opinion, went berserk and wreaked havoc everywhere. He charged that no act of the federal government "could justify your people in your attempts to cut our throats, sack our cities, tear up our railways, destroy our locomotives, etc. etc." Thomson's world had been severely buffeted by the destruction, the loss of Philadelphia's profitable cotton trade, the closing of the Mississippi River, the sagging securities markets, and the collapse of foreign credit; and from his point of view, all for no good reasons.

In concluding his letter, Thomson became more moderate; he pointed out "the Confederates began this contest and they should have the magnaminity when they see that they will have to 'pay too dear for their whistle' to gracefully back down—." He appealed to his former associate to call upon his "heretical friends and get them to propose a national assembly to settle our troubles—," adding upon reflection, "it may be too late in a short time to effect even this." Paradoxically, Thomson wanted the very people that he blamed for the war to bring it to an inconclusive end. He was not sanguine, however, about their willingness or ability to do so; if the war continued, he warned Peters, the Union *"has the power to accomplish its purpose."*[3]

At the very start of hostilities, Thomson was certain the federal forces would prevail if they marshaled their resources quickly and dealt the Confederate armies massing before Washington a decisive blow. The logistical problems of moving troops to the capital from all over the nation, however, were enormous. The capital's only rail link to the north was the B&O's Washington branch, and during the early weeks of the war Garrett was suspected of being a southern advocate. Immediately after the battle of Fort Sumter, however, he contracted to bring Union troops from the West over his road to Baltimore, even though he was far from certain that he could safely carry them through hostile areas of Maryland and Virginia. On April 17 the Virginia state convention increased his miseries by voting secession, throwing portions of Garrett's main line into Confederate hands. Thomson found this development both a boon and a headache as government supply officers suddenly clamored to ship everything over his road and the NC. He hurriedly conferred with Garrett and his business and political ally, Simon Cameron, the new secretary of war. Garrett told Thomson that although his road was blocked from the west, he would spare no effort to send troops on to Washington when they arrived in Baltimore. Thomson was afraid, however, that "the secession of Virginia will carry Maryland with her"; Cameron responded to the possibility by appointing Thomson his personal agent, making him responsible for all transportation to the capital. So began one of the most hectic weeks of Thomson's career.[4]

It was not at all clear to Thomson whether federal troops could be passed through Baltimore without incident and moreover, he and Cameron were afraid their NC would be sabotaged by southern partisans. Cameron, always touchy where his private interests were concerned, ordered federal troops out to protect his road. Their fears were justified; the situation in Baltimore deteriorated rapidly. A mob in the city cut all telegraph communications between the North and Washington, and on April 19 assaulted Massachusetts troops as they were pulled through city streets in horse-drawn railway cars; four soldiers and nine civilians were killed. When Thomson heard of the outbreak he suggested to Washington authorities that "Union men must be aroused to resist the mob." Tensions were running so high in the city that Maryland's governor and Baltimore's mayor took the unusual steps of ordering the destruction of bridges on the NC and B&O to prevent more troops from reaching the city. They also expelled all federal soldiers from the state. Lincoln acquiesced because he was most anxious to keep Maryland from joining the Confederacy.[5]

With Baltimore isolated and communications cut to Washington, Thomson and his counterpart on the PW&B, Samuel M. Felton, a man of great energy and resourcefulness, quickly came up with an alternate route to supply the nation's capital. Felton's road was still operating to Perryville at the mouth of the Susquehanna River, from where troops could be sent by ship to Annapolis, the terminus of the Annapolis and Elk Ridge Railroad which connected with the B&O's Washington branch south of Baltimore. Thomson and Felton started moving troops over the makeshift route even before they received authorization from Washington. Thomson also pressed Cameron to take over the A&ER and the southern end of the B&O's Washington branch and repair the two roads; Felton spoke for Thomson when he promised they could guarantee the railways' operations if the government secured the lines. The PW&B's president summed up the situation succinctly, "it is a question between government or anarchy, and who can hesitate?"[6]

Certainly not General Benjamin Butler and his troops, the first sent over Thomson's stopgap land and water route. Butler arrived in Annapolis to find the A&ER's tracks torn up and, without authority took possession of the road and began repairs. Cameron accepted Butler's *fait accompli* and appointed Scott as superintendent to operate the first military railroad. Scott brought Carnegie and other PRR officers to help restore the line and borrowed equipment from Thomson's and Felton's roads to begin operations. By April 29 the route was open all the way from Harrisburg to Washington and the capital was out of danger.[7]

Thomson, who had not had a decent night's sleep in a week, and who handled a multitude of details day and night in his efforts to bolster the capital's defenses, proudly signing his dispatches "agt. of Sec. of War," physically collapsed on April 27. The strain of the earlier tonnage tax fight and his recent exertions were too much; he was confined to bed for exhaustion and a pulmonary infection. But with Scott still in Washington, he had to take personal charge of the PRR's thorny operational problems caused by an avalanche of traffic. He simply could not let go of the corporate reins even for a few days, and he urgently recalled Palmer, who had followed Scott to the capital, to help him. Two weeks later Magee reported that Thomson was still "quite unwell and will have to remain at home, I think for some days," but added, "the business at the office etc. of the company appears to go on very well—." As weak as he was, Thomson got out of bed to preside over the May 1 board meeting and was back at his office on a regular basis by the end of the month.[8]

The Pennsylvania president's quick and decisive actions to open a route to Washington were largely forgotten when Cameron's war department policies came under close congressional scrutiny at the end of 1861. Garrett and Felton had publicly accused Cameron and Scott of allocating a disproportionate share of government traffic to their own roads, and Scott, as vice-president of the Pennsylvania and assistant secretary of war, was particularly vulnerable to the imputation. Congressional wrath was further aroused when investigators found railways were charging the government higher rates than private interests based upon a tariff schedule Scott had prepared for the quartermaster department's use. The rates in it were essentially those that railway leaders had agreed upon at a Harrisburg meeting in June. Scott later countered at congressional hearings that his schedule only stipulated the maximum tolls that could be levied; other witnesses testified that they assumed the charges were official.

Most damaging to Scott and, by implication, Thomson, was the Committee on Government Contracts' complaint that the Pennsylvania and the NC were defrauding the government by levying the higher local rate on western livestock to Harrisburg. The committee estimated in July 1862 that Thomson's road had increased its earnings by 40 percent, while the NC had doubled its net revenues through overcharges. Scott flatly denied it, stating that government receipts were less than 5 percent of the PRR's gross revenues. The accusation was impossible to prove or refute. The Pennsylvania's net revenues rose by over 40 percent in 1861, but the road kept separate government accounts only for carrying troops. Moreover, although livestock tonnage in 1861 was ten times what it had been the year before, flour shipments rose almost three times faster. Undoubtedly, the Pennsylvania did not lose money carrying the traffic; whether it intentionally gouged the government was another question. Technically, livestock transported from Pittsburgh to the NC at Harrisburg had always been charged local rates, not the lower through rates; Pittsburgh dealers had complained of this discrimination for years. Lack of competition kept local rates high everywhere, and Thomson charged all the traffic would bear knowing the boom was only temporary. But the extra trains he had to operate and the new equipment and facilities he had to provide also pushed up his expenses. Whether through political intrigue or accident of geography, his road captured the bulk of the government's livestock trade and thereby attracted widespread condemnation.[9]

Lincoln, long under pressure to replace Cameron, eased him out of the war department in January 1862 and posted him as minister to Russia. Scott temporarily remained as assistant to the new secretary of war, Edwin Stanton, a much abler cabinet minister and one decidedly more friendly to the B&O interests. The Pennsylvania "crowd" no longer controlled the lucrative war department contracts after Cameron's departure, which ended most of the public abuse hurled at Thomson's road.[10]

Thomson only wished his road was making money as easily as its detractors claimed. The closing of the Mississippi River and the sporadic operations on the B&O brought all the traffic the PRR could handle early in the war's first year. When the fall shipping season began in earnest, an unusually large harvest had to be handled along with the special military trains. By September Thomson's facilities were stretched to their utmost. With fifty to sixty carloads daily in excess of the PRR's locomotive capacity, the general superintendent, Enoch Lewis, lengthened his operating divisions, ran on Sundays, and doubled shifts. By the end of the month, the superintendent of the eastern division reported "that some of our best men have fallen asleep in their trains," because with their longer runs thirty hours on the job and four hours off was not uncommon. In early October, Carnegie, superintendent of the western division, noted morale was low because many of his trainmen "have not visited their families for several weeks."[11]

Despite the furious pace the Pennsylvania demanded of employees, the road was still clogged with traffic in mid-October. The board authorized 100 new cars and as many new locomotives as Thomson thought he needed, but such actions did nothing to relieve the immediate congestion. Resident engineer William Wilson complained that traffic was so heavy that he could not maintain the roadbed, especially on the single-tracked portions of the road where rail deterioration was especially heavy. He noted that the accident rate was soaring and the density of traffic "without a corresponding increase of equipment has no doubt tended to embarrass operations."[12]

The size of the wartime trade and the prolongation of the conflict caught railway managers everywhere by surprise. Although Thomson reacted quickly and improved his facilities to handle the increased traffic, he was shy of investing too heavily lest he be caught after the war with under-used capacity. He did build a 500,000-bushel grain elevator on the Delaware River and lease two Philadelphia wharves to ease snarled port conditions. He enlarged the PRR's stockyards in Pittsburgh but admitted in his 1862 annual report that his road could not handle all the livestock offered for shipment. When he thought an improvement would pay dividends in the future, however, he was much more enthusiastic. He carefully watched developments in the oil region and foresaw that petroleum traffic would enhance his post-war profits. To encourage its growth he bought land on the Delaware River to build storage facilities for coal oil, purchased the Oil Creek Railroad in 1864 to control the crude oil trade, and made special arrangements for the large-scale carriage and tankage of that dangerous commodity. As usual he was looking far ahead.[13]

The unrelenting volume of wartime traffic quickly wore down the PRR's physical plant. Thomson, who always prided himself on operating a first-class property, increased the rate of rail replacement, ordered heavier rails, and personally designed a new device to butt rail ends together on the new second track being laid. By 1863, however, the worn condition of the railbed became alarming. He chronicled a litany of problems in his annual report: the new iron was inferior, locomotives weighed more, heavier cars and higher speeds accelerated rail wear, the cost of rails had shot up, and the shortage of labor and iron was becoming critical. These types of problems Thomson loved, however.

He had kept up with European experiments testing steel rails and steel-tipped iron rails, and under the exigencies of war could defend the cost of ordering 150 tons of expensive cast-steel rails for a trial. He had them installed near stations where the iron variety normally did not last six months. In 1864 he enthusiastically reported that steel, despite its prohibitive cost, had "proved successful upon a scale that would render it of practical value." He was also directing experiments with steel fireboxes to replace the more expensive copper-lined coal fireboxes being used; in fact, by the third year of the war, Thomson demonstrated an obsession for steel. He ordered more steel rails, more steel fireboxes, steel axles for passenger cars, and steel tires for locomotives. By 1866 he had proved that although steel rails cost twice as much as their iron counterparts, they lasted eight times longer, and their quality was constantly improving. Despite the pressures of war, he kept his road on the crest of the technological wave.[14]

Thomson's lot would have been easier had he been able to hire enough labor. The manpower drain caused by the armed forces affected repair and new construction crews more seriously than routine railroad operations. The 1862 draft act exempted locomotive engineers; other trained railway employees were granted a discharge if deemed vital to operations. While his veteran hands were protected, it was almost impossible for Thomson to expand his work force to handle the extraordinary traffic demands. In 1864 his personnel shortage became critical, to the point that, as Thomson reported, "for a time it was impossible to procure for our trains even raw recruits in sufficient numbers." By September the road was so sorely in need of experienced men that the board authorized a European agent to recruit skilled workers overseas. Thomson even considered using company funds to purchase substitutes for his drafted employees, but the war ended before the policy could be tried.[15]

Rampant wartime inflation compounded Thomson's problems. He estimated the cost of railway materials rose 300 percent during the conflict, although prices in general only doubled. Wages lagged behind these increases, rising less than half as fast. Thomson himself fared well; the board raised his salary to $12,000 a year effective July 1, 1862, when it granted an increase to the road's officers. A cost of living adjustment for all employees except managerial personnel the following year raised the company's labor costs 40 percent. Again in February 1865, general salary advances had to be made and acknowledging that the line's officers had not had a raise in two years, Thomson allowed them a 33 percent bonus on their 1864 pay. He was irritated, however, to have to pay what he considered exorbitant wages. In 1864 he groused, "it seems to be a general principle, that as the remuneration of labor is increased, its character and product decreases." Moreover, as he feared, wages remained high after the war while traffic declined, rates fell, and the labor market eased.[16]

Thomson could well afford to pay higher wages during the conflict, for his treasury was swollen with profits. Net earnings rose from $2.3

million in 1860 to $4.2 million in 1865 on gross revenues that increased from $5.9 million to $17.4 million. That profits did not keep pace with receipts was due to the road's unusually high expenses: the result of Thomson's mania for repairs and new machinery, the rising cost of labor and material, and the federal tax on passenger receipts. In 1863 alone, Thomson authorized $1.6 million for construction and new equipment. Until his profits grew embarrassingly large, he sought to plow them back into the property, explaining to disgruntled stockholders that they were only a temporary windfall.[17]

With more than $2 million cash in his treasury, however, Thomson was finding their angry demands hard to ignore by 1863. Nevertheless, he tried. He fulfilled the tonnage tax act requirement that he aid the "commutation roads" and even advanced them additional funds. He paid on the road's debt, not with the depreciating greenbacks, but in gold, despite the fact that he was under no legal obligation to do so. But even with all his expenses and payment of a 9 percent dividend in 1863, the PRR's treasury still held about $2 million in cash on the eve of the 1864 stockholders' meeting. Thomson could no longer postpone the inevitable; the day before the meeting he recommended to the board the distribution of a 30 percent stock dividend on top of a 10 percent regular payment. He issued no other special dividends during the war, but did continue the 10 percent return during the last two years of the conflict, enough to keep his stockholders pleased. From 1862 through 1865, investors in his road received an average return of over 18 percent each year.[18]

Thomson's conservative fiscal policies strengthened his road's postwar competitive position. By paying all dividends, bonded interest, and construction and repair costs from income, and charging off bad stock and bond investments to the same account, he kept his road's capitalization and fixed charges low. At the end of the war he estimated his road was worth $55 million, while its total debt was $15 million below that. He was one of the few railway presidents in the country who could boast to his stockholders that there was nothing "in the accounts of the Company representing fictitious values; on the contrary its property is worth in specie much more than it is represented at upon its books."[19]

Thomson had been lucky, for his road came very near suffering widespread property damage that could have cost him millions to repair. When General Robert E. Lee and his forces invaded the North in 1863 it was widely feared that he would strike at Harrisburg and destroy the Pennsylvania's property in the vicinity. Thomson certainly thought so and immediately moved in June to cut back train service, suspend all through freight traffic, and order all the road's rolling stock rushed to Philadelphia for safety. The PRR's engineers worked around the clock to draw up defensive plans to protect company structures. With his board's authorization Thomson purchased muskets for the workers, who were organized into companies and drilled. PRR scouts were dispatched as far away as Maryland to track Lee's whereabouts and often provided the most accurate information on the enemy's location that General George Meade received.[20]

Confederate troops moved freely across the state by the last week in June, and with the defense forces thrown into confusion, Thomson pressed hard for federal action. He pleaded with Lincoln to declare martial law in Philadelphia and met with friends, including at least one "noted rebel sympathizer," to plot strategy to have General George B. McClellan sent to Pennsylvania "to take military charge of things generally." McClellan, one of the most cautious Union commanders, had been relieved by Lincoln as commander of the Army of the Potomac on November 5, 1862, to be succeeded by Ambrose Burnside and later "Fighting Joe" Hooker, who covered the Union cause with little glory. Rumors were rife that Hooker was about to be replaced, and Thomson had long favored the reinstatement of his old friend, the former vice-president of the O&M. Thomson figured that if he could inveigle McClellan into command of the forces in Pennsylvania, where a major clash was about to occur, the general's reputation could be refurbished; McClellan was not incompetent, only slow, a trait that might have appealed to Thomson. Even after Lincoln replaced "Fighting Joe" with Meade, Thomson had not given up hope. He wrote the president, "In my judgment, it is essential that McClellan be placed in charge of the forces in Pennsylvania not now attached to the Army of the Potomac." Lincoln disregarded Thomson's advice, and the day after Meade repulsed Lee at Gettysburg, Peter Watson, the bright assistant secretary of war, wrote his immediate superior, "Tom Scott and Edgar Thomson will find it harder than ever to manufacture public sentiment to bear upon the President for restoration of McClellan. They would have been far more usefully and patriotically employed in persuading the people to shoulder muskets and fight the enemy instead of signing petitions." Such restraint would have marked Thomson as the only important man in the Union who did not badger the Administration to promote his favorite candidate. The Pennsylvania Railroad escaped Lee's invasion unscathed, although the Confederates destroyed thirty-three bridges on the Northern Central, which General Herman Haupt, chief of construction and transportation on the United States Military Railroads, used his forces to repair. Thomson counted himself fortunate to lose only the freight and passenger revenues for the two weeks and the money he spent on wages and materials for the PRR's defense; Lee, however, was dealt a blow at Gettysburg from which the Confederacy never recovered.[21]

Similarly, Thomson had difficulty recovering from the debilitating pace he had maintained early in the war and suffered a relapse in the spring of 1862. He was so seriously ill by April that he was unable to attend board meetings; when Scott was in town he chaired the deliberations, and when he was away, Josiah Bacon, a Philadelphia merchant, served as president *pro tem*. Thomson's malady, probably a recurrence of his pulmonary problems, lingered far into summer. In May he made plans to go to Europe, but had to cancel them because he did not think he could stand the voyage. Again in June, when he was feeling "much better," he booked passage for July 2. Still not up to par, he postponed his departure until July 16, when his secretary, Robert Lamborn, who had replaced the "Quaker General," William Palmer, reported that Thomson "was in excellent spirits apparently and I think he will be able to stand the voyage quite well." He took Lavinia and his niece Charlotte along for the five-month trip.[22]

Without a doubt, Thomson's 1862 European sojourn was an extended vacation to enable him to regain his health. He had to try, however, to justify it in terms of professional duty. Obediently, his board obliged him by formally requesting in May that he go abroad to sell the Philadelphia and Erie's (P&E) bonds. Those securities symbolized one major reason why Thomson was unable to regain his physical vitality, for amidst all his other wartime activities he bent every effort to construct a major new road. The P&E had been chartered in 1837 to link Philadelphia with Erie, 287 miles across the mountain fastness of north-central Pennsylvania. After innumerable financial contretemps, the railway was only half completed at the outbreak of the war. The hostilities stopped all further construction and, with a heavy load of fixed debts and unmarketable securities, company officials sought to lease their property; Thomson was intrigued. The P&E was building over the only other feasible grade through the Alleghenies and control of it would safeguard Thomson's competitive position in the state. Moreover, if finished, the road would tap the lakes' trade at Erie, enticing some of that traffic away from the New York roads to Philadelphia. In addition, the P&E with its eastern connections would give Thomson another outlet to New York City, which although rather circuitous and not very valuable to him, would at least keep it out of competitors' hands. He also recognized that the lease would be politically wise; many of his own important Philadelphia stockholders owned blocks of P&E stock that had yet to pay their first dividend. Since the state had aided the P&E, he would be able to mollify some of his political critics still outraged by the tactics Scott used in the tonnage tax repeal by helping the state recoup its investment.[23]

The lease negotiations were long and exhausting. Thomson met with P&E representatives in May 1861 while recovering from his first major illness and did not finish negotiating the 999-year lease until the following January. Financially, the agreement was not one of Thomson's crowning successes. Between 1862 and his death in 1874, his company realized a profit from the arrangement only the first two years and the sums were minuscule, while inflation pushed its construction costs $9 million over original estimates. Thomson was unable to sell the P&E securities because of competition from government war bonds; he had to advance construction funds from the Pennsylvania's current revenues. Despite the wartime shortage of labor and material he pushed the construction relentlessly, assigning badly needed men and supplies from his road to the work; he completed the road in mid-October 1864. It was quite a feat, but Thomson was never quite sure it was worth it; he was disappointed when traffic over the P&E remained light and the route never captured a significant share of the lakes' trade for Philadelphia. Furthermore, by 1873 the Pennsylvania was paying $600,000 in annual interest on the P&E's bonds, more than its income from the lease. Strategically, however, he still thought the property a good buy. It buttressed his own road's position in Pennsylvania and to a minor degree discomfited his northern competition.[24]

As the war drew to an end, Thomson could survey his prospects for the coming years with confidence. His policy of plowing earnings back into his property was about to pay dividends. Unlike the Erie, which emerged from the war with a badly worn single track laid with light iron rails, and the damaged B&O, which would take Garrett several years to bring back up to standards, the Pennsylvania had 70 percent more locomotives than it owned in 1861, more than twice as many cars, an almost completed second track, a start at laying steel rails, and almost no floating debt. Moreover, Thomson, now fifty-seven years old, was at the peak of his powers; he was master of his road and optimistic about the future. New opportunities loomed at every hand. He was particularly attracted by the new domestic steel industry, the possibility of building a transcontinental line, and the prospects opening up in the trans-Mississippi West. With the nation poised to rush headlong into the industrial world, Thomson was well positioned as a leading businessman with significant amounts of capital and credit at his command to march in the vanguard. And his greatest triumphs lay before him. He flung his mastery out in all directions from New York City to Utah, from Maine to Mexico, from Georgia to California, and across the Atlantic with dizzying speed. At times the pace seemed almost too brisk for him, particularly as his health became more precarious, but he could not quit. His compelling sense of duty and all his personal inclinations propelled him into the maelstrom that was postwar America.[25]

8

MASTER OF THE WORLD'S LARGEST RAIL EMPIRE

The end of the Civil War signaled the start of a great American industrial boom. Businessmen were ebullient and optimistic, while the government and public were complacent, allowing entrepreneurs their head. In harmony with the national mood and out of a sense of necessity, Thomson embarked on an ambitious expansion program that in nine years more than quintupled the railway mileage he controlled. His empire stretched from the Mississippi River to New York City and down to the Gulf of Mexico with about 6,000 miles of track by 1873, fully 8 percent of the nation's railroads. He became master of the largest transportation company in the world, capitalized at the then unheard of sum of $400 million. Even as he raised and spent hundreds of millions of dollars to finance his ambitious schemes, he kept the dividends flowing regularly; over his tenure as president they averaged almost 10 percent a year.[1]

High profits, regular dividends, and urgent expansion strengthened Thomson's position on the PRR and further eroded the directors' powers. His often incredibly complicated financial dealings, the increasing technical sophistication of the business, and the difficulties of managing a corporation spread out over half a continent overwhelmed the road's part-time directors. Furthermore, by 1869 Thomson had added his four vice-presidents to the board, further solidifying his position. A stockholder's investigating committee in 1874 underscored his complete domination of the company. It complained of his "meager and incomplete" annual reports and deplored "the tendencies in leading officials and managers of railway companies to act as if the property they manage was their own." The committee also realistically placed a portion of the responsibility squarely upon its own shoulders, pointing out that stockholders "transfer the decisions of all important questions to the board of directors." The perceptive report exhibited very clearly Thomson's relentless accretion of powers that enabled him to direct the unrestrained postwar expansion.[2]

The sheer size of the Pennsylvania guaranteed Thomson a national reputation. As master of hundreds of millions in capital, much of it in the hands of influential and powerful individuals, he acquired valuable allies with direct interests in his success who gave him wide support in banking circles, industry, the press, and politics. His ever-widening influence at all levels did not go unnoticed, but the very criticism he attracted only increased his reputation and effectiveness. In 1869, a James Stewart warned Garrett to beware of a powerful railroad clique composed of Thomson, Scott, Cooke, Thomas Durant of the Union Pacific, and Simon Cameron's son, J. Donald, "that intended to capture the U.S. Government," where "the legislation of congress will be made subservient to the behests of the Rail Road Ring." Echoing sentiments of Americans who feared the rise of wealthy men to prominence, he predicted "the time is approaching when this will become a question of national importance, when the very liberties of the people will have to be maintained against the tyranny of the large corporations."[3]

Always shy of publicity and not well known to the public, Thomson personally engendered such fears in very few people. Undoubtedly, Stewart was appalled by some of the startling corporate antics of Thomson's contemporaries that signified the start of a new era. The prewar business world had been characterized by numerous firms of modest size and means; the Pennsylvania, capitalized at $4 million in the early 1850s, was considered awesome. During the war a new generation of business leaders emerged, many of whom took advantage of the conflict to amass questionable gains, and through effort, cleverness, and perhaps luck, some later parlayed their holdings into massive fortunes. They seized upon new industries, advanced technologies, seemingly inexhaustible supplies of natural resources, and displayed an enthusiastic willingness to risk their capital, often reaping huge rewards. Thomson trod the stage with this new breed of American pioneer: men such as Commodore Vanderbilt, the coarse, uneducated enterpriser who late in life gambled his steamboat fortune to capture control of the Central; Jay Gould, the slight, ulcerous, orchid-growing financier whos midas touch sucked unearned profits from wrecked properties; John D. Rockefeller, the fundamentalist Cleveland oil refiner who ruthlessly monopolized his business; Collis P. Huntington, a former Sacramento hardware merchant who, with his partners, Leland Stanford, Mark Hopkins, and Charles Coker (the western "big four"), controlled the Central Pacific, and eventually all other routes to and from California; Jay Cooke, the wealthy purveyor of Civil War bonds; and George Pullman, who made a fortune from sleep and erected a personal fiefdom south of Chicago.

Thomson's older, more sedate business tradition, in which power was wielded with less flamboyance and in more indirect ways, was a precursor of that the new, more voluble breed of entrepreneurs. They too acquired and protected corporate and financial empires, but on a larger and more conspicuous scale than Thomson. Their wealth was so great, they could not be safely ignored by a democratic society; and the attendant publicity they attracted only served to create and sustain the myths of their invincibility. To many Americans, the financial titans of the postwar period exemplified virtues they considered indigenous: daring, strength, intelligence, and inevitable success. The new generation of business leaders, nonetheless, was motivated by many of the ideals that drove Thomson: a passion for hard work; a firm belief that it was furthering the national good; a commitment to progress as measured in dollars, miles, and tons; and a consummate faith in its own abilities.

Marked differences also set Thomson apart from the new breed. The Pennsylvania's president believed that his first responsibility was to his road and its shareholders. Although he expanded the company far beyond its charterers' wildest dreams, he never altered its formal structure of accountability. The mere existence of the 1874 stockholders' investigating committee pointed up that he was ultimately beholden to the road's owners—unlike the new breed of railway leaders who short-circuited such accountability by buying a major interest or securing enough proxies to control their own companies, thereby inviting excesses that eventually swelled the number of people who agreed with James Stewart. Control through stock ownership of such major railways as the NYC, the Erie, and the transcontinentals inevitably led the owner-managers to manipulate their securities for personal ends; they were after all technically accountable to themselves. That Thomson would, like Vanderbilt, Daniel Drew, Gould, and Jim Fisk, sell his own road's stock short, was unthinkable. He bought it for appreciation, confident that his policies would continue to increase its value.

To that end he constantly harped on the need to maintain and upgrade his property. He poured millions of dollars into the Pennsylvania's physical plant after the war, and his improvements were reflected in the attractive prices of his company's stocks and bonds. Thomson derived as much satisfaction from his new equipment and freshly ballasted main line with its steel rails, as he did in reporting ever higher profits. Unlike some of his contemporaries, he maintained that one promoted the other, that his road's unsurpassed facilities kept its earning power above that of his eastern rivals. The figures bore him out. In 1873, the PRR east of Pittsburgh enjoyed gross revenues of almost $40 million, the NYC east of Buffalo, $29 million, the Erie, $20 million, and the B&O, east of the Ohio River, $15.6 million. Thomson could easily afford to enhance, expand, and protect his properties without resorting to financial chicanery.[4]

On a more personal level Thomson lacked the consuming, driving avarice of a Gould, Vanderbilt, Carnegie, or Rockefeller; although he spent his entire career at least indirectly in the pursuit of profit, in keeping with his Quaker background he appropriated, in distinct contrast to his more flamboyant contemporaries, only an infinitesimal portion of his income for personal use. He displayed as much enthusiasm for building and creating, as he did in collecting the rewards. He would not differentiate between his financial talents and his technical abilities. Each augmented and limited the other. This balance, increasingly unique in the postwar world, where specialization was becoming the norm, helped make him an important constructive force in mid-nineteenth-century American economic development.

Thomson's postwar career had a certain desperate pace about it—the quickening of a man who recognized his approaching end, yet had much unfinished business. His health deteriorated badly; from 1866 to his death in 1874, he was free of prolonged debilitating illness only in 1871. His recurring pulmonary troubles affected his heart, and he suffered several heart attacks in his last years. As his health became more problematical, Thomson worked fewer days each year and more often, at his wife's urging, sought diversion from his cares in Europe. Yet when he did work, he labored longer hours, juggled more projects, and undertook larger tasks. His exaggerated sense of duty continued to drive him, and his responsibilities increased as he found it proportionately more difficult to let go and relax.[5]

Although his contemporaries indicated that Thomson became more conservative and deliberate as he aged, his activities belied that assessment. He became financially bolder, sinking great sums into much bigger and often more chancy ventures. The vast resources of his rivals and the accelerated competitive pace provoked Thomson to initiate bold, expansive strategies. He was also undoubtedly affected by the postwar euphoria with its belief that the race went to the swiftest of the strong. Fundamentally, however, he was driven by an inner sense that time was short and that with no children, he would be remembered solely as the Pennsylvania's architect. He frantically sought to finish his monument, a transportation empire linking the Atlantic with important midwestern river cities, and to erect unassailable defenses about it; by the late 1860s that meant command of roads into New York City, the South, and the West and control of all roads which, if captured by hostile interests, might threaten the Pennsylvania's prosperity. These acquisitions cost millions of dollars, many of them borrowed, a policy Thomson was forced to pursue to gain his ends. His headlong expansion filled out the contours of his Pennsylvania as they would endure for the next century, and he would have enlarged his empire further had not the panic of 1873 and a stockholder uprising halted his strenuous efforts.

At the end of the Civil War, Thomson fully expected to return to the straitened conditions of the late 1850s when fierce competition had held profits down even while tonnage increased. To prepare for these eventualities, he advanced funds to numerous feeder lines, calculating that he could always maintain a profit from the local traffic; he enlarged his road's Delaware River facilities and started construction on Philadelphia's Junction Railway to ease car transfer problems there. He also contracted for over $1 million worth of new equipment to handle the coal, oil, and lumber business. At the same time, he curtailed expenses as far as possible, reducing shop and mechanics' wages 15 percent in 1866, paying only the local prevailing salary rate everywhere on the system and spending huge sums for steel rails to lower his maintenance costs. By 1873 his 627 miles of new steel track exceeded that found on any other railway in the nation.[6]

The new rails enabled his road to operate locomotives twice as heavy as the prewar models, pulling longer trains at higher speeds with less roadbed wear. The heavier trains, however, were harder to stop, and Thomson, always watchful for technical improvements, quickly saw the possibilities of George Westinghouse's experiments with an air brake. At the end of 1869 Thomson persuaded his board to allow Westinghouse to demonstrate his innovation on the Pennsylvania. The directors were so impressed with what they saw that they signed a contract with the inventor to equip all the road's cars with his braking system, which enabled the company to operate longer trains safely. Thomson's early adoption of steel rails and air brakes helped hold the road's operating ratio, despite a doubling of tonnage and a vast increase in the size of the system between 1870 and 1873, in the 59 percent range.[7]

Thomson needed all the economies he could effect when traffic temporarily leveled off right after the war. Moreover, Garrett repaired his B&O and sought to reclaim his lost trade; once again there was only enough business for three roads. Worse, Commodore Vanderbilt purchased the Central and then turned on the Erie in an attempt to acquire that property. The titanic battle that started in 1867 between Vanderbilt and Gould for control of the Erie upset all chances for rate agreement in the region. The ensuing rate war that year depressed gross revenues on all lines and set in motion a chain of events that eventually forced Thomson to revise drastically his corporate strategy.

None of the eastern trunk lines owned its midwestern connections. Instead, each relied on corporate friendships to insure steady traffic interchanges. Traditionally, however, the Central was allied with a number of roads skirting the southern shores of the Great Lakes and the Pennsylvania with the Fort Wayne. The Erie had no reliable connections, and its six-foot gauge made transfer of freight and passengers difficult. To the south, Garrett depended upon several small roads and the Ohio and Mississippi to St. Louis and was making plans to build his own Chicago branch. As soon as Gould bested the Commodore for control of the Erie, he set out to disrupt those long-

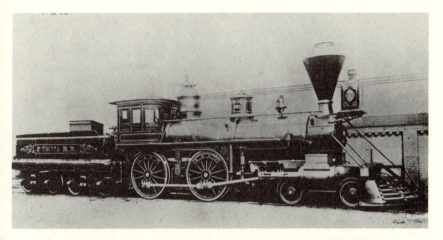

Always a technological pacesetter, Thomson ordered the first experiments with George Westinghouse's air brake conducted on this locomotive. Note the unusual rounded cab. Courtesy of the Division of Archives and Manuscripts, Pennsylvania Historical and Museum Commission, Harrisburg, Pennsylvania.

standing relationships. Whatever else may be said about Gould, he was a man who thoroughly grasped corporate railroad strategy and was something of a genius at executing the bold stroke. He moved in December 1868 to lease the Atlantic and Great Western, another broad-gauged road that cut through the western Pennsylvania oil region and ran southwesterly to Cleveland and Cincinnati, interchanging with numerous lines including the Fort Wayne.[8]

Gould fully understood that all strategy had offensive and defensive components; he was not content simply to gain valuable midwestern connections, he sought to deny them to his competitors. His timing was perfect, for in 1867 Thomson's midwestern friends were feuding with each other, and Gould seized an opportunity to exploit the divisions within the Pennsylvania's extended family. Thomson's problems had begun right after the war when he completed the Pittsburgh and Steubenville to a junction with the Steubenville and Indiana giving him a route from Pittsburgh to Columbus that competed with the Fort Wayne road. Later, when the P&S went bankrupt, Thomson foreclosed and in April 1868 merged the lines into a consolidated road, the Pittsburgh, Cincinnati and St. Louis, popularly known as the Pan Handle route.[9]

President Cass of the Fort Wayne watched Thomson's moves with growing apprehension, and when the Pennsylvania's president sought connections from Columbus to Indianapolis and Chicago, Cass was quick to perceive Thomson's intentions as threatening. He reacted by remonstrating with the Pennsylvania's board, from which he had resigned in 1865, warning that he would build his own line to New York City. Thomson persuaded Cass to delete that threat from his annual report. But Cass went ahead and financed survey crews east of Pittsburgh and invested in a company that Thomson believed was established to build the competing road. Finally, in April 1868 common sense prevailed and the boards of both roads appointed special committees to restore amicable relations; by the end of the year the companies had concluded a friendly compact for the interchange of traffic.

With the Fort Wayne settled down, Benjamin E. Smith, president of the Columbus, Chicago and Indiana Central, an independent western connection with the Pan Handle, became restless as he interpreted the Fort Wayne contract as a threat to his trade. Gould was waiting offstage, watching carefully, and with his unerring ability to spot an opponent's weakness, went after control of Smith's road. Smith, fearful that Thomson was playing Cass off against him, agreed in January 1869 to lease his road to Gould.[10]

Gould's moves caught Thomson by surprise, but even so, he was extraordinarily slow to perceive the threats to his interests despite the ominous portents all around him. He had long been loath to tie up large amounts of capital in midwestern connections when he could acquire dependable allies through traffic contracts. He was so sanguine that he even sold off his road's holdings in the Fort Wayne, assuming that the long history of friendly relations between the lines would continue. At heart, Thomson was simply not an empire builder like Gould. He was molded in a different, more pacific era in which rational men representing commercial interests negotiated mutually beneficial business arrangements. He was slow to recognize the rise of men with personal fortunes so large that they could, at their whim, purchase control of major improvements and upset relations in every direction. Gould, however, had finally touched a sensitive nerve in the Pennsylvania's president. There was nothing that aroused Thomson's ire faster than a threat to his road; it was his family, his monument, and he took full responsibility for its welfare. He had built it, nurtured it, and was inordinately proud of his creation. By contrast, Gould's Erie in the late 1860s stood for everything Thomson despised. It was a poorly maintained, poorly managed, accident-prone railway that served as a handy vehicle for its owner's stock speculations.

When Thomson finally realized the gravity of the situation, he reacted decisively. In a hastily called board meeting on January 11, 1869, he discussed with his directors what should be done. Although they entered nothing in the minutes, it soon became clear that the board gave Thomson a carte blanche to protect the Pennsylvania's interests in any way he saw fit. That meeting was a watershed in Thomson's career; he walked out of it determined on a bold expansion policy to insure that his railroad would never be threatened again. He knew that he must gain control of his vital connections to the west; it had been a fixed principle of his for years that he must never lose his ability to compete for the western trade. Thomson had also long regretted his inability to serve New York City over his own lines. He calculated that now was the opportune time to rectify that problem and squelch any future threats from that quarter. He already knew the important routes that he must have, the Fort Wayne and the Camden and Amboy. He knew too that it would be unprofitable to build his own roads parallel to them. Beyond that he had no specific plans, and Scott heavily influenced his president's thinking. The vice-president, long an unabashed expansionist, engineered the Pennsylvania's takeover of the southern lines, promoted its influence in the Far West and Southwest, and performed the political chores in a dozen states necessary to carry out Thomson's policies.[11]

But Thomson never seriously considered pushing the PRR into the trans Mississippi West. He and most of his colleagues viewed their competitive world in terms of specific regions defined by the great national geographical fault lines. His company was chartered to connect the Atlantic with the Ohio River at Pittsburgh, and until Gould's foray into his territory, Thomson continued to think its primary task was to serve that area. When forced to reexamine his preconceptions, his corporate horizons came to rest on the east bank of the Mississippi River, the western boundary of the adjacent railway balances of power in the Midwest and South. Transportation leaders, including Thomson, until the late 1860s, operated within regional balances of power and bent every effort to manipulate them for their own ends, while content to indirectly influence or coexist with neighboring balances. This was a natural outlook in a nation that was only beginning to throw off its regionalism and create national markets and financial centers. Furthermore, railroad officers, more geographically bound than many other types of businessmen, were slow to evolve national strategies. Thomson had long understood the value of other regions' trade to his own, and as early as the 1830s had been active in helping to develop railroad properties in the West. But he believed that the natural laws of trade would regularly channel products from those areas over the most efficient eastern roads. He found he could live and prosper with the modicum of stability and security the regional balances and interregional alliances afforded him.

Gould, who believed otherwise, ranged into every region and intruded upon everyone's territory, prompting many railroaders to take the longer view of their industry. When Thomson did adopt such strategy, he concentrated on improving his position in the major eastern markets between the Atlantic and the Mississippi; the Pennsylvania's penetration into the Far West, where the balance of power was still developing, had to wait. Moreover, Thomson probably could not have stretched his road from ocean to ocean even if he had wanted to. After the war, an increasing percentage of the Pennsylvania's stock was owned by English investors who were only interested in healthy regular returns and appreciation of their securities. They looked askance at all increases in the road's indebtedness. There was also a considerable conservative shareholder element living in the United States who viewed with alarm even Thomson's activities in the East. After seventeen years in the presidential suite, Thomson knew just how far he could push his mastery without endangering his position. He was still fascinated by the prospects in the Far West, but his only recourse was to invest his own money in the new transcontinentals in the hope that someday he could link his Pennsylvania with one he controlled. He almost succeeded in 1872; but his timing was unfortunate. The panic the following year dashed expansionists' hopes everywhere and brought his western schemes to an abrupt halt. The times were never again as propitious, and the bulk of subsequent railroad growth was not in the more settled East.

Thomson had more specific thoughts on his mind, however, when he walked out of the boardroom that cold January afternoon. He first had to foil Gould's attempt to take over Smith's road. Moving with what was for him bewildering speed, he and Scott bombarded that road's stockholders with appeals to overturn their board's lease with Gould. Thomson had his vote by the end of the month and moved immediately to lease the line himself; he was in such a hurry that he acquired it for his Pan Handle route without even examining its physical condition. Eleven days later he told his shareholders that he would have to increase the PRR's capital stock to pay for needed repairs. Thomson refused to operate an inferior property, even if it were leased and not a very valuable one at that. His failure to inspect the line and to assess adequately Gould's threat convinced him that he was overburdened with work. To remove some of the more onerous tasks from his shoulders, he had his board authorize the addition of two new vice-presidents, bringing the company's total to four.[12]

The Pan Handle's lease of Smith's road angered Cass, who revived his plans to build to the Atlantic and approached Gould for help. Nevertheless, Cass was leery of the New York speculator and watched him carefully. Gould, who wanted the Fort Wayne, could not buy enough stock to get it, so he acquired sufficient stock proxies to control the company's approaching annual elections. When Cass realized in February 1869 that Gould was about to wrest his road from him, he scampered back into the Pennsylvania's camp to get help. In this situation Scott's influence in the state legislature paid off handsomely. In just thirty-four minutes, he rammed a bill through both houses and across the governor's desk that changed the tenure of the Fort Wayne's directors so that no more than one-quarter of the board's members stood for election in any year.[13]

Gould had been stopped, but he continued to negotiate with Cass for a traffic interchange between their roads. Thomson, however, was determined to tie the road more closely to his PRR and began talking to Cass about a lease. The Fort Wayne's president demanded harsh terms, but Thomson was resolved to have the line at almost any cost. The 999-year lease that the Pennsylvania's board finally approved on

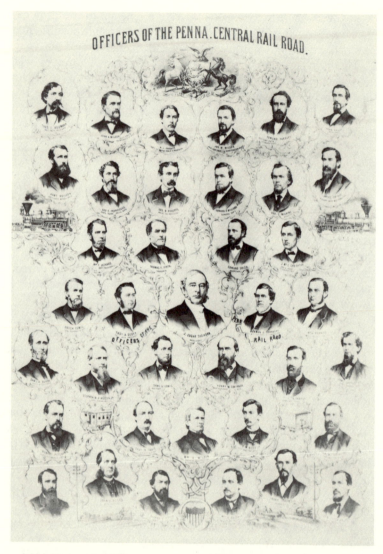

Thomson's talented management team after the Civil War included four future presidents of the Pennsylvania. Courtesy of the Division of Archives and Manuscripts, Pennsylvania Historical and Museum Commission, Harrisburg, Pennsylvania.

May 27, 1869, indeed appeared burdensome. Thomson agreed to pay an annual rental of $1.3 million, equal to 12 percent on the road's outstanding stock, to guarantee the Fort Wayne's three mortgages, equipment bonds, and subsidiary leases. Although he admitted in his annual report that the terms were "onerous," they were agreed to, he explained, only because of the "dire threat" posed to the road. As it transpired, the Fort Wayne paid generous dividends into his treasury for years; Thomson had struck one of his most successful bargains— he gained a greater measure of security and influence in the Midwest and tidy profits.[14]

He also acquired myriad obligations across the region. Cass's road had leased and guaranteed the securities of numerous feeder lines that became Thomson's responsibility when he brought the Fort Wayne into the Pennsylvania's immediate family. Thomson reported in 1871 that under the lease, the PRR became guarantor for $58 million worth of midwestern railroad bonds. While the new roads insured additional connections to Chicago and St. Louis, they also saddled him with superfluous lines that he was contractually bound to maintain. Aside from legal necessity, the only possible rationale he could present for continuing to invest in some of the properties was to keep them out of competitors' hands.[15]

The great consolidation movement in the Midwest, in which Vanderbilt merged the lake shore lines into the Lake Shore and Michigan Southern to give his Central an entrance into Chicago—and Garrett began construction of his own road to that city—moved some of the remaining independent railways in that region to seek corporate havens. One of these, the Little Miami, fell like a ripe plum into Thomson's lap. In February 1870 he leased the road to his Pan Handle, affording that line an excellent route from Columbus to Cincinnati for a rental of less than $500,000 a year. As in the case of the Fort Wayne lease, the Little Miami brought into the Pennsylvania's family six more leased lines.[16]

With the acquisition of the Little Miami, the Pennsylvania's midwestern system, sprawling over Ohio, Indiana, and Illinois, became an administrative nightmare. Some roads, such as the Fort Wayne, were profitable properties; others, such as Smith's, were chronic invalids. No overall operations, maintenance, funding, accounting, and traffic policies existed to govern relations among them and with the parent company. In addition, the responsibility for operating the new roads placed an enormous strain on Thomson and his subordinates. The pressures became so intense that Thomson's health broke in March 1870, preventing him from attending another board meeting until October 3. He took a lengthy leave of absence to rest and recuperate but stayed in Philadelphia, a strong indication that he had suffered his first major heart attack.

It was an inopportune time for him to be out of action, for he had begun working on plans to place all his new western properties under a separate subsidiary corporate structure. Scott assumed the responsibility for organizing the new Pennsylvania Company (PC) and securing its charter in April. The final implementation had to await Thomson's return when he could examine all the prospective arrangements. Finally, on February 1, 1871, the Pennsylvania's board accepted PC stock in exchange for the securities of thirteen roads, ranging from the Fort Wayne and Pan Handle companies to General Ambrose Burnside's Indianapolis and Vincennes—in all over 3,000 miles of railways. To reassure the Pennsylvania's stockholders who worried about their company's pell-mell expansion, Thomson cleverly named the company after the home state and selected Scott as its first president.[17]

At the same time, Thomson's railroad was moving into the South in force. His penetration of that region started in 1867 as a tactical move against the B&O when he decided to build a road to connect the Northern Central at Baltimore with Washington. Thomson had long fought with Garrett, who controlled the only route from Baltimore to the capital, over arrangements for through service between Harrisburg and Washington, and in the midst of the rate war that year, he and J. Donald Cameron, president of the NC, decided to do something about it.[18] Although the PRR indirectly guaranteed the notes of the new Baltimore & Potomac, Thomson did not bother to mention his excursion into the B&O's territory until his 1871 annual report, when he somewhat oversimplistically explained that he wanted to "bypass" the B&O to connect with the Richmond, Fredericksburg and Potomac. This was the first formal indication the shareholders received that consolidation of southern roads under the aegis of the Pennsylvania was already well underway. The campaign was largely the responsibility of Scott, who, with his overpowering nervous energy, adroitly handled all the financing, organizing, and politicking for the PRR. Using the PC as a model, he organized another holding company in 1871, the Southern Railway Security Company, to take possession of the PRR's southern railways. Although never absorbed by the Pennsylvania, it was managed, as Thomson explained to his shareholders the following year, by "gentlemen friendly to our interests and objects." As it transpired, they constituted a veritable horde of "friendly interests," including Cass, Thomson, Scott, J. Donald Cameron, and James Roosevelt of the Hyde Park clan. To calm the fears of his more conservative stockholders, Thomson dryly noted that the PRR "became a shareholder to protect its investment in the Baltimore and Potomac Railroad."

That assertion must have left more thoughtful stockholders somewhat incredulous; for if true, the Pennsylvania's southern venture was a major overkill. Its outlay of about $3 million bought it control of 2,100 miles of railway along three distinct routes: from Baltimore to Charleston; Richmond to Charlotte; and Bristol to Memphis. Thomson's and Scott's invasion of the ex-Confederate states garnered them reams of bad publicity for Scott's high-handed political maneuvering. Many southerners, already sensitive to postwar "carpetbaggers," looked upon the Pennsylvania as the institutional embodiment of that despicable breed, intent on monopolizing the region's transportation for the enrichment of the "bucktails" from Pennsylvania. And there was an element of truth in the accusation; Thomson was so entirely confident of success there that he invested about $150,000 of his own funds in several of the southern companies.[19]

The Pennsylvania's southern campaign was a sideshow, however, in comparison with Thomson's carefully executed expansion of his road to New York City. With the lease of the United New Jersey Railroads (UNJR), he extended his control from the nation's largest port and financial center to Chicago, and in so doing, rounded out the Pennsylvania's principal contours as they existed when it merged with the Central to create the ill-fated Penn Central. The speed of Thomson's eastward expansion indicated that he knew exactly what he wanted. No sooner had he leased the Fort Wayne road, thereby securing his western flank, than he announced that negotiations with the New Jersey roads were underway. He explained to his stockholders that the PRR carried too much freight for the city of Philadelphia to absorb anymore, and connections to other ports had to be sought to handle the increased trade. Thomson had coveted an entrance to New York City after it became obvious to him that the Quaker City had no chance of displacing the New York port, nor of attracting the supportive services and facilities necessary to a major entrepôt for international trade. His principal connection with the northern port was the Camden and Amboy, an all-rail route from Camden to Jersey City, opposite New York. Thomson had alternate links over the Connecting Railway and the Philadelphia and Trenton, and he could also use a more circuitous route across hilly eastern Pennsylvania from Harrisburg. Not one was entirely satisfactory, however; more importantly, none belonged to him.[20]

The UNJR, which included the Camden and Amboy, was Thomson's most important artery to New York. The consolidated company enjoyed a monopoly of the state's traffic long guaranteed by the state legislature but slated to expire in 1869. Protection of their monopoly required UNJR officials to be politically active, yet the monopoly privilege dampened their enthusiasm for improving the company's facilities. As New York City-bound traffic poured over their properties from the PRR and other roads, the UNJR's terminal facilities at Jersey City were overwhelmed. Instead of making necessary improvements, its managers chose to continue paying 10 percent dividends that they financed from a special fund created from the company's wartime excess profits.[21]

Thomson was frustrated over his inability to untangle the traffic snarls at Jersey City, and on the same day that his board adopted the PC contract, he lectured it on the benefits of acquiring the New Jersey roads. Bewildered by the rapidity with which their corporation was changing, the directors postponed action, but Thomson could not delay; he reversed his usual procedure of playing his cards close to his vest and prodded his directors with a public announcement that he was exploring the possibility of a lease.[22]

While Scott handled the political duties in the New Jersey legislature, Thomson dickered with UNJR representatives. It was a touchy situation for many prominent New Jersey citizens opposed leasing their ex-monopoly to what they considered a foreign one. Finally, on April 26, 1871, Thomson brought a firm proposal to his board for its consideration. As he later admitted, the Jersey company also demanded "onerous" terms that he could justify only by the "dire necessity" of reaching the Hudson River over his own tracks. Thomson paid liberally for the privilege; in return for the 999-year lease, he agreed to continue the 10 percent dividends and guaranteed its bonded indebtedness. Cleverly, he required the Jersey company to issue 22,500 shares of new stock and to turn them over to the PRR for use in developing new terminal facilities on the Harsimus Cove property in Jersey City. That tract was the last large undeveloped area on the waterfront, and in Thomson's eyes, one of the principal attractions of the whole arrangement. For his outlay, he acquired 172 miles of railroad, sixty-six miles of canal, and fifteen smaller companies.

The price was considerable, so high that four directors had the temerity to vote against the lease, but Thomson had greatly strengthened his road's competitive position. Although the contract was not profitable until 1889, he gained an outlet to the Atlantic's premier city that a later generation of PRR managers nurtured in the Thomson era, led by Alexander J. Cassett, would improve by tunneling into the very heart of New York City. Only the Central actually had physical connections in the city in 1871. The Erie, like the PRR, had its terminal across the Hudson River. Moreover, Thomson's eastern expansion gave him a more powerful voice in railway rate-making councils and strengthened his bid to maintain rate differentials favoring his native Philadelphia.[23]

With the Erie under the ministrations of Gould, the Central controlled by the unpredictable Vanderbilts, and relations with Garrett barely civil, Thomson found that struggle more difficult every year. The unceasing trunk line hostilities drove down charges relentlessly; in 1865 the through rate stood at almost three mills per ton mile and dropped in steady increments to only 1.3 mills in 1874. It was a tribute to Thomson's skills that, as his income per unit fell by almost 60 percent, he was able to pare his costs and quintuple his tonnage to maintain high dividends. No matter how efficiently he operated his road, nor how severe his economies, he could not hope to maintain his level of profitability without arranging fixed rates. That goal became even more elusive after the war when a new competitive element, express companies, was introduced. These private firms solicited business, routed freight over the trunk lines in their own cars, and took the responsibility for schedules, insurance, and delivery. In a much criticized move, Thomson reluctantly emulated his New York competitors in 1865 and contracted with the Union Line, a private transporter, to ship western freight exclusively over the PRR. Rumors that the real owners of the express company were the Pennsylvania's managers, who were skimming profits off from the PRR, refused to die. And there was an element of truth in them, at least on the face of it, for one backer, William Thaw, was Scott's financial ally, and another, Henry Houston, was the Pennsylvania's general freight agent. Scott also may have held an interest, but if he did, it was in someone else's name. Thomson did not; he expressed his hostility toward such firms, both publicly and privately, and as soon as possible, his road bought the express company's rolling stock and handled its trade through the PRR's freight department. Right after the war, however, he found the private companies valuable because many of his western connections lacked enough cars and the Union line's rolling stock made a crucial difference. But the all-encompassing scope of the lines' activities, their private nature, and dependence upon commissions, made it exceedingly difficult for railway presidents to enforce rate agreements.[24]

Garrett complicated railroad diplomacy by refusing to contract with express companies. Moreover, beginning in 1866 he balked at treating with the other presidents as long as they refused to cut their ties with the private concerns. His favorite tactic that year was to attend the "Big Four" meetings to demand a vote on the subject and, after losing, to walk out. The situation worsened in 1867 when Thomson, usually allied with Garrett, offered him a monopoly of the traffic in the Ohio River territory if Garrett would give up his plans to build a branch line to Pittsburgh. When Garrett expressed "surprise" at the offer and not so politely turned it down, a rate war broke out that lasted the remainder of the year; this conflict led Thomson to build the Baltimore & Potomac to compete with the B&O for the Washington traffic. The trunk lines continued for the rest of the decade to fight for traffic as tonnage levels grew, but not at a rate fast enough to keep all four roads operating at capacity levels. The presidents regularly met to set rates and just as regularly refused to adhere to the treaties they had signed. The recession of 1869 added to all the presidents' woes, and, although Thomson was able to keep his dividends between 6 and 10 percent during the period, it was becoming ever more difficult to squeeze profits from the falling rates. By 1871 that strain caused

Thomson willingly to become associated with one of the more nefarious schemes of that era, the South Improvement Company, an attempt by refiners and railroads to monopolize the oil industry.[25]

The SIC was one of the many ubiquitous creations Scott enjoyed pushing through the pliant state legislature periodically, a company invested with vast authority to hold securities in other corporations. The SIC was a little stranger than most, for although it was passed as a private bill in 1870, with Sam S. Moon, Scott's legislative whiz, and R. D. Barclay, Thomson's private secretary, among others listed as its organizers, it was not printed in the legislative record until 1872, after it had become a *cause célèbre*. What Scott initially had in mind for the new company is unclear, but in 1871 he decided to use the charter to stabilize the chaotic oil trade that was becoming ever more important to the PRR's fiscal well-being.[26]

Scott hoped to create a huge pool combining with the major eastern trunk lines and several large refiners to raise rates on crude and refined oil to profitable levels, regulate tonnage, and curb overproduction in the industry. On January 2, 1872, Standard Oil; Lockhart, Frew and Company of Pittsburgh; Warden, Frew and Company; Atlantic Refining Company of Philadelphia; and Jabez Bostwick in New York City organized the SIC for the refiners. Later in the month Thomson and the presidents of the NYC, Erie, Lake Shore, and Atlantic and Great Western signed contracts with it. Railway officials divided up the traffic with 45 percent going to the PRR and 27.5 percent each to the NYC and Erie systems. The SIC refiners agreed to pay higher posted rates with the guarantee of rebates that ranged from 25 to 50 percent. All outside firms had to pay the full tolls. If the SIC had stopped there it would have simply been another attempt to rationalize the competitive situation. But the company's promoters had larger dreams; the railroad's contracts stipulated that SIC oil companies would receive a drawback, equal to their rebates, on all oil shipped by competitors. Moreover, the railroads had to deliver regular reports on the oil shipped over their lines to SIC's managers allowing them to keep abreast of their competitors' dealings. The scheme's scope was awesome. Once implemented, it would have quickly given a few companies control of the petroleum industry. SIC officials had not reckoned, however, with the outrage their doubling of crude oil rates would cause in the oil region. Rumors of the combination were soon sweeping through the oil fields, and on February 25 when the higher rates were posted prematurely, the public outcry in western Pennsylvania was immediate. Rallies were held; a boycott was initiated; and petitions were presented to the state legislature demanding a free pipeline bill, a measure Scott had always managed to bottle up in committee; and there was a move to rescind the SIC's charter, which no one could find listed among the laws. The producers threatened violence and a congressional investigation of the attempted monopoly. Peter H. Watson, president of the Lake Shore and as president of the SIC, the hapless target of all the wrath, suffered the destruction of his oil tanks in the region. The public's ire remained unabated even after Watson was forced out of SIC's presidency.

When Scott was approached by a producers' committee on March 18, he admitted the PRR's contract with SIC was unfair and offered the protesting producers a chance to come into the combination. Under intense pressure, Scott finally met with other trunk line officials and the producers' committee at the Erie's offices on March 25, 1872, where the railway representatives agreed to break their contracts with the SIC and sign an agreement with the producers that lowered oil rates and forbade all rebates. Later, congressional testimony by Henry Flagler, however, confirmed that Standard Oil began receiving rebates only a week after Scott signed with the producers.[27]

Although Thomson's role in the formation of the SIC was slight, for he was enmeshed in negotiations for the UNJR lease, unquestionably, he supported Scott's brainchild, having long favored collusion and cooperation as rational alternatives to unregulated competition. The fact that he was the first railway president to sign a contract with the SIC only served to emphasize his backing. And, his directors must have endorsed the arrangement, at least tacitly, as they omitted any mention of the SIC in their minutes. When Scott was forced to abandon the audacious scheme, he left the PRR again at the mercy of the large oil firms' demands for rebates, insured the return of costly monthly tonnage fluctuations, and guaranteed steadily falling oil rates.

While the railroads attempted to impose order on the oil trade, the overall competitive situation in the East eased. The next seventeen months were the postwar salad days. After the 1869 recession lifted, economic growth across the country was phenomenal. Huge quantities of material poured across all the trunk lines giving them almost all the traffic they could handle. Although competition for some commodities remained keen, average rates per ton mile fell at a slower pace. On the PRR these reductions were offset by traffic increases that averaged 20 percent in 1872 and 1873, and pushed the road's net earnings from $6.2 million in 1870 to $8.6 million in 1873. This rate of growth was more than sufficient to allow Thomson to keep his stockholders appeased and continue his amazing expansion program. He even quit carping about low rates in his annual reports.[28]

By early summer 1873, Thomson could well afford to be pleased. The PRR under his mastery enjoyed the control of secure connections in every state south of New England and east of the Mississippi River, save Florida, Louisiana, and Wisconsin. Some components of his system were weak, but his overall profits left enough funds to maintain the railways to his exacting personal standards and to strategically defend the properties. He had nurtured a transport colossus, generating in his last full year as president almost $25 million in gross revenues from the parent company alone. Over the rails he so laboriously located in the 1840s, his employees worked 879 locomotives and 18,219 cars of all descriptions.[29]

All this had been built at considerable personal cost. For years Thomson had been a slave to his own creation, caught up in its multitudinous affairs, unable to let go. The larger it grew, the harder he worked, and the more his health suffered. The wonder of it all was that he found the time and energy to oversee all the Pennsylvania's affairs, and at the same time to promote numerous private speculations ranging from Canada to Mexico and seemingly everywhere in between. His ventures made him a millionaire several times over and involved him with wealthy promoters from all over the nation, thereby increasing his invulnerability in the PRR's councils. An established national figure in the business world, he achieved his stature without acquiring the reputation of being a parvenu, as did many of his contemporaries. Although he belonged to an older, more sedate generation of businessmen, he changed during the postwar years, most noticeably in his increased willingness to engage in businesses more closely associated with his ever-growing railway empire. Yet he survived the onset of rampant industrial capitalism with his personal reputation for probity intact. By adapting the techniques he had mastered and refined in his earlier years, he prospered mightily in the industrial era.

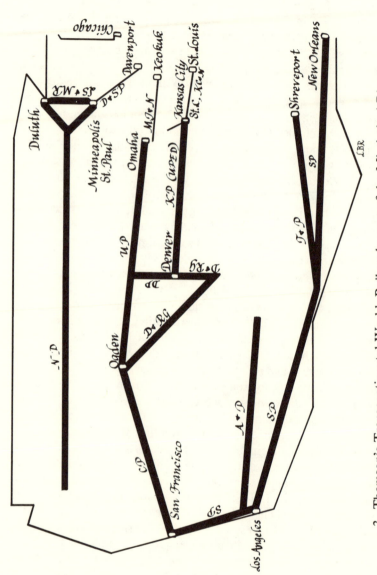

3. Thomson's Transcontinental World: Railroads west of the Mississippi River.

9

NUMBERING
HIS MILLIONS

Thomson's personal wealth never approached that of some of his contemporaries. His nemesis on the NYC, Vanderbilt, left an estate of some $70 million in 1867. Gould passed sums through his pockets that would have staggered Thomson. And Carnegie amassed personal holdings of very close to half a billion dollars. By contrast, Thomson's own worth was modest indeed. His estate evaluation in 1874 showed that his stocks and bonds would have brought less than $1 million on the markets, $987,278 to be exact; he was also due slightly over $300,000 from numerous loans. His assets, less his personal effects, house, real estate, and the family farm, had a market value in May 1874 of just about $1.3 million.

These figures woefully understated the earlier values of his personal securities and his importance as a businessman. His estate was probated in compliance with state law just eight months after the bottom had fallen out of the securities' markets, thereby rendering worthless what had been lucrative investments less than a year earlier. Moreover, he had just sold off many of his more solid securities to prop up Scott's Texas & Pacific. The known par value of his bond holdings alone was almost $1 million, while they were carried on his estate at less than half that figure. And it was obvious that 1,284 shares of the Northern Pacific at $1.00, the Denver & Rio Grande at less than three dollars a share, the Alexandria & Fredericksburg at $1.00 for 300 shares, and the Kansas Pacific at two dollars a share, were all equally undervalued. His holdings in only five companies accounted for three-fifths of the $543,718 value the court placed on all his stock, yet he owned over 88,000 shares in 116 separate businesses.[1]

At his zenith in the early 1870s, Thomson was probably worth about $5 million. With this relatively small holding he exercised an exaggerated influence over the contours of American economic development. He parlayed that $5 million into control of between $750 million and $1 billion of capital. The majority of it, of course, $400 million, was in his own PRR, but at various times he was important in transcontinental properties, the coal industry, the oil business, iron and steel manufacturing, bridge companies, numerous land firms, manufacturing concerns, and construction companies. On a much smaller scale he dabbled in life insurance, general mining projects, the lumber business, and mineral explorations.

As a prominent officer on the Pennsylvania, Thomson's private ventures and his professional duties were always inextricably interwoven. From the first, his wealth and financial reputation had advanced in direct proportion to his road's growing prosperity and influence. By the war Thomson was a recognized figure in major eastern and overseas financial centers, but he was also well aware that he owed his distinction as much to his high office as he did to his uncanny ability to exploit investment opportunities. He clearly profited, at least indirectly, from all his positions, taking advantage of the opportunities they afforded him; but he always tried to maintain a line between his private and public responsibilities. As he grew older and business mores changed that line became less distinct—although it was still much clearer than those of other postwar contemporaries.

When Thomson returned north in 1847 and immediately began speculating in lands lying along the Pennsylvania's still secret right-of-way, picking up where he had left off in Georgia, he indicated his own thoughts about financial proprieties to his fellow speculator, James M. Bell. The exchange occurred after Bell, without divulging specifics, invited Thomson to invest in a project. Thomson assumed that commonly held moral precepts governed such matters when he replied, "I presume of course the object would not be an improper one for me to embark in, connected as I am with Penna Rail Road or you would not suggest it." When Bell revealed the venture was an iron furnace and rolling mill, Thomson, who would later invest in several such concerns, answered tartly, "it would not be *right* for me to enter into the speculation." A little later he turned down another chance to make money when he refused to invest in land on which he would have to locate a depot to realize a return. He put it squarely to Bell, "I must not only be pure in these matters but seem so also—."[2]

In later years Thomson pontificated less and less about "purity" as he embarked upon speculations that sometimes depended upon his road's good will for their success, supplied the Pennsylvania, or promised to connect with some PRR property. He believed that any private endeavor that promised to enhance the Pennsylvania's earnings potential and did not directly involve its credit or good name, was permissible. In addition, he invested in and encouraged others to support the private development of any new technology that might become useful to railways, regardless of whether the company became a supplier of the PRR or not. He thought personal speculation in the Pennsylvania's own stocks or bonds, or those of its lessees or affiliated lines, however, was strictly wrong; Thomson always drew a sharp line there. In 1871 he refused to trade his Philadelphia and Erie bonds for the more salable Allegheny Valley Railroad bonds he held in his treasury which Carnegie was going to place in London for the road. In a rare moment of introspection Thomson wrote the wry Scotsman telling him no and explaining, "if I had adopted a different rule I might have ere this numbered my millions, but as it is I have an abundance to meet my simple habits of life and I have no wish to change them."[3]

Continuing what had worked so well in the South for him, he drew freely upon the talents of bright, brash subordinates for his private speculations. As he grew older, he became increasingly comfortable only with partners drawn from the Pennsylvania's extended family. While individually they may not have been terribly wealthy, their combined assets, reputations, and connections made them collectively a financial force to be reckoned with. Thomson stood at the center of the tight little circle of capitalists that radiated outward from his office that owned investments across the nation; they became known as the "Philadelphia interests." The managers of the nation's biggest corporation, Thomson, Scott, their protégé, Carnegie, and sometimes Houston, formed the core of the group. Herman Lombaert and Edmund Smith frequently risked their spare capital, and members of the Pennsylvania's extended family also were often primary figures among the Philadelphia parties. Cass, son of the former presidential nominee Lewis Cass, was an invaluable asset, for his was a prominent voice in the Democratic Party. Thaw, John McManus, a prominent iron master, Felton, John A. Wright, John Scott, and William Palmer, who by the late 1860s was busily making his own fortune in the West, rounded out the list of principals with direct connections to the PRR. The Philadelphia interests often attracted outsiders with interests in the railroad. Bankers Jay Cooke, Anthony Drexel, and J. P. Morgan, the young son of Junius Morgan, the London banker with whom Thomson dealt for years, Matthias Baldwin, and George Pullman, who certainly were not disinterested parties where any railway was concerned, and several other prominent financiers who occasionally allied with the Philadelphians. Their ties to Boston, New York, and Baltimore capitalists were not strong; they were more often rivals. Instead, they tended to work closely with entrepreneurs in Chicago, St. Louis, Ohio, and Minnesota, who sought profits and power in their areas. Although the Philadelphia interests were constantly shifting, Thomson, Scott, and Carnegie stood at the heart of the group. Their financial assets made them equal to other major regional investment groups: the Joy and Forbes combinations in Boston and the Vanderbilt and Gould cabals in New York. Thomson's office on the PRR and his position within the Philadelphia combine extended his sway far beyond the limits of his own financial resources.

After the war Thomson strengthened his position by raising and using other people's money. He survived panics and frequent recessions without default; he was successful more often than not and his credit always remained first-rate. Most importantly, in an era before the institutionalization of financial markets, he had the reputation for being as good as his word—which was why he often took so long to pledge it. As the PRR's president, he had an entrée into the nation's leading financial houses and many of the greatest international banking firms. He drew on these resources and his wide circle of acquaintances to raise large amounts of money when he needed them. And by the late 1860s, he was constantly approached by promoters of fledgling projects seeking his imprimatur to furnish them with instant credit.

As he became more important and involved in more schemes, Thomson found it difficult to keep abreast of his speculations as they spread across the North American continent. He relied increasingly on others to organize and manage the projects he capitalized because he simply did not have the time or energy to take into hand a tithe of his enterprises. After the war he was less often an owner-manager; more frequently he fulfilled many of the functions of a private banker. He helped combine regional capitalists to underwrite large ventures in which active management was delegated to others. He often placed his seal of approval upon various securities by serving as trustee and placing them with his financial allies. More and more, he and his colleagues provided lines of credit to keep work on their projects progressing and Thomson learned the hard way that he often had to ante up large sums to protect his initial investments and that involvement in one project usually meant that he had to support another half-dozen auxiliary enterprises to insure the principal venture's success. All this cost a great deal of money, and Thomson spent sums in the last decade of his life that he would never have imagined possible before the war. The stakes were commensurately greater, but so were the risks. Thomson prospered, and in so doing he helped supply the burgeoning American economy with desperately needed capital in an era that lacked organized marketing structures and a strong central banking system.

On a smaller scale, he was a precursor of later men such as Morgan, Rockefeller, Harriman, the Mellons, and other entrepreneurs. Thomson differed from them, however, in that he was primarily a builder. He enjoyed seeing something productive rise where nothing had existed before. He had little interest in rescuing and refinancing businesses, although he could do it as his handling of the Fort Wayne indicated, nor did he merge properties on anything like the scale that would come later. Instead, he helped to capitalize and construct many of the improvements these men would subsequently take hold of and reorganize. His vision and money helped weave together the national economic fabric that the next generation would recut and embroider with gilded thread.

Thomson's holdings at his death were broadly representative of his lifelong financial interests. The detailed rendering of his estate, neatly entered in a professional hand, represented only what he owned at the instant of his death; it is in fact a very thin vertical slice of his career. While it may not be accurate to limn a full-length financial portrait from that one-dimensional silhouette, it is the only extant complete rendering of his affairs for any moment in his life. At first glance the tally shows just how wide-ranging and speculative his interests were. His personal horizons were not limited by considerations of stockholder tolerance, directors' provincialities, and outsiders' faith in his road's securities. His purview extended from coast to coast, limited only by his resources, ability to persuade others, and economicfactors over which he had no control. It is the final statement of a man who on the whole was successful, although peppered liberally with failures, the dry dust of wasted dreams, "1,600 shares Bainbridge Oil—$2.00; 36 shares Maysville & Big Sandy RR—75¢; 80 shares Live Oak Copper Co.—appraised @ nothing," that only make Thomson more human. There was probably a story behind the Live Oak Copper Company and the others, but we shall never know it.

A closer look at the time-slice shows that at his death Thomson was still basically following the same business techniques that he had honed in Georgia. The columns of holdings indicate that he was still attracted by businesses located near a railroad in which he held an interest. He made it easier for himself by buying into so many roads; in a fine hand, an unknown scribe listed them all: "Eastern Shore RR, Wilm., Columbia & Aug. RR, Bell's Gap RR, Lawrence RR, Michigan Lake Shore RR, St. Louis, Kansas City & Northern RR," the list runs on and on. The reckoning catalogs twenty-five identifiable railway holdings, although his letters indicated that he took shares in at least thirty-three after the war, not counting the transcontinentals. The bulk of them were located roughly along a line from Lake Superior to Missouri where Thomson took advantage of the chaotic competition among numerous small, underfinanced roads, all aspiring to become major links between the eastern trunk lines and the new transcontinentals. Not all were in that area though. Behind such deceptively innocuous entries as "Lake Superior & Miss. R., Ill. & St. Louis Bridge, and Mexican Pacific," lay thousands of hours of work and worry and the blasted hopes of grand schemes concocted in better days.[4]

Thomson had high expectations for the postwar period, and he got off to an early start; in the last year of the war, he, Scott, and two friends, invested in a railway scheme near Milwaukee. Perhaps they were too early. A year later, Thomson's former private secretary heard it was "a clean loss of $350,000 hard cash to [the] four parties." But Thomson continued to watch developments in the area, carefully looking for a chance to siphon some of the Lakes' trade away from his New York rivals by tapping it at its source. He was most interested in capturing the rich iron-ore traffic for his PRR because its potential for the domestic steel industry appeared unlimited. It was the storied West all over again, chock-full of valuable untapped riches needed by eastern industrialists to sustain America's rampaging growth.[5]

Railroads and land later lured Thomson back into the region. He became interested in plans to build the 150-mile Lake Superior and Mississippi River Railroad to connect the tiny frontier village of Duluth, on the western edge of Lake Superior, with the bustling St. Paul community on the Mississippi River. Between the two were virgin pine forests, but the LS&MR's promoters had wrangled a congressional grant for over 1.6 million acres of the valuable timberland. Thomson expected that the road would attract the western lakes' trade and bring it down the Mississippi from where it would be sent eastward to the Pennsylvania over connecting roads. He guessed that the eastern terminus of the unbuilt Northern Pacific might be located at St. Paul, thereby enhancing his strategic position in the region by making his LS&MR a vital connecting link between the transcontinental and the lakes.[6]

Robert Lamborn, acting as Thomson's secretary, reported in August 1867 that Thomson, Scott, Felton, the London merchant and financier Gilead Smith, and several others had come up with "a Scheme" to build the railway. True to his prewar form, Thomson sent his secretary out to reconnoiter the situation and within six weeks the Philadelphia interests had subscribed almost $500,000. Thomson indicated his confidence in the road's future by putting between $20,000 and $100,000 of his own money in it, but not all who were invited were so sanguine about prospects in the northern piney woods. Edmund Miller, a vice-president of the PRR, must have been approached on a particularly bad day. He refused, declaiming, "I have concluded that if I were to turn hatter, men would be born without heads."[7]

The following summer Thomson inveigled Jay Cooke with his bond-marketing wizardry into the enterprise. Cooke was already speculating in Minnesota lands and in mid-1868 he gazed upon Duluth's half-dozen frame houses, its land office, and its schoolhouse—the whole village; his biographer claimed his "imagination was fired—." He also inspected the LS&MR's thirty completed miles and agreed to take a few of the road's bonds. They proved to be an entering wedge. Cooke had trouble placing the bonds in Europe because Bismarck and Napoleon III were hurling taunts at each other, but he sold over $2.5 million worth through newspaper advertisements to optimistic American investors who cared not a whit about continental diplomacy.[8]

That fall, after recovering from an earlier summer illness, Thomson brought some of the Philadelphia interests out in his private car to northern Minnesota to check on their road's progress. Lamborn described it as "a 33 day picnic—" conducted in an "exhilarating" atmosphere. He told Palmer "even Mr. Thomson gained 8 lbs. while on the trip of 3600 miles of almost continental strolling." Thomson must have been in rare form for Lamborn noted, "it was pleasant to see the old gentleman throw off his customary reserve and for once in his life forget that his existence was shackled by 100,000 gross tons of Iron bands." Thomson was relieved to do something other than swap stocks and write accusatory letters to Garrett, for as Lamborn observed, "he entered into the questions of engineering and construction on the road with the vivacity of a man of forty."[9]

The trip was Thomson's last happy memory of the venture; it proved only troublesome after that. Rival railroad and grain interests in Chicago, Milwaukee, and St. Paul took alarm at the incursion of outsiders into their territory and fought back with their own railway projects to insure that the grain trade would continue in its old channels. To try to attract crops to Duluth's undeveloped port, the Philadelphia investors financed construction of grain elevators, three branch roads, and formed a company to operate slate quarries along the Lake Superior line to furnish needed traffic; Thomson even contributed toward a Duluth library in his quest for community goodwill. Nothing worked; traffic was so light the road had difficulty even meeting the interest on its bonds.[10]

By 1869 the only real hope Pennsylvania speculators had left was the sale of their lands along the route and in Duluth. The Lake Superior and Puget Sound Company, possessor of one of the more grandiose corporate names, and the Western Land Association, handled the sales. Cooke assigned 50,000 acres to Gilead Smith, who organized an emigrant company, as was fast becoming the norm on land grant railways, to entice settlers from Britain and Germany. Smith reported that Thomson "promptly put coupon tickets & orders at my disposal & the cooperation of . . . all his ticket agts from Castle Gardens [sic] to Topeka." Control of the Pennsylvania certainly had its advantages, for Smith in referring to Thomson's ability to mobilize resources halfway across the continent, concluded "this peculiar feature no one on this side of the Atlantic enjoys."[11]

Despite all the Philadelphians' money and effort, the LS&MR lacked the strategic location and the support facilities to divert the grain trade from its regular channels. Moreover, the whole project ran afoul of local political interests active in the area. And despite Cooke's and Thomson's best attempts to sway public opinion through the local newspapers, and their petitions to congress for financial aid, they were still viewed locally as monopolistic interlopers. To salvage whatever they could, Cooke and Thomson in 1871 had the managers of the Northern Pacific, one of their transcontinental ventures, lease their Minnesota speculation. Through this deal Thomson lost his chance to acquire control of the upper Midwest's traffic, but he did have the NP's guarantee of his bonds, for whatever that was worth, and the LS&MR's huge land grant.[12]

While he was struggling with the Minnesota venture, Thomson was also promoting a strikingly similar land speculation 1,400 miles to the east in northern Maine. Somehow he became interested in a small, unfinished oddly named line, the European & North American Railway. The road had been chartered in 1850 to connect Bangor with Vanceboro, located on the state's boundary with New Brunswick. Across the border, building from there to St. John was the European & North American Railway of New Brunswick. Like the LS&MR, the E&NA was slated to traverse almost in its entirety unsettled Maine wilderness—which did little to enhance its financial prospects. Nevertheless, in 1868 Thomson allied with Ohio capitalists, Benjamin E. Smith, a Columbus banker and president of the CC&IC, and the former Ohio governor William Dennison, a useful political ally who was active in numerous midwestern speculations, to take control of the E&NA. The bait was the state's grant of 500,000 acres to the road made in that year and an earlier subsidy of another 1.5 million acres. Moreover, there was a sweetener; an appropriations bill was pending before Congress to pay long-standing Maine claims arising from its loss of territory in the 1842 Webster-Ashburton Treaty that settled the state's northern boundary. Thomson was anxious to acquire a share of the bounty. He wrote Congressman Covode, the PRR's old friend, in June 1868, that "this sum will go towards the construction of a Railway . . . in which I have a material interest—I look upon the project as of great National importance!" In a rather curt closing, Thomson ordered "please endeavor to have it retained."[13]

The Philadelphia interests formed the expected land corporation, in which Thomson bought about 3,000 shares, that issued $2 million of first mortgage bonds on the road's land to finance construction. Thomson linked the land company's sales and emigrant solicitation efforts with his Lake Superior scheme and dumped both into Smith's lap in London. Smith disposed of the land-grant bonds which enabled Thomson and his allies to complete the road in 1871 and to merge it with the Canadian extension a year later.

If he followed his usual routine, Thomson purchased the land-grant bonds at a large discount and dumped them as soon as the road was finished. He may well have received National Land Improvement Company stock as a bonus when he bought the bonds and thereby shared in the profits of the land sales without investing a dime. Aside from the designs Thomson had on the land grant, he had few other aspirations for the E&NA. His adventure in Maine was purely speculative, the type of enterprise he only rarely entered. Usually his projects were interrelated, and ultimately, most led back to his own PRR.[14]

Such was the case with his schemes to control Mexico's railroads. Thomson's interests south of the border grew out of his attempts to make the Kansas Pacific a true transcontinental serving the interests of the PRR. The idea to push south to Mexico City to capture the nation's trade had been floating around since 1866 when the Philadelphia interests decided to locate their KP along the Mexican border to skirt the southern end of the mountain barrier and thence northwest to the coast. With this southerly deflection, they hoped to pick up, as Lamborn explained, the political support of the South and "all the Arizona & New Mexico and Southern California interests." The South in 1866 was without influence in Congress because the representatives of the so-called "Johnson governments" had not been seated and Radical Reconstruction loomed just over the horizon after the Republican congressional victories that fall. Such minor political inconveniences did not daunt the Philadelphia parties. They counted upon the early readmission of the southern states through what Lamborn called Cooke's "grand financial scheme for regenerating the South." The Philadelphia banker proposed to attach "to the bills reported by the Reconstruction Com. a plan for loaning the people of the Southern States (as they accept the [14th] amendment) $150,000,000 through National Banks secured on lands & factories etc." By this device, "he would thus start the wheels of trade and by kindness win them over." Lamborn neglected to explain that the arrangement would have been extremely profitable for the Philadelphia interests.[15]

The tense diplomatic situation between the United States and Mexico was an added inducement to venture into Mexican affairs. While Americans were distracted during the Civil War, Napoleon III had launched a foray into the western hemisphere by placing Maximilian of Austria on a new Mexican throne. Soon after Appomattox, William Henry Seward, secretary of state, began pressing Napoleon to withdraw his puppet, and by early 1866 Seward was making lightly veiled threats of American intervention. There was widespread public support for an invasion, and the Philadelphia parties hoped to exploit the sentiment by appealing to "all the uneasy element in the army & elsewhere which wants Mexico & war," to support a congressional subsidy to build the KP to the Mexican border so as Lamborn put it "we would be on the north edge of Mexico in time to command her system of rail roads as soon as she falls to us and these roads are necessitated." Moreover, Thomson was confident he could secure backing from Thaddeus Stevens, the Pennsylvania Radical Republican who had emerged as a congressional leader, because as Palmer later wrote, Stevens "thinks there would be a better chance to obtain a subsidy for the northern line from Lake Superior if we struck southward." And of course, there were the more mundane financial considerations. The Philadelphia parties acknowledged "we would soon be in the mountains with a double subsidy. We would be near enough [to] Mexico to secure Indian labor." Such were the political and economic machinations necessary to secure a grand design.[16]

Yet the whole intricate plan failed to materialize quite as its sponsors hoped. The United States refrained from intervening in Mexico;

Maximilian fell before a Mexican firing squad in 1867; Cooke's "grand financial scheme" was ignored; Stevens, bogged down in congressional Reconstruction, died the following year; the South remained politically impotent; and the Philadelphia parties were unable to build a successful KP-NP-LS&MR coalition against the UP to push all their subsidy demands through Congress. The basic idea, however, never died; it was just delayed.

Later, General William S. Rosecrans, Palmer's former commanding officer, worked to wring a railroad concession from the new Juarez government in Mexico and tried to raise capital in the United States to build the railway. When the general approached Thomson in 1871, he found a ready listener. The Pennsylvania's president sent him to see Palmer, and the two men easily reached an understanding; Rosecrans was to secure Mexican financial aid for a road from El Paso to Mexico City to be built by the Denver and Rio Grande (D&RG) to its three-foot narrow gauge specifications. This involved Thomson because the agreement would not be with the D&RG but with the Union Contract Company, a Philadelphia concern formed by Thomson, Palmer, and their allies to build the D&RG. If the Mexican roads were built, the Pennsylvania would gain access to a large southwestern rail system that would include Scott's Texas and Pacific, the D&RG, and Mexican Railways. The construction profits would go to the Philadelphians.[17]

When Palmer inspected the proposed location of the Mexican road that year, dodging bandits all the way, he found that the national government had no land to grant the railroad and wondered whether the line would ever generate enough traffic to make it pay. Nevertheless, survey crews began work, and Rosecrans won a promise of financial support from Juarez to build the first 300 kilometers. Unfortunately for Thomson and his friends, Juarez died in July 1872, and Sebastian Lerdo de Tejada, his successor, was less disposed to support Rosecrans. The Mexican Congress deadlocked over the issue, and in April 1873 Palmer went to Mexico City to lobby the subsidy bill through himself. He even tried to get President Grant to broach the topic on a visit to Lerdo, but he refused. In May, a rival Texas concern was granted the concession. Palmer's failure was not as disheartening as it might have been, for the panic that fall shattered everyone's Mexican plans, and the Philadelphia parties rushed to save other more important enterprises. Palmer was reported to have written, after Cooke's banking house closed its doors, that he was "very anxious now *not* to hear of success" in Mexico. Although Thomson made nothing in Mexico, he probably recouped his expenses from building the D&RG and the land companies affiliated with that road. But his dream of a rail empire south of the border evaporated in the economic malaise of that year.[18]

Thomson's schemes, no matter how far-flung, tended to overlap, intersect, and fold back upon themselves. This propensity was nowhere more evident than in his less spectacular, but consistently more profitable, interests in coal properties located in his native state and in the new fields being opened in Illinois, Colorado, and Missouri. The coal business had fascinated Thomson from his days as chief engineer when he tramped through the western Pennsylvania coal country locating his road. His estate reflected that fact; coal stocks were the second biggest group of securities listed in his inventory. As usual, he was drawn to coal properties situated along the Pennsylvania's line or that of some western road in which he had an interest. He enjoyed threefold benefits from these private speculations: an assured income, influence in an industry that remained the province of the small producer, and a source of local traffic for his railroads.

Until 1851 Thomson had concentrated on investing in real estate ahead of his construction. With a finished road in the offing that year, however, he changed his investment strategy and shifted his funds into areas with potentially valuable natural resources, especially coal and timber, showing his willingness to modify proven practices in light of new developments. To raise the larger amounts of capital necessary to buy land and underwrite businesses to extract the resources, he allied with Haupt and several of his wealthy Philadelphia directors, men who were also in a position to advance his professional career, and began to liquidate his southern holdings, particularly his stock in the Georgia Railroad, to pay for his subscriptions.

In 1851 Thomson invested with a large Pennsylvania Railroad stockholder, James Magee, in coal and timber lands between Altoona and Clearfield. They organized the Clearfield Coal and Lumber Company and built a plank road from company lands to the Pennsylvania. In the same locale, Thomson joined with Haupt, Tom Scott, Simon Cameron, Magee, and at least one Pennsylvania director,

George Howell, and bought into the Allegheny Coal and Railroad Company. Capitalized at $1 million, the concern bought mining and timber privileges on 40,000 acres and purchased another 28,000 acres outright. Haupt directed timbering operations along Moshannon Creek and oversaw production in the company's coal mine three miles from Tipton. The Pennsylvania's high coal rates, however, depressed sales and severely cut into the profit margins of its principal customer, Magee's Philadelphia Gas Works, which the Pennsylvania served. Hounded by disputed land titles, bad management, low production levels, lack of capital, and a debt load over $100,000, the company became insolvent around 1858, just before Thomson lowered coal rates on his road. But given a generous 1854 stock offering and the fact that the company's stock still commanded $10 a share as late as 1856, the Pennsylvania's president probably realized a comfortable profit from the concern.[19]

Thomson soon sold his holdings in the Clearfield region to invest in the booming Pittsburgh coal fields. His flagship corporation there was the Westmoreland Coal Company, which by mid-decade had sold 40,000 shares of stock. Although Thomson was not a registered shareholder, probably because his road purchased its coal from the firm, he undoubtedly had a large investment in it, for his secretary, Palmer, kept the company's books in Thomson's office. Moreover, the nine most important Westmoreland stockholders, who owned over half its outstanding shares, were also the largest shareholders in Allegheny Coal. Thomson's interest was probably held by Magee, Horatio Burroughs, and Scott.[20]

The Westmoreland concern prospered during the war and the fact that director John Covode was a prominent Radical Republican did little to hurt the firm's business. It expanded its markets into the West and shipped its coal over the Fort Wayne to Chicago. It grew even faster in the postwar period; its output rose from 90,000 tons in 1857 to 280,000 tons eleven years later. On a capitalization of only $600,000, it paid $120,000 in dividends in 1868, still leaving the company a cash surplus that year of $750,000. Thomson profited not only from the dividends but from the $1 million the company paid his Pennsylvania yearly for the privilege of shipping its coal in its own cars over his road. Palmer's comment on the firm's performance, "pretty fair isn't it?" said it all.[21]

Once he invested in an area, Thomson had the habit of expanding his interests there, perhaps to spread his risks. Although the Westmoreland concern was a raging success, it had its dark days during the 1857 panic and Thomson bought into a nearby company, Pittsburgh and Youghiogheny Coal, acquiring nearly a thousand shares at an almost 70 percent discount. The firm also attracted him because it was located along his Pittsburgh and Steubenville Railroad destined to become part of the Pan Handle route. Backed by Thomson, Scott, Palmer, Carnegie, and the Pennsylvania's legal counsel John Scott, the P&Y initially did well. During the war it branched into the oil business. For unknown reasons, however, it filed for bankruptcy in 1868 obviously catching Thomson and Carnegie unaware, for afterward they met to settle their accounts in the business. Thomson's other major coal investment in the region, the Youghiogheny Coal Hollow Company near the Pittsburgh and Connellsville Railroad, was a much more prosperous outfit. In the dark days of 1874 it still employed 300 miners digging gas and coking coal which was shipped over the Pennsylvania, and its securities held up remarkably well.[22]

Thomson ventured even farther west in pursuit of coal lands before the war. In 1856 he took a flyer in the Coal Valley Mining Company on the Rock River twelve miles from Rock Island, Illinois. The firm owned mineral rights to 920 acres, all mortgaged to Thomson to secure the bonds of the Rock Island & Peoria Railroad in which he had an interest. Palmer reported a year later that Thomson could expect to earn about $67,000 a year from the mines when their coal was shipped east over the Pennsylvania. Palmer was also quick to note that there would be a large local market because a wood shortage and the lack of flowing water would force businesses to rely upon steam power.[23]

Closer to home, Thomson and his friends bought control of the Lehigh Coal and Navigation Company after the war. Their disposition of the firm indicated how much more indistinct the line between Thomson's private affairs and corporate position had become by 1868. He, Scott, and Felton, were all parties to the purchase. In April Palmer heard that he was about to be offered the firm's presidency, and was advised to take it. Charles Hinchman, a longtime friend, explained that it "is owned by people who will soon learn how to appreciate you." Palmer's uncle suggested he see "old dignity" and ask

Thomson what he thought of the offer, and Lamborn pressed him to take it, arguing that Felton was funneling large amounts of money into the company. Palmer at last refused, and the Philadelphia interests unloaded the concern neatly by leasing it to the UNJR just before the PRR, in turn, leased that company. Through the two leases in 1871, the PRR became the guarantor of the LC&N's outstanding liabilities. The coal company's railway later became a valuable asset to the PRR serving its Hazelton Coal properties. Certainly, the Pennsylvania parties lost nothing by the whole transaction and probably realized substantial gains.[24]

Thomson did not always win in the coal business, nor did he always follow his usual proven investing procedures. Sometimes he suffered unmitigated financial disasters as he did with the Karlhaus Coal and Lumber Company. Sometime after the war he purchased at least 10,000 shares in the firm that eventually brought his widow exactly one dollar. He also advanced the company funds and cosigned its notes in conjunction with several men who were not prominent in any of his other speculations. One of these men, Robert Patterson, was a fascinating fellow—a Thomson with elan. A major-general in the army, he fought in the War of 1812, the Mexican War, and closed out his career chasing Rebels. At age 70 he started buying textile mills, made a fortune, and in his eighties was cosigning notes with Thomson. Despite the actuarial tables, his paper depreciated only about 10 percent in the depression.[25]

Thomson's third largest block of stocks was concentrated in the oil industry, a short-lived enthusiasm of his that in all instances, save one, turned out like his Karlhaus investment. His 30,660 shares in thirteen oil concerns had an appraised market value in 1874 of only $2,104. Although he followed his usual bent and invested early in numerous firms at large discounts, he still failed to reap the expected whirlwind of profits. Undoubtedly, he was attracted by the technological novelty of the business and the possibility of securing a high volume of traffic for his road, as well as by the chances for private gain. He was never interested in refining or marketing; rather, like most other observers he thought that the oil industry would develop like the coal business with numerous small producers scrambling for a share of the market. Therefore he scattered his investments, and at least one firm was organized right in his office. The Bright Oil Company was formed in

June 1866 with Thomson acting as president and, unlike most of his other petroleum ventures, probably continued active into the 1870s, for his 6,600 shares were valued at $1,000 in 1874. The Columbia Oil Company, in which he risked only $17,500 turned out to be a bonanza. Capitalized at $2.5 million, it owned a farm on Oil Creek in Venango County from which it extracted 1.25 million barrels of crude between 1861 and 1873, paying out $3.5 million in dividends, a full $1 million in one exceptional year; Thomson enjoyed returns of at least 400 percent before the company collapsed in the depression. Still, he had not reckoned with Rockefeller's Standard Oil capturing control of the nation's refining capacity, accomplishing what Thomson hoped to do in the railroad industry by other means, rationalization of the business. Although he realized some early profits from oil, he held his investments into the period when the chances for additional gains had all but disappeared. Moreover, his interest in the oil business was a little out of character; it was one of the few instances when he invested his money in an industry that the Philadelphia interests had no realistic chance to control.[26]

But his investments in the oil business showed again that Thomson was quite willing to risk his funds. He was far from being as stodgy as his contemporaries would have us believe and certainly was not immune to the speculative fevers that swept the country periodically. Thomson's enthusiasm for the gold and silver mines so popular toward the end of the war for example, was almost boundless, but like his experiences in the oil business, not very enriching. As early as 1864 he had joined with Scott to buy extensive silver lands in the Arizona Territory. Whether they made money from them or not is questionable, but they did figure prominently in the Philadelphians' schemes in the West, Southwest, and Mexico. They even helped determine the route of the KP, for Palmer claimed in 1866 that "Col. Scott advocated the Southward deflection, not because he considers it the best route, . . . but because it leads in the direction of his mines and property." Thomson scattered his mineral risks widely, buying Colorado gold, Maryland gold, Nevada silver, Susquehanna gold, and something called Philadelphia & California gold stocks. He was smart enough not to sink a lot of money into such speculations—he knew how risky they were; in 1874 his 6,730 shares in seven mining firms were worth a grand total of $3.[27]

Steel was a lot more valuable. With his heavy investments in railroads and coal, it was only natural that Thomson should become involved in that new industry; it was a perfect interlock with many of his other interests. With his passion for steel, he joined right after the war with his friends in the Quaker City to construct a Bessemer plant along the Pennsylvania's line at Harrisburg. They put up at least $500,000 of capital and the PRR awarded an initial $200,000 contract for steel rails to the new Pennsylvania Steel Company. Felton took the firm's presidency; although he was producing by mid-1867, he could never raise the necessary funds to expand his plant to meet demand. Finally, Thomson, who was heavily engaged elsewhere and could not take a direct hand in the business, reacted in an uncharacteristic manner and persuaded the PRR's directors to invest directly in a concern of his, probably on the grounds that the steel mill furnished a high volume of local traffic in coal, coke, ore, and steel that his road could ill-afford to lose. In 1871 the board purchased a majority control in the firm, securing the value of Thomson's interest, but at the same time it retained a profitable customer and a valuable nearby source of steel rails.

On a smaller scale, Thomson took a flyer in something called the National Iron Company that went under with the 1873 debacle and made a major investment in the Brady Bend's Iron Company. Brady's was a flourishing postwar concern, and Thomson enjoyed a decent return on his investment of over $50,000. The firm worked four furnaces near his Westmoreland mines, employed over 600 miners, and poured about 32,000 tons of pig iron a year. The company owned local ore lands but became increasingly dependent upon Lake Superior ores, which helped account for Thomson's attraction to that region; one more instance in which he pursued the interrelationships between his coal, iron ore, lumber, transportation, steel, and iron-producing properties. The Bend concern, however, collapsed in the 1873 panic before Thomson had time to unload his holdings. At his death they were valued at just two dollars.[28]

The remainder of Thomson's involvements in the industry were all in conjunction with Carnegie's many fertile schemes. After the war Carnegie was drawn exclusively into the steel business via iron production, iron fabrication, and construction industries. Thomson supplied financial backing for Carnegie at every step; he had a father's fondness for the plucky little Scotsman, who remained an intimate member of the Philadelphia interests long after he left the Pennsylvania's employ. Moreover, Carnegie needed Thomson who was in a position to provide contracts and preferential rates for his multifarious enterprises. Even though Thomson was more willing by the late 1860s to invest in firms doing business with his railroad, he was still wary of doing it too openly. He usually placed his holdings in Carnegie's, Scott's, Barclay's, or some other name and assumed a public posture of neutrality in dealing with his own firms.

When Carnegie returned from abroad in 1866 bubbling with enthusiasm over the idea of attaching steel heads to iron rails, Thomson, whom Carnegie described as "the great pillar in this country of steel for everything," bought into the process. So began a sequence of interlocking investments that in their complexity baffled all but the most astute insiders. Thomson also took shares in Carnegie's Union Mills and loaned the Scotsman money to enable him to buy into a lease of the Superior Iron Company's furnaces in conjunction with both Tom and John Scott and Andrew Kloman, an early partner of Carnegie's. Thomson's Union Mills investment was most profitable because that company supplied the iron for another of Carnegie's creations, the Keystone Bridge Company. Organized in 1865, the company was from the first closely identified with the Pennsylvania. An early member of its board and later president was J. N. Linville, a former PRR engineer; and Thomson himself held about 5 percent of the firm's shares in his wife's name.[29]

Thomson missed out on Carnegie's premier creation, but it was not because he was not offered a chance. Ever superstitious, Carnegie feared embarking upon any large project without Thomson's and Scott's backing. When he organized Carnegie, McCandless and Company to build a new Bessemer steel plant at Braddock, Pennsylvania, he employed the most overt kind of flattery to entice the Pennsylvania's president into the concern. He asked Thomson to allow his name to be used for the new mill, explaining "that there is not one of our party who is not delighted that an opportunity has arisen through which expression can be given, however feebly, to the regard they honestly entertain for your exaulted character & career." Carnegie wanted money, and Thomson knew it. He wrote back, "as regards the Steel Works, you can use the name you suggest, . . . [but] I have not funds at present to invest." Carnegie was cornered. He named his mill the Edgar Thomson Steel Works and the honor cost Thomson nothing. But he hardly could have guessed what a steel empire the hard-driving Carnegie would build over the next quarter of a century.[30]

Thomson's iron and steel concerns functioned as suppliers for his most important new postwar interest—construction companies. Although he had invested in two such enterprises earlier, the Hoosac Tunnel and the Western Transportation Company, both were oddities created by special circumstances. He, Scott, and two others in 1856 had invested $60,000 in Haupt's construction company that had a contract to build the Troy and Greenfield Railroad in Massachusetts, a project that included boring a five-mile tunnel through the Hoosac Mountain. Thomson bought in because he was a close friend of Haupt's and had vague notions that the Pennsylvania could extend its influence into New England through control of the T&G. The contract was jinxed from the start with technical problems, political interference, and a shortage of working capital. Haupt almost went bankrupt in the 1857 panic, but survived to repay Thomson and his partners their principal with interest. Thomson still owned 106 shares of the T&G, however, and was owed over $36,000 by Haupt's construction company when he died. To the west of the PRR, the WTC was chartered in 1856 for the express purpose of constructing and operating the Pittsburgh and Steubenville Railroad. Thomson stayed in the background as treasurer of the firm and two years later turned even that job over to Palmer. During the war Thomson sold a majority interest in the concern to his Pennsylvania, probably because the WTC owned enough securities to control the unfinished road, and finally completed the line in 1865. Thomson, Scott, and their allies who owned the 45 percent of the construction company's stock that remained in private hands shared the profits.[31]

Although Thomson had always had frequent opportunities to invest in contracting companies that built his roads, he resisted the temptation. Yet after the war when the public began to question the propriety of railroad managers investing in such firms, Thomson began to do so and continued the practice even after the Credit Mobilier storm broke. Many of his larger speculations, such as the transcontinentals and the Iowa roads, were building far ahead of demand, and he had no prospect for an early return on his capital from the lines' operations. If he was to recoup his expenditures, he had to do so in the construction phase. Moreover, since construction companies took stocks and bonds as payment, such investments were an effective way to gain control of new railways. In more remote areas, he had to launch his own construction firm just to get the work done. In a nation hell-bent on flinging rails down everywhere he could justify such methods on the grounds that such an arrangement hastened financing and insured direct control over the quality of the finished work. The construction company device was also a golden opportunity for the unscrupulous to rake-off profits and get out before promoters discovered that the finished road's earnings were insufficient to cover its bloated indebtedness. While Thomson was never so accused, largely because he built his own roads or those of the Philadelphia interests, and never lines owned or leased by the Pennsylvania, he nevertheless courted such charges.

Allied with his Philadelphia friends, Thomson showed a distinct postwar weakness for construction firms with bridge contracts at the major western river crossings. The great postwar transcontinentals ran west from the Missouri River while the eastern trunk lines terminated at the Mississippi. Railroads located between the watercourses were intensely competitive; the region constituted a major fault in the nation's evolving railway network. Isolated by unbridged rivers, the railroads were highly prized plums for any eastern road. Control of the bridges across the two rivers would put the Philadelphia parties in a position, like the feudal barons of earlier times, to exact tolls on all merchandise crossing the country and at little cost to manipulate the regional balance of power. Thomson was also enamored with bridges. The intricately engineered structures arching over the wide expanses of water would long stand as enduring monuments to the technical excellence of his age and to his own passionate interest in structural mechanics. Western bridge contracts promised large orders for his and Carnegie's iron works, and opportunities for speculating in nearby lands, approaches, and connecting roads offered the lure of quick gains. Moreover, the sale of bridge companies' securities promised high commissions. And at the heart of it all, Thomson's road stood to increase its share of the western trade.

By the late 1860s Thomson was a major investor in bridge concerns at Dubuque, Keokuk, Davenport, and St. Louis, all attempting to span the Mississippi. The bridge at St. Louis, a city vital to his PRR, was the most important. Thomson had been active in that area before the war when he had purchased 3,000 acres fronting on the Mississippi and Missouri rivers. When Palmer inspected the tract in September 1859, he wrote back "the soil was a black mould as rich as the Delta of the Nile—and like it, subject to annual overflow." Low, swampy, and reputedly unhealthy, the land had been bypassed, although only twenty-five miles from St. Louis. It was infested with squatters, whom Palmer described as "thieves and scoundrels," and his traveling companion wore a brace of Colt revolvers while visiting the area. It was not clear exactly what Thomson intended to do with the land, but it had immense potential value.[32]

In 1866 Thomson, Carnegie, and Scott inveigled the PRR's bridge engineer, Linville, into a position as chief consultant to Captain James Eads, the military engineer responsible for the design and execution of the St. Louis structure. As a director of the Keystone Bridge Company, which bought its iron from the Union Mills, Linville was a valuable insider. As expected, the Keystone company easily won the contract and Carnegie, trading on Thomson's financial stature, marketed the St. Louis bridge company's $4 million first mortgage bond offering for a commission of $50,000. Thomson bought at least $160,000 of the bridge concern's stock.[33]

Thomson's interest in the area was part of a larger overall plan; he was suffering from an acute case of transcontinental fever and, while he had invested heavily in several, his PRR had no direct connections with any of them. He envisioned the St. Louis bridge as a potential gateway to the Plains—if he could secure control of a road to that city. Thus in 1867 his secretary noted that "a subscription has been started at the P.R.R. Off. to build a road from St. Louis to Terre Haute." The St. Louis, Vandalia and Terre Haute Railroad, in which Thomson invested personally, gave him a wholly owned road between those cities when the 158-mile line was completed in 1870. West of St. Louis, Thomson bought into the St. Louis, Kansas City and Northern that would give the Pennsylvania access to the UP over connecting roads and link up directly with his KP.[34]

The bridge was the key to his intricate design, but construction on it was continually delayed, and the structure was not opened until he lay on his deathbed. Eads was a perfectionist intent on building his own monument. Despite the holdups, Thomson reaped large profits from the $150,000 stock bonus "which accompanied St. Louis Bridge Bonds," most of which he disposed of by 1873. His overall strategy in the bridge affair was imaginative and well-coordinated with his transcontinental investments; only the hard times that swept the nation just as he was on the verge of success, doomed his attempts to consolidate his position west of St. Louis.[35]

Farther upriver, Thomson engaged in a similar undertaking at Keokuk where he had also owned land before the war. The venture was a complicated, interlocking financial arrangement among the bridge company, the Iowa Contracting Company, and the Missouri, Iowa, and Nebraska Railroad; although separate entities, all had the same principal backers, Thomson, Scott, and Carnegie. Thomson was still looking for a secure route out to the transcontinentals and the MI&N was designed to link Keokuk with Nebraska City, which in 1867 was about to be connected with Fort Kearney on the UP. In a scheme designed to warm any capitalist's heart, the Pennsylvania interests organized the Iowa Contracting Company to build their railroad and, of course, Carnegie's Keystone firm received the contract for the bridge superstructure. That way the profits stayed in the family and the PRR could acquire a trans Mississippi ally. Moreover, when the bridge bonds were offered for sale in March 1869 they carried with them a 50 percent stock bonus. The Pennsylvania interests took $600,000 of the bonds at 85 and paid for them with the interest they received on the bonds paid from outsiders' subscriptions. As Carnegie noted, "this arrangement saves us from advancing money." Thomson ended up with huge holdings in the bridge firm's stocks and bonds, MI&N stock, and local government bonds. At his height in 1871–72, he owned almost $650,000 worth of securities in the immediate region; by buying early and controlling all aspects of the venture, he probably paid an average of less than ten cents on the dollar for his holdings.[36]

The bridge was finished in May 1871, but the company's prohibitive charges and opposition from other roads in the area, left it standing idle. Thomson hypothecated many of his Keokuk securities to capture control of the UP and, after they were returned, held on to them because he foresaw a bright future for the bridge, contracting company, and railroad in conjunction with his other interests in the

KP, D&RG, and his Mexican schemes. The depression of 1873, however, caught him with a fistful of Keokuk securities that he was unable to unload. The bridge and ICC bonds held their values in the downturn, but the MI&N securities plummeted.[37]

Upriver at Rock Island—Davenport, the Philadelphia interests repeated the same arrangements that had served them so well farther south, except they did not attempt to gain control of the bridge company. They remained content with securing the contract for the bridge's superstructure. Having done so by 1871, they organized a contracting firm, the Davenport & St. Paul Construction Company, to build a railway connecting the two cities. The railroad issued $6 million in mortgage bonds, naming Thomson and Governor Dennison as trustees, and Carnegie assumed responsibility for placing the securities abroad.

Thomson hoped that a southerly connecting road to the major transcontinentals would revive his Lake Superior and Mississippi River Railroad's sagging fortunes. The D&SP was too late, however, to save it, a fact Thomson must have recognized, for his enthusiasm for the Davenport project was never very intense; he purchased only 150 shares in the construction company. Yet that small speculation cost him most dearly. Carnegie placed a large block of the D&SP's bonds with the Sulzbachs in Frankfurt, Germany; but soon after, bickering among the road's managers and the depression drove the railway into bankruptcy. The Sulzbachs sued in 1874 to collect on the defaulted bonds and their suit dragged through the courts for another decade. Finally in 1884, a federal court of appeals held that Thomson, as a trustee for the mortgage, was liable for the full amount and charged his estate $800,000 in a settlement with the plaintiffs—a stiff penalty considering that Thomson had also lost money in the venture. By the time construction began on the railroad, the Lake Superior project had already been tucked under the NP's wing. From Duluth to Davenport, Thomson gained little more than grief.[38]

Just before his death Thomson found a bridge scheme with much greater potential, one that would satisfy his latent desire to tap New England's markets for his PRR. Local interests in Poughkeepsie had organized a bridge company, and by early 1873 Thomson and Carnegie were seriously considering buying it out. As much as Thomson coveted the connection, the financial drain of Scott's Texas adventure made him extraordinarily cautious. Nevertheless, Carnegie pushed hard, appealing to Thomson's well-known weakness for any idea that promised to increase the Pennsylvania's revenues. "In a short time the traffic, crossing the Bridge, will be enormous," Carnegie promised, "& without such an outlet you must, year, by year, lose ground in your struggle for the New England traffic." Thomson's resistance weakened as they worked out an alliance with the Reading Railroad to spread the costs and to alleviate fears among London lenders that the Pennsylvania may have expanded too fast. In June he joined Carnegie, Scott, and others, and invested $100,000 in a $1 million pool to acquire the company.[39]

The agreement with the Reading was short-lived. Thomson decided that the PRR should have sole control over its New England connection and announced that he was going to build a new railroad from Harrisburg to the Hudson. The Pennsylvania interests raised another $1 million, and Thomson sent survey crews into the field to locate the line, which would parallel portions of the Reading. Thomson was attracted by the vision of expanded markets for his coal companies and the prospect of building the new road close to the South Mountain Iron Company in which he had an investment. The newspapers reported that the Pennsylvania parties spent close to $1 million grading portions of the Pennsylvania, Poughkeepsie and Boston Railroad before the panic halted all work. By 1874 all the Philadelphia interests had unloaded their securities; the bridge was eventually built and served for almost a century, but the PP&BR was never completed.[40]

Thomson's partnership with Carnegie and the other Philadelphia interests was not confined to bridge and railway contracts. He entered into other speculations with them that, like the Poughkeepsie bridge scheme, blurred distinctions between private and corporate interests. Back in 1858 Thomson had met Thomas T. Woodruff, inventor of the sleeping car, and had examined his innovation. From that chance encounter the Philadelphia investors created a nationwide company that reaped them large profits. Thomson passed his impressions of Woodruff's product on to Scott, who organized a sleeping car company, later bought by Thomson, Scott, and Carnegie, to operate the cars over the Pennsylvania to compete with the Central's service. The new firm paid handsome dividends until 1862 when, with a number of rival companies in the field, it had difficulty raising capital to build all the cars it needed. Carnegie, still backed by Thomson and Scott, reorganized the concern as the Central Transportation Company and with a monopoly on sleeping car service over the PRR and its subsidiary lines, went after the contract to operate its cars on the new transcontinentals. The CTC's managers watched apprehensively, however, as George Pullman's rival Palace Car Company obtained contracts on western roads and even the right to operate over the NYC.[41]

When the UP sponsored a meeting in New York City in early 1867 to hear proposals from sleeping car companies, Pullman and Carnegie were both there. Carnegie saw the Chicagoan for the formidable foe he was and suggested they combine their resources to submit a single proposal. Carnegie finally enticed him into the newly formed Pullman Pacific Car Company by naming it after him, and they jointly signed an agreement with the UP in midyear. UP officials demanded a percentage of the company and Oliver Ames, president of the transcontinental, was given 2,600 of the 5,000 shares to hold in trust. Carnegie, Scott, and probably Thomson, controlled another 1,200 shares. By 1869 Carnegie had also contracted with the Central Pacific, although the managers of that road demanded the right to operate the cars; in that year the CTC returned a 17.8 percent profit. The following January Carnegie consolidated his sleeping car interests by leasing the CTC to the Pullman Company. He and Scott promptly began purchasing additional Pullman shares. Thomson bought 250 shares in the name of Barclay and then traded his Union Mills stock to Carnegie for still more Pullman. Carnegie was still bullish on the stock in March 1872, writing Thomson, "I wish to put myself on record as advising you to arrange for a large interest in the Pullman Co . . . The investment will yield not less than 18%–22% cash the remainder surplus." Thomson may have complied, but his growing commitment to Scott's Texas and Pacific probably forced him to let the opportunity pass—even at 18 percent. He did buy almost $1 million in Pullman stock and bonds for his road, however, and it turned out to be a fortunate investment. At his very last PRR board meeting Thomson used the securities to shore up his road's crumbling financial position.[42]

He did not miss the opportunity, however, to turn a tidy profit from Carnegie's telegraph business. Western Union, founded in 1856, achieved domination of the industry in the early postwar years and was plagued by numerous small firms established for the express purpose of harassing the giant and forcing it to buy them out. In 1867 Carnegie joined the sport when he organized the Keystone Telegraph Company, probably with Thomson's and Scott's hidden backing and promptly received permission to string his wires on the Pennsylvania's poles for a nominal yearly sum per mile. With this valuable concession, Carnegie immediately contacted one of the larger remaining independent telegraph firms, the Pacific & Atlantic Company, and less than two weeks later merged with it in a stock trade that tripled the value of his Keystone holdings. In a neat twist, Carnegie then formed a company to string telegraph wires for the P&A for a fee of $3 paid in that company's stock for each $1 of actual construction cost.[43]

With the resources of a larger company at his disposal, Carnegie attempted to do battle with Western Union. He received Scott's permission to string wires along the Pennsylvania's new midwestern connections, but made little headway against Western Union's domination throughout the rest of the country. The P&A was a money-maker though, paying dividends of 37.5 percent in its first three years. But after 1869 profits relentlessly declined as its managers squabbled among themselves, and in 1872, Carnegie approached Western Union officials offering to sell the P&A. As was his custom, he struck a very advantageous deal giving P&A stockholders a profit of two dollars a share. Western Union officials, realizing their company was already overcapitalized, had second thoughts about absorbing all the P&A stock, but Carnegie quietly got rid of his own and that of his PRR friends, including Thomson's entire holding of 450 shares, before they changed their minds. The 1873 panic halted the exchange and Carnegie instead leased his company to the larger firm. Thomson was forced to sell his Western Union shares late in 1873, but he undoubtedly counted his gains from all the transactions. His ability to influence the awarding of contracts had made Carnegie's schemes profitable in the first place, for the only asset of value Carnegie had to offer was his contracts with the Pennsylvania. Ironically, however, Carnegie's companies enabled him and Thomson altruistically to proclaim they were fighting to restore competition to the telegraph industry.[44]

Of the remaining shares listed in Thomson's estate rendering, only those in manufacturing concerns and various land companies held any value. Perhaps the most interesting and the only one from which Thomson personally realized profits directly from the war effort, was his large interest in the American Stove and Holloware Company. It is the only recorded instance in which Thomson became financially involved with a relative; in this case he put up $62,000 to enable his nephew, Edgar, to buy into the concern in 1863. During the war the company produced shot and shell for the Union forces. One of the partners withdrew from the concern a year after the peace and four years later the assets of the two remaining partners were transferred to the Pennsylvania's president. Thomson reorganized the company and went public with it, purchasing a 25 percent interest for himself; he also served as its president during 1870 and 71. Thomson must not have thought highly of his nephew's business abilities as he squeezed him out of the firm. The new company's factory covered an entire Philadelphia city block and manufactured various types of cooking stoves, plain and enameled holloware; and it did a small machine casting business. It was a successful enterprise; in the depths of the 1873 depression, its stock held its value and the company grossed close to $500,000 dollars a year.

Thomson also made fairly substantial investments in two basic railway equipment industries, the Union Car Spring Company and the Hamilton Steeled Wheel Company, a firm that made iron wheels with steel wearing surfaces that was probably an offshoot of his interest in attempts to bond a steel head to an iron rail. Thomson's investment in that process and his shares in the American Anti Incrustation Company, both attested to his willingness to pioneer in capitalizing interesting technological possibilities. His real estate investments were always offshoots of his railway interests, and at his death he still owned shares in four companies, all but one organized to develop and market large land grants. Land company stocks held their values quite well during the financial downturn because they were backed by tangible assets; only his Boston and Lake Superior Land Company shares depreciated to nothing, thanks to the demise of the parent venture.

Thomson also invested in a few more sedate securities less directly related to the railway business, although they comprised a small proportion of his final holdings. His three bank stocks, appraised at $13,000, accurately reflected his peripatetic financial interests. He still owned thirty-five valuable shares in the National Bank of Augusta left from his southern sojourn, fifty shares in the Louisiana National Bank he picked up somewhere, and 100 shares in a firm called the Guaranteed Trust and Safe Deposit Company. Life insurance companies in the immediate postwar period were still novel investments with fairly high risk factors associated with them. His 378 shares of American Life Insurance & Trust Company, worth almost $19,000 in 1874 were obviously a solid investment; his 100 shares in the North American Mutual Life Insurance Company, valued at thirteen dollars each, were not quite as gilt-edged. Thomson's investment in Howard Fire & Marine Insurance Company was a total loss, as was his interest in the Hope Mutual Insurance Company, a firm that had little left in the depression when its shares traded for .0025 cents each. None of these companies did business with the PRR.[45]

In the last decade of his life, Thomson refined the investment procedures he had learned in the South. He still preferred to enter a project on the ground floor, but over the years he became more adept at using other people's money. Repeatedly, he took advantage of stock bonuses offered to make corporate bonds more desirable, sold the shares while their prospects were still bright, and held the other securities for collateral and appreciation. Through these techniques he was able to turn his funds over quickly, and as a rule, at a profit. That was how he was able to command so much capital given his modest fortune. The velocity of his money was awesome; he kept his funds always moving from one project to another, rarely advancing large amounts for long periods. In many respects his was a paper empire, one in which securities begot more securities. In this sense he was a classic speculator, but with an important difference; Thomson built things with his paper. His native haunts were not the investment houses, but the drafting rooms. To him stocks and bonds were a means to an end, not an end in themselves. And he liked to see his projects well-constructed. After he bought properties for the PRR, he frequently informed his stockholders that he would have to spend more of their money to bring the acquisitions up to his standards.

Thomson was really a rare combination of tinkerer and hardheaded businessman. Like many other bright, ambitious men, he dreamed of building great things, of reaching for the ultimate, in his case, a coast-to-coast railroad. He was consumed with a passion for transcontinentals, and he pursued them with unrelenting zeal. With the exception of the CP and the Southern Pacific, he invested in every transcontinental begun in his lifetime. He even tried to build his own, the KP, and failing in that, he bought up the UP. For one, short, glimmering moment, Thomson controlled a railroad empire that stretched from New York City to Ogden, Utah where the UP met the CP. It was as close as he was to get, a lot closer than anyone before, to control of a system of roads linking the Atlantic to the Pacific. The energy and time Thomson devoted to transcontinental strategy and finance after the war, especially in light of his duties on the PRR and his manifold personal investments, was truly prodigious. He paid a high price for his ambition. His health buckled and then broke, but he dreamed the large dreams.

10

IN QUEST OF
THE PACIFIC

Thomson's transcontinental ambitions knew no bounds. Never satisfied simply to exercise his influence in the ruling councils of one giant, he once controlled roads building simultaneously over the northern, central, and southern routes. He wanted all the Pacific basin trade funneled across the Horseshoe Curve. He would then dominate all the regional railway balances of power, and by denying his rivals the trade, he would have the security he ardently sought for his road. Most significantly, he could fundamentally alter the American railroad map, removing the regional discontinuities that bedevil the industry to this day.

The Pennsylvania president's western strategy was fatally flawed, however. By the postwar era a regional group the size of the Philadelphia interests no longer commanded sufficient assets to construct and control several transcontinentals simultaneously. From 1866 to the depression, they never had fewer than two Pacific roads in hand and usually three. In addition, Thomson and his friends moved into the western arena just as the nation's political climate changed. Had they been able to secure government guarantees for their roads' securities, direct subsidies, and better land grants to stretch their resources, they might have emerged as America's premier financial group. But public opinion was rapidly turning against such largess, particularly after the well-publicized shenanigans of some eastern railway leaders. And it did not help that the fights between the various transcontinental interests in congressional cloakrooms deadlocked the national legislature.

The business world was rapidly changing by the late 1860s, a fact

Thomson sometimes sensed rather than understood. He was already carrying too many burdens, and the thousands of miles that separated him from the various transcontinental headquarters and construction crews made it impossible for him personally to oversee his interests. Every single one of his Pacific projects suffered severe managerial and organizational problems. In the cases of the Kansas Pacific and the Northern Pacific, they crippled the enterprises. Organization was one of Thomson's strong points, and he fumed as squabbling officials a half a continent removed frittered away his funds. His closest Philadelphia associates could not take hold of the work either; they had their own business cares aside from their joint speculations. Scott, well over a decade younger than Thomson and seemingly robust, was only a few short years away from a debilitating physical breakdown; Cooke's banking business was activity enough for three men; Baldwin's locomotive works was inundated with orders; Carnegie was juggling projects halfway across the globe; Pullman was busy with his own growing empire; and Palmer was laying the foundation for one of Colorado's great fortunes. None of the parties could give full attention to the investments. They became dependent upon others, outsiders who often pulled them into ancillary enterprises that squandered assets. As long as Thomson, Scott, Pullman, and Baldwin refused to pledge their companies' credit and continued to fund ventures valued at hundreds of millions of dollars solely on their personal lines of credit, their postwar chances for success across the West were slim. The future belonged to the rising generation of enterprisers who, with their banking allies, could control eight- and nine-digit sums; businesses were becoming so large and ingesting such great quantities of money, that informal regional investment groups, linked by blood, marriage, and friendship, could no longer reasonably expect to succeed on that scale.

Nevertheless, Thomson could never shake the lure of the West. Visions of its lucrative traffic flowing over his Pennsylvania's rails haunted him while the sheer scope of the ventures out on the Plains excited him. His investment methods had always been more attuned to the nation's developing areas—he needed a business frontier. Out there he could still go into schemes early at large discounts, help build useful improvements, and with a little luck reap substantial profits. Moreover, there was the attraction of land, something basic, tangible, known. The huge grants appealed to Thomson's sentimental side, awakened childhood instincts nurtured at his father's knee, the sentiments that prompted him to buy and keep the family homestead. He was responsible for opening up millions of acres to European farmers, enabling others to start anew, while using the income from the sales of these lands to build his roads and augment his profits. When the scarcity of men and materials during the Civil War dampened enthusiasm for a transcontinental, Thomson publicly supported the chartering of the Union Pacific. Although he served on its board for a year, he took no active part in its organization; he had problems enough operating the PRR. As the hostilities wound down to their inevitable conclusion, his interest in transcontinentals quickened. Instead of throwing his reputation and energy behind the UP, he grasped an opportunity to construct and control his own Pacific road in an effort to become master of the country's first coast-to-coast rail system.

The vehicle for Thomson's aspirations was a small Kansas railroad, the Union Pacific Eastern Division, probably so named to confuse potential investors, which had rights under the 1862 Pacific Railway Act to build from the Missouri River to the 100th meridian. Two years later, the little road was granted twenty alternate sections of land for each mile of track laid, a government loan, and most importantly, permission, if it reached the 100th meridian first to connect with the Central Pacific, which would have made it the first transcontinental. In 1864, John D. Perry, president of the Exchange Bank of St. Louis, captured control of the company, but beset by a shortage of operating capital, unable to pry the first installment of government bonds out of the new Johnson administration, and pestered by legal difficulties, he approached Thomson and Scott about the possibility of their taking an interest in the work. The Pennsylvanians talked to their Ohio financial allies and agreed to invest only if they took it over. Perry balked, but in the face of continuing difficulties the next year he sold Thomson, Scott, Baldwin, and their friends an equal share in the concern for $1 million. Thomson, however, won de facto control with the right to name the odd director. To insure reliable inside information about the project, he installed Palmer as the firm's treasurer and Charles Lamborn as its secretary. For once the Philadelphia interests may have negotiated too fine a deal; Palmer reported, "the St. Louis parties think Scott drove a pretty hard bargain." The ill-feelings between the two parties lingered for years and ultimately determined the project's fate.[1]

Thomson was excited by prospects of capturing a transcontinental for only $1 million. Had the 1864 amendment not offered the possibility of supplanting the UP, however, he would not have entertained the idea. But as matters stood by mid-October 1865 the future appeared bright, for only a shade under 20 percent of $1 million he stood to gain, even if another foot of the road was never built, a share of the almost 500,000 acres of land already ceded the road for completing its first forty miles. As Palmer smugly put it, "there is some danger of our becoming a large landed proprietor." Considerations of personal profit, however, paled before the tantalizing prospect of operating his trains through to San Francisco.[2]

To achieve that goal the UPED's crews would have to outbuild the UP's. When Thomson and his friends took control, they thought they could advance their railhead about ten miles per month, enough, they reasoned, to outstrip the UP. But Thomson badly underestimated the resources and determination of his rivals. While the UPED's construction plodded along right on schedule, the UP's forces caught up and the following year outdistanced their Kansas competitor by eighty miles. Strangely, the Philadelphia parties did not exert any pressure to speed up the work until late summer, and by then it was too late. To the north chief engineer Grenville Dodge's crews had made railway construction an art. They laid 265 miles in only nine months in 1866 and by year's end were averaging three miles a day. Worse, on October 6 the UP's gangs spiked down their rails across the hallowed 100 meridian, giving them important political and psychological advantages in the race for the Pacific; Congress, however, had removed the stipulations that had made that line legally meaningful in determining which company would become the first transcontinental.[3]

The UPED's slowness was a manifestation of internal troubles plaguing the company. The split between the St. Louis and the Philadelphia interests widened, and in large measure Thomson was at fault for not ending the paralyzing dispute; he never took charge, instead he sat by and watched the internal bickering tear the concern apart. When his Philadelphia friends, upset at the slow rate of progress, proposed to Thomson in May 1866 that he take the road's presidency and allow his trusted protégé Palmer to attend to its duties, Thomson demurred. Lamborn reported Thomson, who had been ill that spring, told him that "he was never able to hold a *nominal* position and he always would work." Instead, Thomson suggested that Carlos Greely, an ally of the St. Louis parties, replace Perry as president and that Palmer assume the vice-presidency "to do the outside work." Thomson's departure in July for Europe left all the internal problems in limbo until his return.[4]

While railway matters drifted in 1866, the road's subsidiary National Land Company made money. The firm had 6.4 million acres to sell and sent its agents abroad to lure emigrants out to Kansas. The UPED investors were principals in the land speculation as well, and while Thomson was in Europe he talked up western opportunities wherever he went. He was quick to note the effect of American letters that were "fostered by their relatives who have gone before and send back tales of their success which must seem marvelous to those who live as the German farmers do—." Despite the land company's efforts, the UPED never attracted a great number of settlers, its 10,000 in 1868 was perhaps a representative sample. By 1872, however, it had disposed of almost 500,000 acres at an average price of $3 each. With 3,000 shares in the concern, Thomson certainly shared in the benefits. In addition he speculated on his own account with Baldwin and Scott in Kansas lands.[5]

When Thomson returned from Europe in November 1866, he realized the UPED had lost the race out on the Plains. The Philadelphia interests abruptly changed their strategy and set out to persuade Congress to subsidize a southern transcontinental. Thomson was already interested in Mexican projects and was looking for the easiest route across the continental divide. Some of his partners urged him "to engulf the Missouri Pacific into the greedy maw of the Kansas & Transcontinental boa," as Lamborn put it, but he simply could not be persuaded to put up the money.

Instead, he supported intense lobbying efforts to win a subsidy to build to southern California. All along the way he had to fight strong opposition from the UP, NP, and the Atlantic and Pacific Railroad interests. The A&P was an ambitious line building from St. Louis into the Indian Territory and on toward the coast; ironically Thomson had helped charter the company. Scott's suggestion that all the transcontinentals make common cause to secure subsidies proved impractical. The UPED interests failed to accomplish anything in 1867 but came very close the following year. But it was an election year, and railroad subsidies were becoming controversial so the UPED political forces retreated, confident as Lamborn reported, that "the next session of Congress will be much more liberal than the last and the members will feel less responsibility towards their constituents when the election shall be over." While preparing for the December session, Lamborn was told "it will require $500,000 in money & securities to carry the measure this winter." He confidently predicted, however, "it can be done." He was wrong. Early in the new session the house resolved to grant no further corporate subsidies. And by the end of 1869 it was clear to all concerned that the UPED was never going to become a transcontinental.[6]

The problem Thomson faced early that year was where the road should go; building from somewhere to nowhere was not the way to create a valuable property. Moreover, he was losing interest in the venture. Back at the end of 1868 Palmer had again tried to talk him into taking control of the enterprise. Once more, Thomson, who had just recognized the threat Gould posed to his western connections, refused, this time on the grounds of his health. "I have come to the conclusion," he responded, "that if I attempt to increase my labors & responsibilities that I will soon break down — In view of this, I have concluded that nothing but an overwhelming necessity shall induce me to extend our Control of Railways beyond Chicago on the North and the Mississippi River in the South." Unwilling to put the resources of his friends and his railroad behind the work to build on to the coast, Thomson supported an alternate plan to push the UPED to Denver and from there to connect with the UP at Cheyenne. He also favored changing its name, which had always been a source of confusion, to the Kansas Pacific, an ironic choice just as its promoters abandoned their transcontinental dreams.[7]

Palmer pushed his Mexican-American and Irish construction crews hard and finished the KP to Denver on August 15, 1870. On the last day his gangs laid over ten miles of track in as many hours, eclipsing the UP's record: a symbolic victory at best. Thomson's profits from the railway and land company must have been on the order of $250,000, but he failed to get what he wanted most, a transcontinental. Settling for half a loaf must have galled him—especially since his neglect to intervene decisively in the company's affairs in 1866 had contributed to its failure to reach the Pacific. But he did not withdraw his investments from the region entirely after the KP was finished. He went on to invest in the Denver Pacific and the Denver and Rio Grande.

The KP splayed when it reached the foot of the mountain barrier at Denver. The DP branched north to the UP, and the D&RG, the remains of the promoters' dreams for a thirty-fifth parallel transcontinental, went south skirting the eastern slope of the Rockies with the goal of a possible extension into Mexico and a connection with the Southern Pacific for access into California. Early in 1869 the KP parties were busy making arrangements to buy the DP from the UP and finish it. Thomson drove a hard bargain in return for his participation in the venture. He was enmeshed in negotiations in the East to lease the Fort Wayne and was in no mood to be pleasant. At the KP's annual meeting in April, Palmer had been elected a director and given responsibility for finishing the road to Denver; only after that did Thomson and his friends agree to help finance the DP.[8]

The eastern parties invested $250,000 in the road, with Thomson, Baird, and McManus footing the largest subscriptions, each risking $40,000. As usual, the Philadelphia parties bought into the construction company, Thomson 8 percent and Scott 5 percent. Yet even before construction started in September, Thomson was having second thoughts about the project. The pace he kept was beginning to exact its toll. He was tired, intermittently ill, and increasingly worried because he could no longer personally oversee his widespread investments. Furthermore, the economic portents in the late summer of 1869 were not good, thanks to Gould's and Fisk's machinations in the gold market, and Thomson was unusually wary; he finally demanded in late August that someone take $15,000 of his DP subscription. Josiah Reiff, a Palmer confidant, wrote Palmer that Thomson "had positively concluded for himself not to go into any new enterprises," adding, "I think he is laboring under a slight attack of the blues." It became worse. He surprised everybody a week later when he announced that he wanted to withdraw from the DP entirely. Lamborn reported on September 8, "Thomson told me today that he will under no circumstances go into another outside affair. He had put his foot down, and if he were to see a vase of gold at the end of a new rail he would not now go for it." Apparently Thomson's new found reluctance was not all of his own making, for Lamborn concluded, "it is a promise made his wife." While it was likely that Lavinia was concerned over Thomson's deteriorating health, it was more probable that he had decided to get out of the DP and KP projects altogether. Within a year he sold his interest in the DP and held only a few KP securities.[9]

He did not withdraw from the area entirely. Instead he took one more flyer in Colorado to promote his land and mineral interests there and to please Palmer, who like Carnegie, was positively superstitious about entering any project without at least the nominal backing of his former patron. Thomson still had large holdings in the KP's National Land Company and in the Central Colorado Improvement Company, which owned large tracts of land all over the territory. When Thomson learned that Palmer's proposed D&RG would open up these lands and connect with Mexican railways, he was interested. He invested in the road's stocks and bonds, bought heavily into the Union Contract Company which built the railroad, and along with Felton became a trustee for the company's first mortgage bonds. Felton's presence indicated that the whole party of Philadelphia interests were principals in the firm; Baldwin, for example, received the contract for the road's locomotives. Construction began in mid-summer 1871 on the three-foot gauge line and by the 1873 panic it was completed just south of Pueblo, Colorado, where all work was halted for lack of funds.[10]

Just before the economic downturn, Thomson, who had not been feeling well since May and who was extremely worried over rising interest rates and the shortage of venture capital, took his last vacation. Ostensibly, it was an excursion to promote the D&RG among prominent eastern financiers, but Thomson probably joined at his wife's insistence that he take in western vistas and try to forget his cares. Palmer put the party up at the Manitou House in Colorado Springs, where the visiting moguls chipped in to subsidize an amateur theatrical on July 9 for the benefit of the local Episcopal church. Charlotte played the dormouse in *Alice's Adventures in Wonderland* and then demonstrated her versatility by appearing as Ophelia in something the newspaper labeled *Artist's Dream*. A gushy local editor reported that she "wore her willows very gracefully." The newspaper noted parenthetically "that a couple of Ute chiefs" also attended the performance. Thomson, Lavinia, and Charlotte went on to Salt Lake City and probably to San Francisco. The leisurely vacation worked wonders for his health. He returned home brimming with his customary optimism and remained relatively robust into the following spring. He needed all the inner resources he could muster, however, for Cooke's failure that fall, after he overextended his credit in the NP, a project in which Thomson had a significant interest, precipitated the depression that brought most of the Pennsylvania president's ventures crashing down.[11]

Aside from Scott's Texas and Pacific, the NP was perhaps the most speculative of all Thomson's transcontinental schemes. Projected to build far in advance of settlement through some of the roughest terrain in America from Duluth to Puget Sound, it was always a financial runt. Chartered in 1864 and given a federal land grant, the company lay dormant until the late 1860s when it was revived by New England capitalists. Thomson, with his extensive interests in the Lake Superior area, realized by 1869 that his dreams for the KP were not to be fulfilled, so he joined with Cass and bought two seats on the NP's board for the Pennsylvania interests. That same year, Cooke, who was attracted by the road's large land grant, the company's only tangible asset, gained control of the project. He organized a pool to buy $5 million of the NP's gold bonds and divided it into twelve separate subscriptions, that together constituted a 50 percent ownership of the railroad. Each subscription cost just under $500,000 and accompanying the bonds were stock bonuses totaling $41 million to be paid as the construction advanced. Lamborn described the NP bonds as "very pretty" and noted that Cooke had sold $50,000 worth of them to Chief Justice Salmon P. Chase in his quest for political preferment.[12]

The Philadelphia parties bought into the pool even before the subscriptions were offered to the public in January 1870. Thomson's personal share was in the order of $70,000, or one-eighth of a one-twelfth interest. That Thomson thought of the NP as a logical extension of his other speculations in the area became evident when he brought Gilead Smith into the project to recruit settlers for the NP's lands. Thomson promoted the NP opportunity widely among his associates. Scott took an interest of course, and was reported to be "enthusiastic about it." Thomson even suggested to Lamborn, who was not wealthy, that he sell his other interests or borrow money, because he should not pass up a valuable chance to "go in on the ground floor," a favorite phrase of Thomson's. The Pennsylvania's president confidently predicted that "the parties in it are so strong that the thing will be carried through if there is any possible way of doing it. The control is to be in Phila.," almost the exact words he had used to describe the UPED project in 1866. The large element of risk and an indefinite accountability, however, were serious enough to deter many large capitalists whose support the NP desperately needed. The entire subscription was taken, but there were few prominent names on the list, and Cooke put up the money for many of those who did agree to take shares.[13]

Nevertheless, with what funds he had available, Cooke started construction on February 15, 1870. At the same time, he petitioned Congress for permission to issue bonds on the company's lands, since it had nothing else to mortgage. The construction crews' steady progress west of Duluth, along with the high costs of a political campaign, soon exhausted the initial $5 million subscription. Moreover, funds were needed to equip and operate the newly completed portions of the line. Cooke decided to promote a $100 million first mortgage bond issue to cover all expected costs. It was a staggering undertaking for a private house of his size, especially in a market that was already glutted with speculative transcontinental securities. Furthermore, it bonded the NP at a rate of $50,000 per mile, higher than any such road. As a result, the bonds sold slowly and at heavy discounts, while calls upon Cooke to carry the work rose rapidly. By January 1871, the NP was overdrawn $600,000 at his banking house.[14]

Thomson recognized the project was foundering because nobody seemed able to prevail upon the road's managers to curb their profligacy. To keep his house afloat, Cooke resorted to advancing his depositors' funds to the railroad. Worse, the NP was not attracting sufficient traffic to make its completed sections pay, and the Philadelphia parties further burdened the road by unloading their unprofitable Lake Superior road on it. Cooke and his allies had to spend precious dollars buying and building lines that meandered southward to central Iowa in search of traffic. This condition of things continued through 1872. By late the next summer, Cooke's financial position was extremely precarious as bond sales continued to dwindle and money became progressively tighter. In desperation he turned to Congress for help. With Thomson's support he joined with Scott, who controlled the T&P, to request a $40,000-per-mile federal guarantee for the NP's bonds. The whole scheme was little more than a pipe dream; the Credit Mobilier scandal had burst over the capital with its revelations of avarice in the nation's highest councils and had all but immobilized the political process. Few politicians dared support any resolution that smacked of a giveaway to railroads. It was a measure of the Philadelphia interests' growing desperation that Cooke continued to push the bill. He forwarded their appeal to Congress, stating that "Scott, Thomson & all the big bugs of the Penna. R.R. & Texas & Pacific have signed below us on behalf of the Roads." A million distinguished endorsements, however, could not have passed the proposition in 1873.[15]

To his credit Cooke carried the NP as long as was humanly possible. When many frightened investors started selling their NP bonds late in 1872, he bought heavily. Quite possibly Thomson sold, but if so he probably delayed unloading until mid-1873 when he was strapped for funds to shore up the T&P. His strong support for Cooke's petition to Congress early in that year indicated he was still hopeful, but the tightening money markets squeezed Cooke so severely that he was finally forced to admit insolvency and close his doors on September 18. Thomson could only watch as his NP holdings depreciated to near worthlessness. His total losses were in the range of $50,000, not frightful given the stakes he was playing for, but untimely to say the least.

If Thomson could have mustered more resources in the twenty-four months preceding Cooke's failure or if he had contracted his own obligations and concentrated on the stronger transcontinental projects, he would have emerged without question as the most prominent railway personality of his generation. As it was, he came within a hairbreadth of that distinction, when for one glorious year, 1871, he was the master of the Union Pacific. He had secured connecting roads across the Midwest to Chicago and St. Louis, and with the UP he had acquired a lever, as Carnegie needlessly reminded him, for "keeping the lines between Omaha & Chicago in attitudes friendly to the Pennsylvania Railroad." His takeover of the UP marked an important step in the American railway business; since the Civil War, the more powerful and advantageously located lines had assiduously absorbed the less fortunate. By the early 1870s, at least four well-financed parties stood poised to push their domains into the Far West: the Joy interests in Boston, who were already strong between the Mississippi and Missouri rivers; the Vanderbilts, after they extended their NYC into Chicago; the predatory Gould; and Thomson's Philadelphia interests. But Thomson and his allies made their move first and caught their competitors by surprise. When the news of their takeover of the UP leaked out in February, *The Railroad Gazette* confidently predicted that Thomson's PRR would "control all the transcontinental traffic for many years to come."[16]

The editors of that esteemed trade journal, however, were better reporters than prognosticators. The very methods by which Thomson and his friends captured control of the troubled road made it impossible for them to maintain their position. They had grasped the opportunity that appeared in December 1870 when the federal government demanded that the land-grant railways start repaying the interest on their subsidy bonds. The news drove UP securities so low that the road's managers could not raise money to fund the railway's first mortgage coupons due January 1, 1871. Into the breech stepped UP director and New York shipbuilder and financier, Cornelius S. Bushnell, a man with a reputation as something of a gambler who had personally guaranteed the Union ironclad *Monitor*'s performance during the Civil War. Bushnell and several other directors each personally endorsed notes for the needed money becoming liable for over $600,000. The short-term notes had to be repaid and Bushnell approached Thomson, Pullman, and Scott. By most accounts, Pullman, who operated his sleeping cars over the UP, was first to recognize the chance to capitalize on the UP's troubles. Thomson, just returned from his leave of absence and embroiled in negotiations to organize the PC, lease the UNJR, and establish a steamship company, also found the opportunity enticing. The three men and Carnegie drove a hard bargain. They would raise the money to meet Bushnell's obligations only if he made arrangements to fund the NP's large floating debt, clear up its accounts with the Credit Mobilier, and give the Pennsylvania interests control of the road.[17]

Bushnell did his best to comply. He went to UP headquarters in Boston and purchased $4.6 million of the company's securities at prices far above their current market values to enable the UP to pay off its floating debt. Bushnell then hurried back to Philadelphia where the Pennsylvania parties loaned him the funds he needed to meet his personal obligations taking the bonds and 30,000 UP shares, each with a par value of $100, as collateral. Bushnell also gave Thomson and his colleagues the option of purchasing the UP shares at nine, the price they commanded in late January. Bushnell, applied with the Ames faction on the UP, delivered four of the twenty UP board seats and three of the seven seats on the board's executive committee to Thomson and his friends. Scott was awarded the road's presidency. On January 27, Carnegie wrote a friend triumphantly "you see we have Union Pacific. I go on the Executive Committee in March."[18]

To raise the funds to back Bushnell and take over the UP, Thomson and his colleagues extended their credit to its breaking point, so close in fact, that Thomson indirectly dipped into his road's treasury. Pullman put up at least 1,800 shares in his company, while Thomson, Carnegie, and Scott traded their Keokuk and Hamilton Bridge bonds for $600,000 in Northern Central Railway bonds owned and guaranteed by the PRR, which were more easily hypothecated. Thomson took the NC bonds from the Pennsylvania's sinking fund but only on a short-term basis because his board's financial committee was apprehensive over the PRR's rate of expansion. The Philadelphia interests placed the NC bonds and Pullman's stock with Drexel, Morgan and Company in return for something over $600,000 in cash. To this they added an unknown amount of their personal money, and Bushnell drew on them to pay off the directors' December notes.[19]

Bushnell had been secured by the Philadelphia interests, but he still had to meet a payment schedule for the UP securities he had purchased. That was the problem. The Pennsylvania parties were stretched thin but hated to let go. They had to support Bushnell to retain their control. The UP stock, which soared to nearly thirty when the news broke of the PRR coup, was the only collateral they held that promised to ease their burdens quickly. The 30,000 shares in Carnegie's safe in New York City, however, were nearly 10 percent of the road's outstanding stock and secured control of the UP for the Philadelphia interests. Nevertheless, they were forced to sell it, and most observers believed that the spread between the stock's market price and the Pennsylvania interests' option to buy at nine was simply too enticing for Scott and Carnegie to resist, and one or the other sold out. Thomson was described as being "surprised" when he heard of the sale.[20]

The story does not ring true; Scott and Carnegie would never have attempted such a deed alone. It was their very close personal associations with Thomson and his PRR that gave them much of their clout in the business world. They would not have had the UP in the first place had he not had access to bonds on which they could easily raise cash. The notion that Thomson was the wounded innocent in the sale of the UP's stock arose from two common beliefs about him; that he was careless with his money and that by 1871 he was only the "nominal" head of the PRR, having been eclipsed by Scott. The one thing Thomson was serious about was his money. He often placed large investments in others' names, but they were always trusted associates upon whom he could depend to do his bidding. The idea that he was only a figurehead for powers behind the throne arose from his propensity to push Scott into the public eye to perform the political and financial tasks that he found so distasteful but so necessary. Scott, emerging as a businessman in his own right, traded heavily on his association with the PRR's president and his ability to tap the large pool of capital centered at the road's front office. For Scott to have broken with Thomson would have been sheer madness; Thomson's name clothed him with instant financial respectability. Moreover, Scott was always aware that Thomson was the one man who could destroy his credibility as a businessman by banishing him from the PRR's inner sanctum. That Scott initiated ventures and lured Thomson into them was evident, the Pennsylvania's foray into the South and the T&P enterprise stand as conspicuous examples, but like Carnegie and Palmer, Scott went into no important projects before 1873 without his chief's backing. The principal Philadelphia interests were simply too mutually interdependent to consider selling each other out.[21]

Instead, the Philadelphia parties found that the calls upon their resources to support Bushnell were beyond their immediate means. Thomson and Scott were already involved in the California and Texas Construction Company and were busily buying a rail empire in the South, while all had sundry interests spread across the nation. The nature of their desperate need for cash became apparent at a March 9 UP executive committee meeting held just two days after Scott was elected president, at which he managed to exact $19,000 for "legal expense." It provided no relief. Less than two weeks later the Philadelphia parties began to sell the UP stock and before they were through, they had unloaded over 32,000 shares. Still short, they borrowed from Bushnell and sold off some of their PRR stock. In November Carnegie asked Thomson to make the exchange of $250,000 of the NC bonds permanent, citing their need "to have something which we can sell or hypothecate more readily in order to meet engagements." Scott remembered later that in December 1871, "I was a little embarrassed myself for want of money," when he placed seventy-five worthless Little Rock and Fort Smith Railroad bonds with the UP for a loan of just over $60,000. The UP's president defended the transaction claiming the company owed him that much and more for raising the value of its securities. It was later charged that the bonds were delivered to James G. Blaine as payment for political favors.[22]

Plainly, the Philadelphia interests had overreached their resources. By the end of 1871 they had only 400 UP shares left, and even with their profits of over $500,000 they could not secure all Bushnell's obligations. Furthermore, Carnegie claimed there was a difference of opinion among the partners over a proper course of action; the fact that Pullman used his gains to repurchase UP stock for his own account suggests that not all the parties were willing to go to the wall to see the whole arrangement through. Scott was caught very short of liquid assets at the same time, and Thomson, heeding his C&T calls and enmeshed in the NP and D&RG projects, must have been severely strapped. As late as September 11, 1873, Thomson was still trying to raise money "to secure the payment of Bushnell's note," an indication that the Pennsylvania parties still had UP obligations left on the very eve of the panic.[23]

At the March 6, 1872 UP annual meeting all the Philadelphia parties, with the exception of Pullman were, as Carnegie remembered, "ignominiously but deservedly expelled from the Union Pacific board." To their chagrin, the NYC gained control of the transcontinental and its presidency. Undoubtedly, Scott would have been ousted anyway even if the Pennsylvania interests had not sold out. None of the other UP parties considered Scott's presidency to be in the long-range interests of his company. Scott was an investor in all the other transcontinentals and was the moving force behind the construction of a thirty-second parallel road, the T&P, of which he became president in 1872; his loyalty was not to the UP but rather to the goal of dominating western trade for the benefit of his PRR. The Ames faction apprehensively eyed the Pennsylvanians' invasion of their corporate domain; what strength the UP enjoyed in 1871 as the only completed transcontinental was predicated upon its ability to play eastern connections against one another. Nevertheless, for one brief year, as full of distractions and troubles as it was, Thomson stood athwart all the great transcontinental projects; he was poised to capture the traffic of the West if only he could maintain and advance his lines of control.[24]

Early in 1872 he still had reasonable expectations that he could control the UP, NP, and T&P, along with the KP and D&RG combination, and insure his Pennsylvania Railroad's dominance for generations to come. Had he accomplished the feat it would have been an unparalleled achievement. But he tried to build and rule a transportation empire spanning the western half of the continent using only private funds; he was unwilling or unable to go that last step and commit the PRR's vast resources to the faltering transcontinentals. The two times he did so, with the NC bond exchange and later a similar transaction with the C&T, he was careful to minimize its liabilities. Given his mastery over the PRR, there was no question but that in 1872 he could have advanced his road's funds and credit to at least one of the transcontinentals. A guarantee of the NP's bonds would have advanced their price, relieved Cooke, helped insure the line's early completion, and enhanced the PRR's profits, possibly without advancing a cent. The UP could have been held for less than a couple million dollars. The KP could have been built faster or the D&RG extended into southern California for a reasonable outlay. Daring with his own money, Thomson was more conservative with his stockholders'.

As the year 1872 progressed, Thomson's western expectations faded fast. The KP was already hopeless, the NP by Christmas appeared irretrievable, the UP was lost, and his last major transcontinental speculation was rapidly consuming his personal fortune. The Texas and Pacific, chartered to build along the thirty-second parallel route Thomson had advocated before the war, was Scott's promotion. Thomson never personally took hold of the work, but he lent his good name, his credit, his funds, and finally his endorsements to his vice-president and his friends and stuck by them even in the darkest days of the panic.

Authorized to build a road from Marshall, Texas through El Paso, where it would connect with the D&RG, to San Diego, the company received the last of the great congressional land grants, a potential gift of 16 million acres. Drawing upon his experiences in other such projects, Scott organized the California and Texas Railway Construction Company, capitalized at $10 million, to build his road and sold shares in it to the Philadelphia interests. Thomson bought about 5 percent of the company for $500,000, never expecting to have to come up with that kind of money. Unfortunately, after construction began in October 1872, the C&T rather than the T&P, financed all the work. The initial 10 percent call on the construction company's subscribers, all that they had expected to ante up, was spent long before the first workman put a spade to the ground. Subsequent calls were made, until by the panic, 80 percent had been paid in; in less than two years Thomson turned over $400,000 cash without receiving a cent in return. Worse, in the C&T's efforts to speed up construction to meet the terms of the land grant, it far overspent its means. By the fall of 1873 the company had about $7 million in unsecured debts. Unable to raise any more funds at home, Scott left for Europe in July with a satchel full of T&P securities to try to raise cash on them to ease the C&T's burdens. He needed the money to get the work, which had been halted in 1873 by a drought and an epidemic of "Yellow Jack," under way again.[25]

The T&P bonds were not exactly the most tempting buy on a tightening market. Desperate for securities he could sell, Scott turned to the PRR for relief. Still in Europe, he had a proposal presented at a special board meeting on August 18, from which Thomson was absent, to purchase $2 million worth of the Pennsylvania's Pittsburgh, Cincinnati and St. Louis Railroad stock with a note for that amount drawn on the C&T plus $4 million in T&P construction bonds. The board debated this ticklish request in a rare all-day meeting and finally decided to accept the arrangement, a strong indication that it had Thomson's approval. With solid securities to offer, Scott was on the verge of success overseas when news of the Wall Street panic destroyed his prospects. He hurried home facing ruin.[26]

Cooke's closing caught Thomson short as well; he had been hard-pressed for cash since his takeover of the UP. Almost a full year before the panic, he complained to Carnegie, "I have no funds at present to invest, having been drained by the Texas & California—." His strategy at the onset of the depression was to secure his own personal situation to avoid default and then to support, if possible, his financial allies. He knew full well that repudiation by any of the Philadelphia parties would reflect on his credit and that the C&T was the single greatest threat to their collective solvency. As soon as Scott returned in late September, the prominent parties involved in the concern convened in a hastily called meeting. Dodge, who was ramrodding the T&P's construction, attended the emotionally charged conclave at which the reputations and careers of Thomson, Scott, Thaw, McManus, Baird, Houston, and Carnegie hung in the balance. He reported that the arguments lasted all day and most of the night. They finally agreed that they had to try to save the road, which meant they had to secure the $7 million owed by the C&T. Six of them assumed personal liability for portions of the debt by attaching their endorsements to the C&T's notes. They signed what became known as "three name" and "five name" paper, with Scott, McManus, and Baird taking up $4.5 million and Thomson and Houston adding their names to an additional $1.7 million. They hoped to pay the C&T's remaining indebtedness from their personal assets.[27]

Carnegie, who was building the Edgar Thomson steel works, refused to extend his credit. He feared that his endorsements would destroy his ability to raise money for his steel mill. The Philadelphia interests, however, needed every last resource they could muster. When Scott failed to budge Carnegie, he asked Thomson to bring the canny Scotsman to his senses. On October 3, Thomson came straight to the point, "I think that you should tax your friends, if you have not the means yourself, to meet your calls for the Texas concern." But Thomson also revealed his own long-held inner doubts about the project, "the scheme itself was good enough, but it has been most wofully [sic] mismanaged financially, Scott having acted upon his faith in his guiding star, instead of sound discretion." As he penned those sentiments he must have harked back to a letter he had written Carnegie two years earlier in which he advised his friend to invest in the T&P, "if the concern is not too rotten." It was too late, however, for backward glances. Thomson twisted Carnegie's arm hard, "Scott should be carried until his return, and you of all others should lend your helping hand where you run no risk—." But Carnegie remained unmoved by Thomson's entreaty. His continued refusal to aid the men who had been responsible for his own success opened a wide breach with Scott and to a lesser extent with Thomson. For the rest of his life Carnegie regretted that he abandoned his friends in their hour of need, admitting later that he was a cause for Scott's "premature death." He could have added, for Thomson's also.[28]

His signature on the "five name" notes obligated Thomson for a minimum of $340,000 of the C&T's debts, assuming his four co-signers were able to meet their calls. Moreover, he was assaulted from all sides by distressed friends beseeching him for money. With all his other troubles, he advanced the Karlhaus Coal and Lumber Company some $12,425 in cash and endorsements taking only the firm's notes in return. He helped Bushnell with $10,000 and endorsed an almost equal amount of notes for a company cryptically listed as simply the N&A. But the C&T remained his most worrisome obligation. Calls on his endorsements began almost immediately, and as the markets plummeted, the value of his fortune shrank daily. To hold, Thomson drew heavily upon his reputation for being as good as his word to hypothecate $250,000 of the T&P construction bonds with the London, Asiatic, and American Company. Between October 1 and November 4 he drew 40 percent of it out to meet his C&T obligations. Although it appeared that he could meet all his personal responsibilities, his allies were not so secure. On November 5, a $300,000 three-name note came due which the Philadelphia interests could not pay; it was all over—their grandiose constructions crumbled everywhere about them into heaps of dangerously jagged shards.[29]

Immediately, Scott appointed an attorney to make arrangements for paying the C&T's widely scattered debts. He brought the major creditors together and persuaded them to allow him to retain control of the concern to see what he could salvage for them. So great was the blow to Scott's reputation that he felt obliged to present his resignation to the Pennsylvania's board three days later. Thomson chaired that meeting, but despite the fact that he blamed Scott for the C&T mess and especially for dragging him and the PRR into the disaster (for the $2 million C&T note in the road's treasury was momentarily worthless), he advised his directors to decline Scott's offer as "not necessary or desirable." That was not the half of Thomson's troubles. At that same meeting he was forced to authorize payment of the Pennsylvania's 5 percent, semiannual dividend in script.[30]

Scott's failure to meet his obligations weighed heavily upon Thomson. The two men for years had been closely identified as the prime movers within the PRR-Philadelphia interests, and Scott's protest reflected badly on them all. Cooke's default was more excusable, as he was not so intimately involved in their many ventures. Although Thomson and others survived the panic, if only barely, the Pennsylvania interests' seemingly indefatigable expansion was rudely halted; they proved as vulnerable as other financial groups. Thomson watched in dismay as the NP slid into bankruptcy; the UP, inexorably headed in the same direction, was saved only by Gould bent on cannibalizing the property. The DP went under; the KP and D&RG defaulted on their obligations; the A&P, whose presidency Scott resigned in 1873, fell into receivership; and the T&P survived only by dint of its creditors' forbearance. He had done all he could to save them.

The early 1870s marked the high noon of Thomson's aspirations and influence. After the panic, he was just happy to escape from his transcontinental projects without being declared a bankrupt and to hold on to the Pennsylvania's presidency. For the last eight months of his life, as the world he had so tenaciously labored to build tumbled down about him, he worked frantically to meet his personal obligations, fend off an angry stockholders' rebellion, and shore up the Pennsylvania's deteriorating financial situation.

11

I HAVE
CONCLUDED
TO STOP

While Thomson was frantically attempting to underpin his own erod-ing financial situation, he also had to face threats to his Pennsyl-vania's very solvency. Hanging ominously over everything was the company's floating debt that had bloated to almost $16 million at the time of the panic. Offsetting these unsecured obligations was a cash balance of only $4.4 million. Furthermore, he had to continue to meet large fixed expenses assumed during happier times that included a guarantee of principal and interest for almost $34 million in the bonds of subsidiary companies, many of which could no longer cover their obligations. Thomson's penchant for leasing roads on generous terms had also come back to haunt him. By the panic, the road's lease ex-penses alone were $11.6 million a year, and while some of the lessees regularly returned more than their costs, the majority did not.[1]

Thomson had long recognized the dangers inherent in the PRR's extended financial condition and had sought to float a $35 million consolidated mortgage that represented a lien on the Pennsylvania's holdings of $50 million in securities. The first $10 million of the new bonds were marketed in July 1873 by the London, Asiatic and Ameri-can Company in Britain and sold quickly at 90. The panic, however, killed any chance of placing the rest of the issue. Cut off from the public money markets, he resorted to redistributing the PRR's assets internally to support the weakest properties in his empire. To pre-serve the company's dwindling cash reserves, the directors met five days late on November 7 to vote the semiannual 5 percent dividend be paid in company scrip redeemable in seventeen months. With only a little over $1 million left in the treasury, they had little choice. To increase his maneuverability, Thomson asked his board not to purchase any more securities for the new consolidated mortgage's sinking fund. Probably a test vote, the directors then abolished the sinking fund altogether and released its $9 million in stocks and bonds to Thomson, declaring in a scenario reminiscent of Lewis Carroll, that the mortgage still had first claim to the no longer extant fund's assets.[2]

For the last six months of his life, Thomson engaged in an endless process of exchanging the securities of his defaulted companies for marketable issues kept in the Pennsylvania's vault. He was robbing Peter to pay Paul in the belief that the depression would be sharp and short. The avalanche of plaints grew with each passing day, and not all the companies were the perennial financial cripples; he had to make cash advances to the Northern Central, the Pennsylvania Company, and the Susquehanna Coal Company. It was plain that he was buying time rather than pursuing a policy designed to cure his company's ills when Thomson, from his deathbed, authorized a 5 percent cash dividend that would cost his treasury almost $3.4 million right after his treasurer had reported that he had only $500,000 in his till. To make good the difference, the directors voted to sell off some securities and place $3 million of the consolidated mortgage bonds with Speyer and Company at 85.[3]

Thomson was moved to pay the cash dividend by the acrimonious annual meeting held on March 10 in which his leadership was seriously challenged for the first time. The earlier scrip dividend acted as a catalyst; the shareholders were angry about everything. They questioned whether Thomson's annual reports had been truthful, whether PRR officials were personally profiting from their investments in the captive PC, and demanded an intelligible rendering of their company's assets. All Scott's attempts to explain away the stockholders' mistrust and fears were to no avail. They voted to create an investigating committee to examine all facets of the Pennsylvania's organization and operations. To prevent the PRR's officers from undertaking any new obligations while the committee deliberated, the stockholders voted to prohibit further leases, security guarantees, advancement of funds to other railways, and sale of the Pennsylvania's property. The dictum was so broad, that if followed, it would have destroyed Thomson's efforts to save his empire. After venting all their frustrations, they acknowledged Thomson's mastery by reelecting the incumbent directors.[4]

The board ignored the shareholders' restrictions and continued to shuffle and sell securities to meet the Pennsylvania's obligations. When on May 15 a Boston stockholder demanded that the directors conform with the resolution, the board's reply was so evasive that it must have only convinced its correspondent that the real world had not yet intruded into the boardroom. The directors ignored all his specific charges, recounted the success of the road, and affirmed "it is now the settled policy of the Company not to expand its control of lines," beyond the Atlantic and Mississippi River, unless new connections "can be had with profit to the shareholders." The road's owners had been willing to accept the board's disdainful attitude so long as their company's assets appeared secure and the high dividends continued regularly. Neither was any longer true by 1874; Thomson's annual reports, always short on explanation and long on statistical tabulations, almost incomprehensible to all but accountants and bankers, did little to explain in layman's terms the company's fiscal condition. Stockholder ignorance fed fears that their property had been mismanaged and prompted their rebellion in 1874.[5]

The seven-man investigating committee started work immediately. Although Thomson was in no danger of being ousted from his presidency, the inquiry undoubtedly proved an embarrassment, and he must have observed its deliberations with a combination of apprehension and irritation. His death almost four months before the committee issued its report spared him its condemnation for assuming too much corporate power. Its disapproval of Thomson's expansion into the South and West, however, appeared the product of a depression mentality; stockholders had not complained earlier when he had balanced rapid expansion with high returns. Had Thomson been in Scott's place he would have had no trouble satisfying the commitee's demands to retrench and concentrate on developing the territory east of the Mississippi and north of the Ohio rivers for he had long accepted those as the company's legitimate boundaries.[6]

Thomson's ceaseless activities to forestall the loss of his personal fortune and his professional reputation sapped his physical resources. He had suffered some debilitating illness each year from 1866 through 1870, and again in 1872. Spring of 1873 was one of the few such seasons that he felt reasonably well, and, although very tired throughout that year, he was still reasonably healthy for a man his age with his history of heart trouble. Over the years Thomson's physical problems had affected his moods and activities. He was always much more the financial risk-taker when he was robust; when not feeling well, he drew back and consolidated his gains. Although he never directly equated his health with his economic views, his outlook was repeatedly the bleakest when he was sick. In the spring of 1867, he had written Carnegie: "I have been put into so many things, with promises of good results, that have disappointed my expectations, that I have concluded to Stop—." The following winter also took its toll on his normally upbeat personality; he lamented to Bell, "I find that I have more now on hand to look after than I can do justice to." Shortly thereafter he refused to assume control of the KP and confided to Palmer his fears that if he assumed additional responsibilities "I will soon break down." After he had returned from a tiring trip out to Keokuk in the summer of 1869 he debated whether to support his friends in the DP. Reiff described him as "laboring under a slight attack of the blues;" probably he was exhausted.[7]

Feeling dreadful in the winter of 1868, Thomson even considered resigning his presidency for a career in, of all things, politics. His political views had remained Whiggish after the war. He was a staunch supporter of high tariffs, a cause to which he became more devoted after he invested heavily in iron and steel companies, and he persistently advocated a reduction in the number of greenbacks in circulation and a gradual return to the gold standard. He publicly endorsed the secretary of the treasury George S. Boutwell's 1869 coinage plan that would have removed silver coins from circulation. His social views were equally conservative. Early in 1868 he wrote Covode to applaud Congress' intent to retrench and offered his views on how to solve the problem of unemployment and create demand for manufactured goods. His solution was brutally simplistic: "drive the idle people now in the cities out to the Western Praries [sic]. They now earn nothing," he pointed out, "and as long as high prices continue will stay here living in hope. If they were on the Praries [sic] they would be consumers of domestic manufacturers and producers of grain which is now in consequence of this unnatural distribution of labor so uncomfortably high." Thomson was not one to shirk from coercion, and he predicted that people would be driven out to farms only "by pinching times." Despite the fact that his own speculative ventures depended upon the ready availability of capital, he supported a severe contraction of the currency that would "pinch" hard enough to make prosperous farmers of urban dross.[8]

Thomson's views on the desirability of minimal government, except of course when it was necessary to aid projects that private capital was unable or unwilling to undertake, were common after the war. Just before the Pennsylvania legislature met in early 1869 to select a new senator, he was rumored to be the front runner for the seat. A Pennsylvania editor cheerfully noted after touting Thomson's "purity of character" and his "truly wonderful" administrative ability, that "if the reticence of General Grant is any commendation, Thomson is his peer in that respect." The editor even tried to justify the Pennsylvania's seamy political reputation by arguing "no legislation can be obtained by corporations for the benefit of their interests without it is paid for in hand to the Legislature," but carefully added that nobody would "dare approach him with any scheme of bribery." Thomson allowed the public speculations to continue, evidently deliberating on whether to accept the honor. He knew that he would have no trouble winning, for Scott had perfected the art of legislative manipulation. Finally, he decided not to stand probably because he harbored an innate disgust for the politicians' craft, and he knew that it would inevitably be whispered about that Scott had secured the seat for him. Instead, Scott, with little trouble, arranged for the selection of John Scott, an attorney who was a close ally of the PRR and the Philadelphia interests. Thomson, however, must have been seriously afflicted with an attack of the "blues" to have even considered the office.[9]

The relationship between Thomson's health and his outlook also worked in reverse—he was more apt to become ill when his affairs were not progressing well. His break with Scott in 1873 alone must have been nearly sufficient to cause his death. Since the mid-1850s Scott had been his most intimate and trusted subordinate on the road; he was almost like a son to the elder man. Thomson had always allowed him a great deal of freedom to act on his own initiative, confident of Scott's loyalty and good sense. Moreover, Thomson found the younger man most useful; Scott took the opprobrium for the Pennsylvania's political sins, leaving Thomson his reputation for "purity." And Scott possessed in abundance what Thomson so thoroughly lacked, a pleasant, outgoing personality. Scott was the perfect "front man" for the company; he did the face-to-face negotiating, represented the Pennsylvania's interests in political circles, and promoted the Philadelphia interests' ventures. Sometimes in Thomson's eyes, the effervescent Scott overreached as when a friend noted Thomson "slightly demurrs [sic] at the amount subscribed [to the DP] for him by Col. Scott," and in the case of the T&P.[10]

Scott's failure in Texas was the final denouement. In 1872 Thomson had realized that both he and Scott were too deeply involved in the C&T for their own good. Thomson's caution in this instance, however, deterred Scott not an iota—he continued to borrow heavily wherever he could to push the work until the following summer. When Scott in desperation asked Thomson to save the C&T by loaning it securities guaranteed by the PRR, Thomson had no choice if he wanted to preserve their personal credit. When the panic struck, Thomson, who had already gone farther than he thought prudent, saw no recourse but to pledge his own fortune to secure Scott and the others. His C&T endorsement rendered him possibly liable for as much as $1.7 million, more than he could hope to cover given the disastrous state of the security markets. When the calls on his endorsements started to come in, Thomson convinced himself that his impending ruin was all Scott's fault, and the relationship between the two men noticeably cooled.

Carnegie, meanwhile, was brooding over his decision not to aid his associates. Scott's default only added to Carnegie's guilt and shortly afterwards, when he realized that Thomson was skirting the edge of bankruptcy, he encouraged Scott to put up a security deposit to protect Thomson. Carnegie promised Scott he would guarantee the collateral up to $150,000, in effect making good any of Thomson's losses to that amount. Carnegie's only stipulation, as he later explained to Thomson, was that Scott "should see you and make satisfactory arrangements, based upon bye gones being bye gones, he to abandon all personal undertakings and devote himself to carrying out your views, as he professed himself anxious to do." When Carnegie went to Scott's house to sign the necessary documents, he discovered that Scott had not mentioned the arrangement to Thomson; Carnegie realized then just how strained the relations between the two men had become. The steelmaker refused to have anything more to do with the guarantee, lest Thomson think he was taking Scott's side in the dispute. Not until late January 1874, after Scott had mentioned his "misunderstanding" with Carnegie to Thomson, did Carnegie finally reveal all the details to Pennsylvania's president.[11]

By then, however, the dispute had already been leaked to the press. If Carnegie wrestled with a tortured conscience for letting Scott down in his hour of need, then Scott must have been doubly remorseful because he was primarily to blame for Thomson's appalling financial losses and perhaps even for his death only a few months later. As soon as he could, Scott secured the remaining C&T endorsements in Thomson's estate with securities valued at double their sum, most of which were guaranteed by the PRR. Moreover, he must have been at once relieved and embarrassed when Thomson, certain he was about to die, made no move to deny him the Pennsylvania's presidency. A word from Thomson to the board in May could have shifted his mantle to George Roberts or A. J. Cassatt or any number of prominent personalities, but he held his counsel. With the stockholders' committee beginning its investigation Thomson must have been tempted to make Scott a scapegoat for the road's problems. But there were too many similarities in their backgrounds, too many shared experiences, too many hard fights fought and won, and too many decades of personal friendship that overrode their immediate differences. And Thomson was simply not that vindictive a man. He recognized Scott had made errors of judgment, but he had not deceived him. He still trusted Scott to do what was right for his road.[12]

The breakup of his long friendship with Scott hurt Thomson more than he indicated publicly. He poured out his bitterness to Lavinia; after her husand's death she shunned Scott and willingly divulged the details of the rift and the deep pain it caused Thomson to numerous friends. The Pennsylvania's president had ample time to dwell on the estrangement, for in early April he had another heart attack. He continued to work as long as he was able, but after chairing the April 22 board meeting he could no longer carry on. For several more weeks he tried to dispatch some of his responsibilities from home, but he finally had to give up any pretense of working. His wife later remembered that he had been "suffering" for several months before his death. As he grew progressively weaker it must have dawned on him that he was not likely to shake off the effects of this illness. Perhaps given his troubles, he was not able to. He began to brood over his will drawn in December 1871 that established a trust fund to care for the orphaned daughters of railwaymen who had lost their lives in the service of his company. Twice on his deathbed he changed it. On May 24, he added a codicil: "made in sickness of body, but with a clear understanding," directing that his niece, Charlotte, "to whom I cherish the feelings of a father," be considered his daughter, even if it meant postponement of the trust. He was so weak that evening he had to sign with a pencil. Two days later, after wrestling with the dilemma of providing from his shrunken estate for his family and funding the orphanage, he added yet another codicil stating that he had not meant to order the trust's delay, only that his niece should be taken care of first. His sister-in-law, Charlotte Smith, had to sign for him; he was too feeble even to hold a pencil. With his last testament finally arranged according to his wishes, he died the following evening, May 27, at 11:40 P.M.[13]

Tributes poured in from all over the country. Organizations and corporations passed public resolutions of mourning. Flags in Philadelphia, many raised just for the occasion, flew at half-mast. The Pennsylvania's employees draped his office and all stations along the line in black. Locomotives entering and leaving Philadelphia were hung with black serge. The wake was held at Thomson's house where he lay, fittingly attired in his usual black suit, for three days in a black cloth-covered casket "heavily mounted in solid silver," covered with floral offerings. On June 1 a short service was conducted at his home, after which the PRR's six oldest directors served as pallbearers, placing the casket on the bier that transported it to St. Mark's Episcopal Church for the last rites. Immediately afterward, his remains were interred in the Woodlands Cemetery. For the next twenty-eight years, Lavinia, who always dressed in white at home, visited his grave on the 27th of every month to place a wreath of white roses on his tomb. And on November 27, 1903, she was laid to rest beside him.[14]

Thomson's death gave rise to a spate of newspaper articles speculating on his successor. Most surveyed Thomson's career, mentioned his strained relations with Scott, but predicted that Scott would assume the presidency with little difficulty. On June 3 the PRR's board did the expected. It unanimously selected Thomson's protégé as the company's fourth president. Other Thomson favorites Roberts, Cassatt, and Frank Thomson were promoted, and in later years all reached the presidential suite.[15]

Thomson's estate proved considerably more difficult to settle than the PRR's problems of succession. The root of the delay lay in his uncharacteristically vague will and the numerous lawsuits brought against the estate's trustees. Thomson failed to indicate what proportion of his estate should go toward maintaining Lavinia "in such style as my wife may think best," and compounded the problem with his codicil ordering that Charlotte be treated as his daughter. Until the courts determined the levels of support, nothing could be done about the orphans' trust. Eventually, the courts awarded Lavinia and Charlotte a fixed yearly income, initially $20,500 for Lavinia and $7,500 for Charlotte, that could be adjusted to take into account any changes in "style"; the remainder of the estate was freed for the orphanage.

The claims made against the estate, however, hung like a thundercloud over it. At a court hearing after Thomson's death, the trustees presented an enumeration of Thomson's assets; $1,066,214 in securities, $19,025 in cash, and $300,000 in real estate that included his house and adjacent lots, the family farm, and a summer home, Elbron, in New Jersey. The trustees admitted valid claims against these holdings for $131,298, the bulk of which was $107,000 due the London, Asiatic and American Company for its loan; those presented no real problems as they were freely admitted and could be met. Claims for another $1,445,000, however, if sustained, threatened the estate's very existence and delayed its final closing for almost a decade. The most threatening was the $1 million claim by the Sulzbach Brothers that Thomson, as a cotrustee for the Davenport and St. Paul Construction Company, should be liable for the issuance of bonds "beyond the amount authorized by the progress of the railroad to completion." Defense counsel argued that Thomson as a trustee was only secondarily responsible, but ten years later, Thomson's estate was finally held liable for $800,000. By then, its securities had greatly appreciated, and the trustees had no trouble paying the debt. The remaining claims were settled on a piecemeal basis.[16]

The litigation delayed the orphanage for almost a decade. His favorite philanthropic project had undoubtedly been prompted by his paternalistic feelings toward his employees, his innate Quaker sense of community and family, and his personal experience with Charlotte that made Thomson realize female orphans suffered considerable disadvantages over their male counterparts. He had hoped to open the orphanage before he died. But as Lavinia later related, he had to draw on the money he had set aside for the purpose to meet his obligations during the panic. In 1871 he had purchased the lot adjoining his house to build the boarding school on and planned to use his own home as the administration building. All work was postponed until 1882 when the trust purchased two more houses on Rittenhouse Street and St. John's Orphanage, named for Thomson's patron saint, opened its doors to three girls on December 4. It soon expanded into yet another house and by the end of the century had a capacity for sixteen girls.

Lavinia personally supervised the orphanage until her death, giving liberally of her time and money. The curriculum was traditional for a nineteenth-century girls' school, emphasizing the household arts, sewing, housework, laundry, and cooking, with instruction in music, singing, personal hygiene, and religion. All the girls were required to attend the Episcopal church. When old enough, the orphans took further training at hospitals, teachers' colleges, and business schools to prepare them for a vocation.

The institution grew steadily, and just before World War I the name of the school was changed from St. John's, which had caused no end of trouble because a Catholic orphanage in the city had the same name, to the J. Edgar Thomson School. In 1913, the orphanage's summer retreat, located since 1888 at Elbron, was expanded. The year before, the trustees reorganized their educational program to better prepare the girls to enter public high schools, where many became honor students.[17]

In the 1920s the school's charter was altered. Improved railway safety procedures resulted in fewer fatal accidents, and by 1922 the number of girls had dropped to thirty-six. To fill its facilities, the trustees secured authorization to admit orphan girls of railway men who had died natural deaths. The following year, plans were made to maintain seventy-five girls in their mothers' or guardians' homes. The "extension plan" worked so well that by the crash of 1929, only twenty-four of the 180 girls lived at the new orphanage built in West Philadelphia. Institutional care was discontinued altogether in 1935. By the start of World War II, the foundation, with assets of $2 million, supported 234 girls whose fathers had worked for seventeen different railroads. Through 1980, more than 1,800 girls had received help from Thomson's bequest, and the foundation was still enthusiastically fulfilling his mandate.[18]

John Edgar Thomson was a man luckier than most; he left two living legacies, his orphanage, and his railroad. And he had built well. On the day of his funeral, all the Pennsylvania's corporate offices were closed—except for the treasurer's window. As the priest conducted graveside services at Woodlands Cemetery, a long line of stockholders formed at that window to collect their semiannual 5 percent dividends in cash; nobody spoke. Upon reaching the window they conducted their business in hushed, reverent tones and walked quietly away. Thomson would have been pleased.

EPILOGUE

In January 1975 *Fortune Magazine* established a business Hall of Fame and selected its first nineteen honorees. Although such notables as E. H. Harriman, James J. Hill, and Commodore Vanderbilt were not included, Thomson was prominently featured along with the more widely known Henry Ford, Thomas Edison, and Pierpont Morgan. He would have appreciated the justification for his selection: the editors praised him for setting a pattern of rail construction and organization that was long imitated. They noted he expanded his railroad system from 250 miles to over 6,000 miles as his company's profits rose from $617,000 to $8.6 million during his years in charge; they were particularly impressed by the fact that in large part those profits came from his ability to cut costs, from 1.909 cents per ton mile in 1864 to 0.978 cents in 1873. But Thomson would have been proudest of the editors' personal tribute—their simple declaration that "no scandal touched this man."

Even Thomson, however, would have challenged the editors' conclusion that his workers knew "that promotion was by merit, and that they were all involved in discovering the right way to run a railroad." By the early 1870s railroad managers could no longer view labor simply as another commodity to be purchased, used, and discarded at will. But because Thomson paid his employees wages at least as high as those found on other eastern roads and provided them with working conditions as safe as those on any railway, he was not very sympathetic to his employees' growing demands for the right to organize to determine their own fate.[1]

For all his paternalism Thomson understood that that day was soon coming, for in 1872 the Pennsylvania Company had been forced to recognize the Brotherhood of Locomotive Engineers on its western lines and had promised in its contract that wage changes would be made only after prior consultation with the brotherhood's representatives. When Thomson unilaterally lowered wages 10 percent on the PRR in December 1873, and the PC followed suit, the engineers struck all PC operations in the Midwest. With Thomson's blessings, the PC's managers had the state militias called out in Ohio and Indiana, and the strikes were broken in short order. They were a harbinger of what was to come in the bloody 1877 strikes and riots. Thomson would not have handled the situation very much differently than Scott and Garrett did; they all shared the same general attitudes toward their workers, a strong admixture of traditional complacency colored with a growing sense of distrust and fear.[2]

That outlook pointed up the fateful paradox in Thomson's legacy. He built a great railway located in the industrial heartland of the United States, organized a superbly efficient administration to oversee the daily operating details, groomed several talented men as successors, and left a corporate entity that proved fiscally stable and highly profitable. In fact, he was much too successful. The traditions he established, a strong emphasis on technical knowledge in the front office, promotion from within, and highly structured operating departments, all served the road well in its early years, but those truths were later chiseled in stone by heirs trained at his knee until the corporation became so conservative that it was no longer able to adjust to the changing times.

Like Thomson himself, the PRR's greatest strength was always in things mechanical; until the mid-twentieth century, the road continued to be a technological pacesetter. The sight of K-4 Pacifics charging up the 1.8 percent grade at the Horseshoe Curve trailing long lines of Tuscan red coaches; the Raymond Loewy streamlined GG-1s humming along under the cantenary at over 100 miles per hour, bringing the Broadway Limited in on time; early experiments with electric, gasoline, and diesel locomotives; the rapid postwar dieselization; the new centralized traffic control; and 250,000 freight cars bearing the line's familiar keystone illustrated that Thomson's spirit was alive and well on the road.

A willingness to experiment with organizational and accounting procedures never penetrated the road's front offices. Every single chief officer from Thomson to Stuart Saunders, who presided over the merger with the New York Central on February 1, 1968, was promoted from within the system. Saunders came the closest to being an outsider since he came to the PRR from the Norfolk and Western, but that really was not much of a change for him as the Pennsylvania held a 33 percent interest in that line at the time. Moreover, from Thomson on all, except Scott and again Saunders, who was a lawyer, were engineers or came up through the mechanical departments. Managers were promoted because they understood and had proven themselves adept at overseeing the technical aspects of the business and had during their careers caught the eye of someone in the executive suites—the proven Thomson method; they were, to a man, reliable, loyal, and technically competent. They were never advanced because they sparked ideas, demonstrated originality, or manifested a consistent ability to take the larger view of the industry.

Almost to the very end, they ran the railroad as Thomson would have wanted them to. They kept costs down, property in splendid shape, and dividends flowing regularly. These policies enabled the road to perform heroic service in World War II when it moved twice its prewar tonnage and three times its peacetime passenger load with little increase in its fixed plant and did so with consummate efficiency. Thomson's methods were still effective in coping with conventional operational problems almost three-quarters of a century after his death. But throughout the twentieth century, officials continued to operate the railway as if it still had the monopoly over the transport of people and goods it had had in Thomson's time. The road was singularly ill-equipped, as was the case on many other lines, given its traditions and internal structures, to meet a host of new threats. Increased outside regulation; the rise of strong labor unions that checked management's customary abilities to economize in that area; competition from barges, airplanes, buses, automobiles, and trucks; and a shift of production and markets away from the Northeast; all slowly sapped the Pennsylvania's vitality. The regional fragmentation of the industry, a holdover from the failures of Thomson's generation to create and hold transcontinental empires, stymied the PRR's ability to reach new markets located outside the geographical boundaries Thomson left it. The railroad's managers had forgotten Thomson's exhortations to expand to win new traffic—that dictum was never engraved on the tablets. Instead, they finally decided on a parallel merger with the New York Central, a road in far worse financial shape than the PRR. Thomson's heirs lost faith in the future of their own business and siphoned badly needed funds away from their Pennsylvania, seeking higher returns in outside ventures such as resorts, airlines, and pipelines. Capital improvements on the road were postponed in the hope that the merger would bring the economies that would pay for them.

It was an ill-fated arrangement from the start. Corporate antagonisms dating from the Thomson-Vanderbilt era could not be stilled at the scrape of a pen and while "red teams" and "green teams" struggled to enable the Central's computer to "talk" to the Pennsylvania's, general confusion was the order of the day everywhere on the Penn Central. Perhaps Thomson could have brought something out of it all; certainly, the Saunders and Alfred Perlman administrations could not. The combination lasted less than three years as a private entity before admitting bankruptcy citing liabilities of over $750,000,000 due within the year. Significantly, the last people to realize the severity of the situation were the Penn Central's directors; they had never regained the powers Thomson had taken away from them. Harry L. Eddy, the librarian at the Association of American Railroads, understood what Thomson's reaction to all this would have been, and said it best in a letter he wrote just four months after the bankruptcy, "what has happened to the Pennsylvania in the recent past is enough to cause the old man's portrait to turn its face to the wall in the board room on the 17th floor of Penn Center."[3]

NOTES

Chapter 1

1. A. K. McClure, *Old Time Notes of Pennsylvania* (Philadelphia, Pa., 1905), 1: 133; J. Elfreth Watkins, *History of the Pennsylvania Railroad Company 1846-1896* (Philadelphia, 1896), 1: 337; Herman Haupt, "Reminiscences of Early History of the Pennsylvania Railroad Company," undated twice cited, Pennsylvania Railroad Company, Miscellaneous, Vol. 1, Hill Railway Library, University of Wisconsin.

2. Herman Haupt to John Edgar Thomson, Dec. 9, 1861 cited, Herman Haupt Papers, Sterling Library, Yale University, Box 3; Watkins, *Pennsylvania Railroad*, pp. 328 cited, 338 twice cited, 337 cited.

3. Watkins, *Pennsylvania Railroad*, p. 336 twice cited.

4. Ibid., p. 336 cited; Baltimore and Ohio Railroad collection in the Maryland Historical Society, Baltimore.

5. Watkins, *Pennsylvania Railroad*, p. 336; John Edgar Thomson Passport, Oct. 6, 1854, the John Edgar Thomson Foundation, Philadelphia.

6. Inventory and Appraisement of the Estate of John Edgar Thomson, 1874, Office of Registrar of Wills, Philadelphia; "John Edgar Thomson," *The Penn Monthly* (July 1974): 492-93 cited.

7. Watkins, *Pennsylvania Railroad*, p. 328 cited.

8. Frederick B. Tolles, *Meeting House and Counting House: The Quaker Merchants of Colonial Philadelphia, 1682-1763* (Chapel Hill, 1948), p. 143; Summary of John Edgar Thomson's Career, Thomson Foundation, Philadelphia.

9. Frederick B. Tolles, *Quakers and the Atlantic Culture* (New York, 1960), pp. 59-69; Daniel J. Boorstin, *The Americans: The Colonial Experience* (New York, 1958), pp. 33-34; Tolles, *Meeting House and Counting House*, p. 47 cited.

10. Tolles, *Meeting House and Counting House*, pp. 63-73; The Will of J. Edgar Thomson, Deceased, December 20, 1871, codicil dated May 24, 1874, cited, The Historical Society of Pennsylvania, Philadelphia.

11. Watkins, *Pennsylvania Railroad*, p. 327; Inventory and Appraisement of the Estate of John Edgar Thomson, 1874.

12. Watkins, *Pennsylvania Railroad*, pp. 327-28.

13. J. L. Ringwalt, *Development of Transportation Systems in the United States* (Philadelphia, 1888), p. 69; John Hill Martin, *Chester (and its Vicinity) Delaware County, in Pennsylvania. . .* (Philadelphia, 1877), p. vi.

14. Summary of John Edgar Thomson's Career, Thomson Foundation, p. 1; Watkins, *Pennsylvania Railroad*, p. 328.

15. Watkins, *Pennsylvania Railroad*, p. 328 cited; Thomson to Samuel Dickey, Mar. 30, 1831, Roads and Travel Notes Box, The Historical Society of Pennsylvania, Philadelphia; Simon Cameron Papers, The Historical Society of Dauphin County, Harrisburg (hereafter cited as Harrisburg Cameron Papers).

16. Watkins, *Pennsylvania Railroad*, p. 328.

17. Stephen E. Ambrose, *Duty, Honor, Country: A History of West Point* (Baltimore, 1966), p. 122.

18. Thomson to Lemeul P. Grant, Sept. 20, 1846 cited, Lemeul P. Grant Papers, the Atlanta Historical Society, Atlanta, Box 1, Folder 1.

19. Obituary of John Edgar Thomson, *New York Times*, May 29, 1874.

20. Henry V. Poor, *Manual of Railroads of the United States, 1869-1870* (New York, 1869), p. xxvi; George Rogers Taylor and Irene B. Neu, *The American Railroad Network, 1861-1890* (Cambridge, 1956), p. 4; Caroline E. MacGill, *History of Transportation in the United States before 1860* (Washington, 1917), p. 387.

21. Avard Longley Bishop, "The State Works of Pennsylvania," *Transactions of the Connecticut Academy of Arts and Sciences* 13 (Nov. 1907): 170-75, 186-88, 191; Carter Goodrich, *Government Promotion of American Canals and Railroads, 1800-1890* (New York, 1960), pp. 64-65.

22. Daniel Hovey Calhoun, *The American Civil Engineer: Origins and Conflict* (Cambridge, 1960), pp. 53, 167-69; Mark Aldrich, "Earnings of American Civil Engineers, 1820-1859," *The Journal of Economic History* 31 (June 1971): 409.

23. William Hasell Wilson, *Reminiscences of a Railroad Engineer* (Philadelphia, 1896), p. 6.

24. Ibid., pp. 6-8; Summary of John Edgar Thomson's Career, Thomson Foundation, 1.

25. Bishop, "State Works," p. 193.

26. *The National Cyclopedia of American Biography* (New York, 1897) 7: 492-93.

27. Bishop, "State Works," p. 196; Wilson, *Reminiscences*, p. 11.

28. Wilson, *Reminiscences*, pp. 11, 17; Bishop, "State Works," p. 210; Henry Varnum Poor, *History of the Railroads and Canals of the United States of America* (New York, 1860), p. 558.

29. Watkins, *Pennsylvania Railroad*, p. 329; Wilson, *Reminiscences*, p. 11; Ringwalt, *Transportation Systems*, pp. 74, 76-77.

30. Watkins, *Pennsylvania Railroad*, p. 329; John F. Stover, *American Railroads* (Chicago, 1961), pp. 18, 21; Alfred W. Bruce, *The Steam Locomotive in America: Its Development in the Twentieth Century* (New York, 1952), p. 21.

31. Wilson, *Reminiscences*, pp. 13-16; Stover, *American Railroads*, p. 26.

32. Thomson to Dickey, May 30, 1831 twice cited, Roads and Travel Notes Box, Historical Society of Pennsylvania, Philadelphia.

33. Poor, *History of Railroads and Canals*, pp. 487-88, 476-77; MacGill, *History of Transportation*, p. 392.

34. Watkins, *Pennsylvania Railroad*, p. 329 cited; Bruce, *Steam Locomotive in America*, pp. 21-26.

35. Thomson to Col. Simpson Torbert, Nov. 26, 1832, Coryell Papers, Historical Society of Pennsylvania, Philadelphia; Poor, *History of Railroads and Canals*, pp. 519-35; Wilson, *Reminiscences*, pp. 11, 17; Watkins, *Pennsylvania Railroad*, p. 329 cited.

Chapter 2

1. Georgia Historical Commission Marker #121-8, 744 Broad Street, Augusta.

2. U.S. Congress, House, *Abstract of the Returns of the Fifth Census*, 22d Cong., 1st sess., 1830, Doc. No. 269, p. 24; J. D. B. DeBow, *Statistical View of the United States, A Compendium of the Seventh Census* (Washington, 1854), p. 212.

3. Mary G. Cumming, *Georgia Railroad & Banking Company, 1833-1945* (Augusta, 1945), pp. 12-13, 14-15 cited; Ulrich B. Phillips, *A History of Transportation in the Eastern Cotton Belt to 1860* (New York, 1908), p. 221; Joseph B. Cumming, *A History of Georgia Railroad and Banking Company and its Corporate Affiliates, 1833-1958* (n.p., 1971), p. 3-4; Augustus Longstreet Hull, *Annals of Athens, Georgia, 1801-1901* (Athens, 1906), p. 100.

4. M. G. Cumming, *Georgia Railroad*, pp. 15-16, 27; Minutes of the Directors of the Georgia Railroad and Banking Company, Mar. 29, Apr. 2, May 31, 1834, Office of the Georgia Railroad Bank and Trust Company, Augusta, Georgia (hereafter cited as Directors' Minutes).

5. Forest G. Hill, "Government Engineering Aid to Railroads Before the

Civil War," *Journal of Economic History* 11 (Summer 1951): 242; *Athens Southern Banner*, May 31, 1834; Directors' Minutes, June 5, June 28, 1834, Aug. 23, 1834 cited.

6. Directors' Minutes, Oct. 11, 1834 cited; Watkins, *Pennsylvania Railroad*, p. 329; Nellie Peters Black (ed.), *Richard Peters: His Ancestors and Descendants* (Atlanta, 1904), pp. 18, 20; *Extension of Wadley Lease Indenture* (St. Louis, 1973?), p. 24.

7. M. G. Cumming, *Georgia Railroad*, p. 21; Directors' Minutes, Oct. 11, 1834; Watkins, *Pennsylvania Railroad*, p. 328; Black, *Richard Peters*, pp. 25-26; *Athens Southern Banner*, Jan. 8, 1835.

8. *Athens Southern Banner*, Jan. 15, Feb. 12, Mar. 5, Mar. 12, 1835; Black, *Richard Peters*, pp. 20, 21.

9. Directors' Minutes, Apr. 14, Aug. 4, 1835; *Athens Southern Banner*, Apr. 30, June 18, Sept. 17, 1835.

10. Directors' Minutes, Sept. 8, Oct. 24, Dec. 30, 1835; *Athens Southern Banner*, May 20, 1835.

11. W. K. Wood, "The Georgia Railroad and Banking Company," *Georgia Historical Quarterly* 57 (Winter 1973): 545; M. G. Cumming, *Georgia Railroad*, pp. 26-27; *Athens Southern Banner*, Jan. 7, Jan. 14, Feb. 18, Mar. 17, Apr. 21, Apr. 28, 1836.

12. Report of the Engineer in Chief, Apr. 30, 1836 cited, Minutes of the Georgia Railroad Stockholders' Meeting, Office of the Georgia Railroad Bank and Trust Company, Augusta, Georgia (hereafter cited as Stockholders' Minutes); Directors' Minutes, Mar. 26, 1836; Richard E. Prince, *Steam Locomotives and History: Georgia Railroad and West Point Route* (Wyoming, 1962), p. 13.

13. Directors' Minutes, Apr. 5, 1836; *Athens Southern Banner*, June 18, 1835 cited; Report of the Engineer in Chief, Apr. 30, 1836, Stockholders' Minutes.

14. Report of the Engineer in Chief, Apr. 30, 1836, Stockholders' Minutes.

15. Directors' Minutes, Mar. 26, Aug. 2, Sept. 20, 1836; *Athens Southern Banner*, July 30, Aug. 6, Nov. 26, 1836; Milton S. Heath, *Constructive Liberalism: The Role of the State in Economic Development in Georgia to 1860* (Cambridge, 1954), pp. 266-67.

16. *Athens Southern Banner*, May 26, Dec. 10, 1836, Jan. 21, Feb. 4, Feb. 11, Mar. 11, 1837; Directors' Minutes, Aug. 30, 1836.

17. Engineer's Report, May 2, 1837 cited, Stockholders' Minutes.

18. Ibid.; Directors' Minutes, Oct. 25, 1836, Feb. 28, 1837; *Athens Southern Banner*, Nov. 26, 1836 cited, Dec. 24, 1836.

19. Directors' Minutes, Jan. 17, 1837, Sept. 20, 1836; Engineer's Report, May 2, 1837, cited, Stockholders' Minutes.

20. Augusta *Constitutionalist* reprinted in *Athens Southern Banner*, May 6, 1837 cited, Dec. 30, 1837.

21. Directors' Minutes, May 17, 1837 cited, Feb. 21, May 23, July 4, Aug. 4, Aug. 22, Nov. 28, 1837; Peter Temin, *The Jacksonian Economy* (New York, 1969), p. 113.

22. *Athens Southern Banner*, May 27, 1837; Directors' Minutes, Oct. 10, 1837, Feb. 5, Jan. 2, July 14, Oct. 2, Dec. 11, Dec. 25, 1838, Jan. 1, 1839.

23. Thomson, *Report of the Engineer in Chief of the Georgia Rail Road and Banking Co.* (Athens, 1839), pp. 9, 15-16 cited.

24. Directors' Minutes, Jan. 22, 1839 cited, July 30, 1839, Jan. 29, June 11, July 16, 1839.

25. Ibid., Feb. 5, July 30, Sept. 10, Oct. 8, Oct. 9, 1839, Jan. 15, 1840.

26. *Athens Southern Banner*, Sept. 13, Oct. 12, Oct. 26, Nov. 16, 1839; Thomson, *1840 Report*, pp. 6 cited, 7.

27. Thomson, *1840 Report*, pp. 3-5, 8, 9.

28. *Athens Southern Banner*, May 15, 1840; Black, *Richard Peters*, p. 22; Directors' Minutes, May 13, Sept. 8, 1840, Jan. 12, May 12, 1841, May 11, 1842, Oct. 10, 1843.

29. *Athens Southern Banner*, Feb. 29, Sept. 4, 1840, Feb. 5, 1841, Mar. 4, 1842; Black, *Richard Peters*, p. 22.

30. *Athens Southern Banner*, Dec. 10, Dec. 17, 1841, Mar. 31, 1843.

31. Directors' Minutes, Jan. 15, July 14, Oct. 13, 1840, Jan. 12, 1841.

32. Thomson, *1841 Report*, 4-7; 1841 Stockholders' Minutes cited.

33. 1841 Stockholders' Minutes cited.

34. Directors' Minutes, May 12, 1841, June 15, 1841 cited, Dec. 14, 1841, Feb. 8, 1842.

35. Thomson, *1842 Report*, pp. 3 cited, 4-5, 8, 9, 11-12.

36. 1842 Stockholders' Minutes cited.

37. E. Merton Coulter, "John Pendleton King," *Dictionary of American Biography*, ed. Dumas Malone, Vol. 5 (New York, 1932), p. 395; Directors' Minutes, Feb. 11, Mar. 6, 1845, Jan. 20, 1847; *Athens Southern Banner*, Mar. 20, May 22, 1845.

38. Directors' Minutes, June 14, Dec. 27, 1842, Mar. 14, 1843; Dorothy Adler, *British Investment in American Railways, 1834-1898* (Charlottesville, 1970), p. 24.

39. Thomson, *1843 Report*, passim, p. 4 cited; Directors' Minutes, Aug. 15, Oct. 10, 1843; *Athens Southern Banner*, Oct. 22, 1835; 1843 Stockholders' Minutes.

40. Directors' Minutes, Aug. 15, 1843, July 9, 1844; 1844 Stockholders' Minutes.

41. Directors' Minutes, July 30, 1845, Apr. 14, July 31, 1846.

42. *Decatur Watchman* reprinted in *Athens Southern Banner*, Aug. 14, 1845 cited; M. G. Cumming, *Georgia Railroad*, p. 67 cited; Black, *Richard Peters*, p. 23 cited.

43. Black, *Richard Peters*, p. 25; M. G. Cumming, *Georgia Railroad*, pp. 66-68; Thomson to Grant, Sept. 12, 1845 cited, Grant Papers, Box 1, Folder 1.

44. *Reports of the Directors and of the Engineer-in-Chief of the Geo. R.R. and Banking Company, to the Stockholders in Convention. May 13th, 1846* (Augusta, 1846), p. 11 cited; Directors' Minutes, Nov. 10, 1846 cited, Dec. 8, 1846 cited, Feb. 9, 1847.

45. Minutes of the Directors of the Pennsylvania Railroad, Apr. 9, 1847, Feb. 3, 1852, Office of the Secretary of the Penn Central Railroad, Philadelphia (hereafter PRR Directors' Minutes); Thomson to Grant, Dec. 22, 1847, Grant Papers, Box 1, Folder 1; Thomson to W. P. Sawyer, May 26, 1851, Thomson Letterbook, The Pennsylvania Historical and Museum Commission, Harrisburg, Pennsylvania; 1852 Stockholders' Minutes; *Reports of the Directors Etc. of the Geo. R.R. & Bank Co. to the Stockholders in Convention* (Augusta, 1851, 1852), pp. 31, 30.

Chapter 3

1. 1837, 1841, 1842, 1847 Stockholders' Minutes; *Reports of the Directors, Etc. of the Geo. R.R. & Banking Co., to the Stockholders in Convention, 1851, 1852, 1853, 1854*, (Augusta, 1851, 1852, 1853, 1854), pp. 31, 30, 29, 27.

2. Thomson to Grant, Jan.?, 1846 cited, Apr. 8, Dec. 8, Dec. 13, 1846, Grant Papers, Box 1, Folder 1.

3. Thomson to Grant, Jan. 13, 1841, Feb. 12, 1842 cited, ibid.; *Athens Southern Banner*, May 27, 1837.

4. Thomson to Grant, Feb. 12, 1843 first two citations, Apr. 10, 1842 cited, May 20, 1842, Grant Papers, Box 1, Folder 1.

5. Thomson to Grant, Nov. 28, 1846 cited, June 6, 1847, Sept. 22, 1847 cited, ibid.

6. Thomson to Grant, May 20, 1842 cited, ibid.; Allen G. Bogue, *From Prairie to Corn Belt: Farming on the Illinois and Iowa Prairies in the Nineteenth Century* (Chicago, 1968), pp. 170-71; Directors' Minutes, Jan. 22, 1839, Oct. 11, 1834; 1839 Stockholders' Minutes; Thomson to Grant, Aug. 24, 1844, Grant Papers, Box 1, Folder 1; Summary of John Edgar Thomson's Career, Thomson Foundation.

7. Thomson to Grant, Oct. 4, 1845 cited, Grant Papers, Box 1, Folder 1.

8. James M. Russell, *Atlanta, Gate City of the South, 1847 to 1890* (Forthcoming); Black, *Richard Peters*, p. 21; Thomson to Grant, June 23, 1844 cited, Feb. 1, 1844 cited, Feb. 5, 1844 twice cited, June 11, 1846, Grant

Papers, Box 1, Folder 1; Thomson to J. T. Jackson, July 1, 1850, Thomson Letterbook.

9. Thomson to Grant, July 29, 1845, Sept. 24, 1845, Oct. 17, 1845, Dec. 8, 1846 cited, Sept. 22, 1847 cited, Grant Papers, Box 1, Folder 1.

10. *Athens Southern Banner*, Apr. 28, Sept. 24, 1836, and Apr. 20, 1839; Directors' Minutes, Feb. 28, 1837, Feb. 5, 1838, Mar. 9, 1841, Aug. 15, 1843, Apr. 9, 1844; Ringwalt, *Transportation Systems*, p. 120; Phillips, *Transportation in Cotton Belt*, pp. 365-66; Thomas D. Clark, "The Montgomery and West Point Railroad Company," *Georgia Historical Quarterly* 17 (March, 1933): 293-97.

11. James F. Doster, "The Georgia Railroad & Banking Company in the Reconstruction Era," *Georgia Historical Quarterly* 48 (March, 1964): 1-12; Thomson to Grant, June 12, 1845 cited, July 29, 1845, Aug. 3, 1845 cited, Sept. 10, 1845, cited, Grant Papers, Box 1, Folder 1.

12. Thomson to Grant, Sept. 12, 1845 cited, Sept. 24, 1845 cited, Grant Papers, box 1, Folder 1.

13. Thomson to Grant, Oct. 4, 1845, Oct. 17, 1845 cited, Oct. 20, 1845 cited, Nov. 2, 1845, Dec. 1, 1845, ibid.

14. Thomson to Grant, Apr. 8, 1846, ibid.; Directors' Minutes, Apr. 14, 1846; Thomson to Grant, May 14, 1846 cited, Grant Papers, Box 1, Folder 1.

15. Thomson to Grant, June 11, July 7, July 14, Sept. 20, Dec. 13, May 14, 1846, Feb. 5, 1847 cited, Grant Papers, Box 1, Folder 1.

16. Thomson to Grant, Sept. 22, 1847 cited, Nov. 22, 1847 thrice cited, ibid.; Directors' Minutes, June 12, 1849.

17. Directors' Minutes, June 12, 1849, Feb. 9, 1847; Thomson to Grant, Oct. 1, 1851, Grant Letterbook, Vol. 1, Box 3, the Atlanta Historical Society; Thomson to Grant, Dec. 22, 1847, Grant Papers, Box 1, Folder 1.

18. James H. Grant to L. P. Grant, Apr. 17, 1846 cited, Grant Papers, Box 1, Folder 2; MacGill, *History of Transportation*, 471; *Athens Southern Banner*, Dec. 23, 1845; Directors' Minutes, Nov. 10, 1846; Thomson, *Report to the Commissioners on The Nashville and Chattanooga Rail Road* (Nashville, 1847).

19. MacGill, *History of Transportation*, p. 471; Phillips, *Transportation in Cotton Belt*, pp. 285-86; Thomson to Grant, Dec. 22, 1847 cited, Grant Papers, Box 1, Folder 1; Directors' Minutes, Apr. 11, 1848; 1848 Stockholders' Minutes; *Before Railroads: A Contemporary View of the Agriculture, Industry, and Commerce of the South in the Forties* (Nashville, 1928?), pp. 3-6.

20. Inventory and Appraisement of the Estate of John Edgar Thomson, 1874; James H. Grant to L. P. Grant, Mar. 20, 1849 twice cited, Grant Papers, Box 1, Folder 2; Thomson to Grant, Oct. 1, 1851, Grant Letterbook, Vol. 1, Box 3.

21. Gilvert E. Govan and James W. Livingood, *The Chattanooga Country*,

1540-1962: From Tomahawks to TVA (Chapel Hill, 1963), pp. 164-66; Phillips, *Transportation in the Cotton Belt*, pp. 176, 270; "James P. Boyce," *Dictionary of American Biography*, ed. Allen Johnson, vol. 1 (New York, 1927), p. 523.

22. Robert R. Russell, "The Pacific Issue in Politics Prior to the Civil War," *Mississippi Valley Historical Review* 12 (Sept., 1925): 187-201; William D. McCain, *The Story of Jackson: A History of the Capital of Mississippi, 1821-1951* (Jackson, 1953), 1: 60; Jackson *Flag of the Union*, Aug. 12, 1853; Directors' Minutes, July 11, 1852; Thomas A. Marshall to Thomson, Aug. 26, 1852, Thomson to Marshall, Sept. 2, 1852, Haupt Papers, Box 1; Haupt, *Report of the Final Location* . . . (Philadelphia, 1853), pp. 16-17.

23. Marshall to Simon Cameron, May 5, 1854, Harrisburg Cameron Papers; *American Railroad Journal* 27: 141, 31: 187; Haupt to Cameron, Sept. 5, 1854, Harrisburg Cameron Papers; Directors' Minutes, Sept. 12, 1854.

24. Phillips, *Transportation in the Cotton Belt*, pp. 369-71; Marshall to Cameron, May 5, 1854, Harrisburg Cameron Papers.

25. U. B. Phillips, "Alexander Hamilton Stephens," *Dictionary of American Biography*, ed. Dumas Malone, vol. 9 (New York, 1935), pp. 569-71; Thomson to Alexander H. Stephens, n.d., all citations, William Jackson Palmer Papers, Colorado State Historical Society, Denver.

26. *Philadelphia Evening Bulletin*, July 8, 1859; Thomson to Samuel Barlow, Jan. 23, 1860 cited, Samuel Barlow Papers, The Huntington Library, San Marino, California.

27. Thomson to John Covode, Feb. 25, 1860 all citations, John Covode Papers, The Historical Society of Western Pennsylvania, Pittsburgh; Roy F. Nichols, "The Kansas-Nebraska Act: A Century of Historiography," *The Mississippi Valley Historical Review* 43 (Sept. 1956): 199-203; Henry Cohen, *Business and Politics in America from the Age of Jackson to the Civil War: The Career Biography of W.W. Corcoran* (Westport, 1971).

28. *Athens Southern Banner*, July 2, Aug. 20, 1841, Apr. 17, 1845 cited, Dec. 16, 1845.

29. *Reports of the Directors . . . 1843*, pp. 6-8 cited.

30. *Report of the Engineer in Chief . . . 1842*, p. 7; *Reports of the Directors . . . 1845*, p. 18; Haupt to Thomson, Dec. 9, 1861, Haupt Papers, Box 3.

31. *Report of the Engineer in Chief . . . 1842*, pp. 4-5; *Fourth Annual Report of the Directors of the Pennsylvania Railroad Co. to the Stockholders, December 31, 1850* (Philadelphia, 1851), pp. 42, 52-54. (All Pennsylvania Railroad Annual Reports hereafter cited as *PRR Annual Report*.)

32. *Athens Southern Banner*, Mar. 21, 1844.

33. Albert Fishlow, *American Railroads and the Transformation of the Ante-Bellum Economy* (Cambridge, 1965), pp. 134-40; Milton S. Heath,

"Public Railroad Construction and the Development of Private Enterprise in the South Before 1861," *The Journal of Economic History*, Supplement 10 (1950): 41; Goodrich, *Government Promotion of Canals and Railroads*, pp. 270-71; James A. Ward, "A New Look at Antebellum Southern Railroad Development," *The Journal of Southern History* 39 (Aug. 1973): 409-20.

34. Report of the Engineer in Chief, Apr. 30, 1836, Stockholders' Minutes; Thomson to Grant, June 12, 1845 cited, Sept. 12, 1845, Grant Papers, Box 1, Folder 1.

35. Thomson to Grant, May ?, 1846 cited, Nov. 11, 1846 cited, author's italics, Feb. 5, 1847 cited, Grant Papers, Box 1, Folder 1; Thomson to Richard Peters, Sept. 19, 1861, in the Nellie Peters Black Collection, University of Georgia Libraries, Athens.

Chapter 4

1. J.D.B. DeBow, *Statistical View of the United States* (Washington, 1854), p. 192; James W. Livingood, *The Philadelphia-Baltimore Trade Rivalry, 1780-1860* (Harrisburg, 1947), p. 162.

2. Julius Rubin, "Canal or Railroad? Imitation and Innovation in the Response to the Erie Canal in Philadelphia, Baltimore, and Boston," *Transactions of the American Philosophical Society* 51, Pt. 7 (Nov. 1961): 13-18.

3. H. W. Schotter, *The Growth and Development of the Pennsylvania Railroad Company* (Philadelphia, 1927), pp. 17-18.

4. Rubin, "Canal or Railroad?" p. 16; Bishop, "State Works," pp. 196-99, 247-48.

5. McClure, *Old Time Notes*, p. 128; Terrence Brooks, *The Pennsylvania Railroad: The Early Days* (Los Angeles, 1964), pp. 1-2, 4; George H. Burgess and Miles C. Kennedy, *Centennial History of the Pennsylvania Railroad Company* (Philadelphia, 1949), pp. 38-39, 42; William Bender Wilson, *History of the Pennsylvania Railroad Company: With Plan of Organization, Portraits of Officials, and Biographical Sketches* (Philadelphia, 1899), 2: 233-35; Thomson to Grant, early April 1847 cited, Grant Papers, Box 1, Folder 1; Minutes of the Board of Directors of the Pennsylvania Railroad, Apr. 9, 1847, Office of the Secretary of the Penn Central Railroad, Philadelphia.

6. Thomson to Board of Canal Commissioners of Pennsylvania, May 12, 1847, RG-17, Misc. Reports and Documents, W2C-20, Pennsylvania Historical & Museum Commission, Harrisburg, Pennsylvania; Thomson to Grant, June 6, 1847 cited, Grant Papers, Box 1, Folder 1.

7. PRR Board Minutes, June 9, July 28, 1847; *1st PRR Annual Report*, pp. 5-6.

8. Thomson to Grant, Sept. 22, 1847 cited, Grant Papers, Box 1, Folder 1;

PRR Board Minutes, Aug. 25, 1847; Thomson to Merrick, Sept. 20, 1847 cited, Thomson Letterbook; *1st PRR Annual Report*, p. 6.

9. PRR Board Minutes, Feb. 2, 1850, Apr. 30, 1851.

10. Thomson to Grant, Nov. 22, 1847 cited, Dec. 22, 1847 cited, Grant Papers, Box 1, Folder 1.

11. *1st PRR Annual Report*, p. 28; Thomson to Merrick, Aug. 14. Aug. 18, 1848 cited, Thomson Letterbook.

12. PRR Board Minutes, Apr. 11, May 16, 1849; Thomson to Norris & Brooks, May 5, May 19, 1849, Thomson Letterbook.

13. Thomson to Merrick, July 26, 1849, Aug. 13, 1849 cited, Thomson Letterbook.

14. Thomson to Grant, Dec. 22, 1847, Grant Papers, Box 1, Folder 1; Eliza Cope Harrison, *Philadelphia Merchant: The Diary of Thomas P. Cope, 1800-1851* (South Bend, 1978), p. 547; Thomson to Grant, Mar. 29, 1848 cited, Thomson to James Grant, May 25, 1848 cited, Grant Papers, Box 1, Folder 1.

15. *2nd PRR Annual Report*, p. 13.

16. PRR Board Minutes, May 23, 1849; Thomson to William C. Patterson, Dec. 11, 1849, Thomson to Merrick, Sept. 20, 1847 cited, Thomson Letterbook.

17. Thomson to Patterson, Dec. 19, 1848 cited, Thomson Letterbook.

18. Haupt, "Reminiscences," p. 7; PRR Board Minutes, June 8, Aug. 20, 1849.

19. Haupt, "Reminiscences," p. 7; W. B. Wilson, *Pennsylvania Railroad*, 2: 236-37; PRR Board Minutes, Aug. 22, 25, 1849.

20. Thomson to Bell, Nov. 26, 1849 cited, James M. Bell Papers, Duke University, Durham, N.C.

21. McClure, *Old Time Notes*, 1: 134; Burgess, *Pennsylvania Railroad*, p. 54; Haupt, "Reminiscences," p. 8.

22. Burgess, *Pennsylvania Railroad*, p. 55; Schotter, *Pennsylvania Railroad*, pp. 30-31.

23. Thomson to Board of Canal Commissioners, May 12, 1847, RG-17; Thomson to James Burns, Dec. 14, 1848, Thomson Letterbook; Thomson to J. A. Gamble, Dec. 10, 1850, RG-17; *4th PRR Annual Report*, p. 15.

24. *4th PRR Annual Report*, pp. 49-52; PRR Board Minutes, Mar. 5, Apr. 16, June 25, 1851.

25. *4th PRR Annual Report*, p. 8 cited, 25; PRR Board Minutes, Feb. 27, May 23, May 29, 1850.

26. PRR Board Minutes, July 17, Oct. 23, Dec. 4, Dec. 18, 1850; Thomson to David Brown, Oct. 7, 1850 cited, Thomson Letterbook; *4th PRR Annual Report*, p. 10.

27. PRR Board Minutes, Jan. 2, Mar. 1, 1851.

28. *5th PRR Annual Report*, pp. 15, 41; Thomson to Patterson, Apr. 21, 1851 cited, Thomson Letterbook; Thomson to Bell, June 5, 1851, Bell Papers; Thomson to Grant, Oct. 1, 1851 cited, Grant Letterbook, Vol. I, Box 3.

29. *4th PRR Annual Report*, p. 31.

30. Burgess, *Pennsylvania Railroad*, pp. 785-86.

31. PRR Board Minutes, Oct. 22, 1851; Herman Haupt, *Reply of the General Superintendent of the Pennsylvania Railroad to a Letter From a Large Number of Stockholders of the Company Requesting Information in Reference to the Management of the Road* (Philadelphia, 1852), p. 12 cited; PRR Board Minutes, Feb. 19, 1851 cited; Herman Haupt, "How J. Edgar Thomson Became President of the Penn. Railroad Co. (in 1852)," pp. 1-2, Association of American Railroads, Economics and Finance Library, Washington, D.C.

32. PRR Board Minutes, Oct. 15, 1851 cited, Oct. 22, Oct. 29, Nov. 5, Nov. 26, 1851; *Philadelphia Evening Bulletin*, Jan. 3, 1852.

33. PRR Board Minutes, Oct. 22, 1851 cited.

34. Haupt, "How Thomson Became President," p. 5 cited.

35. Haupt, "Reminiscences," p. 17 cited; PRR Board Minutes, May 12, July 3, 1851.

36. Merrick to Editors, *Philadelphia Bulletin*, Jan. 3, 1852; Unidentified newspaper clipping, Jan. 3, 1852, Herman Haupt Scrapbook, p. 44 cited, in possession of Mrs. Susan Haupt Adamson, Washington, D.C.; Haupt to Thomson, Dec. 9, 1861, Haupt Papers, Box 3.

37. *5th PRR Annual Report*, pp. 24-29.

38. Haupt, "Reminiscences," pp. 15-17.

39. PRR Board Minutes, Feb. 3, 4, 1852.

Chapter 5

1. Calculated from PRR Board Minutes, Vols. 2-6.

2. PRR Board Minutes, Feb. 23, 1870, Jan. 26, Mar. 22, 1871.

3. Thomson to John W. Garrett, Feb. 12, 1859, B & O Collection.

4. James A. Ward, "J. Edgar Thomson and Thomas A. Scott: A Symbiotic Partnership?" *The Pennsylvania Magazine of History and Biography* 100 (Jan. 1976): 37-65.

5. PRR Board Minutes, May 12, 1852; Thomson to Bell, Feb. 11, 1852 cited, Feb. 28, 1852 cited, Bell Papers.

6. Schotter, *Pennsylvania Railroad*, p. 34; *6th PRR Annual Report*, p. 11; PRR Board Minutes, Apr. 3, May 31, June 23, Sept. 1, Sept. 16, 1852.

7. PRR Board Minutes, Oct. 20, 1852, Sept. 16, June 24, Aug. 17, 1853.

8. Ibid., Nov. 9, 1853.

9. Ibid., Apr. 19, Aug. 23 cited, Sept. 6, Dec. 20, 1854, Feb. 28, June 6, 1855; Schotter, *Pennsylvania Railroad*, p. 41.

10. Summary of John Edgar Thomson's Career, Thomson Foundation; Lavinia Thomson's Scrapbook, ibid.; Palmer's Diary, Oct. 1857, Palmer Papers; Burgess, *Pennsylvania Railroad*, p. 298.

11. *9th PRR Annual Report*, p. 7; Watkins, *Pennsylvania Railroad*, pp. 4-5 cited; Burgess, *Pennsylvania Railroad*, p. 67.

12. *PRR Annual Reports*, 1850, 1855, 1860; *14th PRR Annual Report*, p. 4; *12th PRR Annual Report*, p. 25; Burgess, *Pennsylvanaia Railroad*, p. 799; PRR Board Minutes, May 5, Nov. 6, 1856, May 5, Nov. 2, 1857; *11th PRR Annual Report*, p. 5; Gerard Ralston to Palmer, Mar. 12, 1858, Palmer Papers.

13. *11th PRR Annual Report*, pp. 48, 61; *9th PRR Annual Report*, p. 42; *13th PRR Annual Report*, p. 5; *12th PRR Annual Report*, p. 18; Palmer to Thomson, Sept. 3, Sept. 7, 1855, June 19, 1856, Palmer Papers; PRR Board Minutes, Apr. 20, 1859.

14. Palmer to Isaac Clothier, July 20, 1859 cited, in Clothier, *Letters: General William J. Palmer* (Philadelphia, 1906), pp. 30-37; *13th PRR Annual Report*, 21; *14th PRR Annual Report*, pp. 27, 34; Burgess, *Pennsylvania Railroad*, p. 713.

15. *13th PRR Annual Report*, p. 21; *Philadelphia Evening Bulletin*, July 1, 1859.

16. Anna J. Reynolds, "The John Edgar Thomson School: The Past, Present, and Future" (unpublished mss, Thomson Foundation), p. 2 cited.

17. *Report of H. Haupt . . . on the Expediency of aiding the Ohio and Indiana and the Fort Wayne and Chicago Rail Road Companies to Complete their Roads* (Philadelphia, 1854), pp. 15, 21, 29; PRR Board Minutes, Sept. 21, 1852, May 19, July 6, 1854.

18. PRR Board Minutes, Mar. 31, June 14, July 23, 1856; Burgess, *Pennsylvania Railroad*, p. 177.

19. Thomson Obituary, unknown newspaper, 1874, Lavinia Thomson's Scrapbook, Thomson Foundation; PRR Board Minutes, Mar. 17, Apr. 14, 1858, Aug. 18, 1862; *12th PRR Annual Report*, p. 12; *Philadelphia Evening Bulletin*, Aug. 3, 1858, May 2, 1859; Palmer to Ralston, Oct. ?, 1858, Ralston to Palmer, Feb. 18, 1859 cited, Palmer Papers.

20. PRR Board Minutes, June 13, 1860; Schotter, *Pennsylvania Railroad*, p. 51; Burgess, *Pennsylvania Railroad*, p. 181; Thomson to Barlow, Mar. 2, 1860, Barlow Papers.

21. PRR Board Minutes, Apr. 7, Apr. 28, Sept. 21, Dec. 22, 1852.

22. PRR Board Minutes, June 3, 1852, Apr. 25, 1853, Nov. 24, 1856, Feb. 17, 1858; *10th PRR Annual Report*, p. 23.

23. PRR Board Minutes, June 22, Aug. 17, Dec. 3, 1853; Schotter, *Pennsylvania Railroad*, pp. 62, 77; *12th PRR Annual Report*, p. 12.

24. Alfred D. Chandler, Jr., "The Railroads: Pioneers in Modern Corporate Management," *Business History Review* 39 (Spring 1965): 34 cited; Leland H. Jenks, "Early History of a Railway Organization," ibid., 35 (Summer 1961): 153-70.

Chapter 6

1. Schotter, *Pennsylvania Railroad*, pp. 7-8; Burgess, *Pennsylvania Railroad*, p. 93; *4th PRR Annual Report*, p. 21.

2. Thomson to Seth Clover, Aug. 14, 1854 cited; Thomson to the Board of Canal Commissioners, Oct. 16, 1854 cited, RG-17; Thomson to Covode, May 22, 1855, Covode Papers; Schotter, *Pennsylvania Railroad*, p. 44.

3. PRR Board Minutes, May 27, Aug. 16, 1852; Thomson to Bell, June 21, 1852 cited, Bell Papers.

4. Harrison, *Diary of Thomas Cope*, pp. 552 cited, 495 cited; PRR Board Minutes, Jan. 28, Mar. 22, 1852, and Jan. 5, Jan. 21, 1853.

5. PRR Board Minutes, Jan. 6, Oct. 27, Nov. 10, 1858; Thomson to Bell, Nov. 16, 1858 cited, Bell Papers; McClure, *Old Time Notes*, 1: 140.

6. Bishop, "State Works," pp. 278-80; PRR Board Minutes, Mar. 22, Apr. 3, 1852, May 20, June 24, July 6, Aug. 17, Sept. 3, 1853, Feb. 8, Mar. 23, Apr. 25, 1854; Burgess, *Pennsylvania Railroad*, p. 94.

7. PRR Board Minutes, May 18, June 6, 1855, Jan. 21, 1857; Burgess, *Pennsylvania Railroad*, pp. 76, 94-95; Thomson to Andrew Curtin, Dec. 20, 1855, in Bishop, "State Works," p. 255; *9th PRR Annual Report*, pp. 14-18; Thomson to Bell, Mar. 18, 1856, Bell Papers.

8. Thomson to Bell, Jan. 23, 1858 cited, Bell Papers; Bishop, "State Works," p. 256.

9. PRR Board Minutes, Aug. 5, Oct. 10, 1857.

10. Ibid., Jan. 6, Feb. 3, May 24, 1858; *Philadelphia Evening Bulletin*, Feb. 10, 1858; McClure, *Old Time Notes*, 1: 485; Burgess, *Pennsylvania Railroad*, p. 98; *12th PRR Annual Report*, p. 20.

11. Bell to Thomson, Nov. 2, 1858, Bell Papers; PRR Board Minutes, Oct. 27, Nov. 10, 1858, Jan. 5, 1859, Mar. 21, 1860; Burgess, *Pennsylvania Railroad*, p. 98; Samuel Richey Kamm, "The Civil War Career of Thomas A. Scott" (Ph.D. dissertation, University of Pennsylvania, 1940), pp. 15-16; William H. Russell, "A Biography of Alexander K. McClure" (Ph.D. dissertation, University of Wisconsin, 1953), pp. 227, 228; McClure, *Old Time Notes*, 1: 480-85.

12. McClure, *Old Time Notes*, 1: 507, 511; PRR Board Minutes, Mar. 7, 1861; Burgess, *Pennsylvania Railroad*, pp. 106-22.

13. Kamm, "Tom Scott," pp. 8-9; Burgess, *Pennsylvania Railroad*, pp. 128-36.

14. Scott to Cameron, June 28, 1860 cited, NCRR Agreement, Oct. 12, 1860, Scott to Cameron, Dec. 24, July 31, 1860, Cameron Papers, Library of Congress; Kamm, "Tom Scott," p. 10.

15. Burgess, *Pennsylvania Railroad*, p. 138; PRR Board Minutes, Dec. 18, 1861.

16. *14th PRR Annual Report*, p. 4.

17. Thomson to Barlow, Aug. 12, 1858 cited, Barlow Papers.

18. Haupt, "Reminiscences," p. 23 cited.

19. *12th PRR Annual Report*, p. 19 cited.

20. Thomson to Garrett, July 1, 1859 cited, B&O Papers; Thomson to Barlow, Sept. 6, 1858 cited, Barlow Papers; Thomson to Garrett, Feb. 19, 1859 cited, B&O Papers.

21. Thomson to Garrett, July 6, 1859 cited, July 13, 1859 cited, B&O Papers.

22. Thomson to Clement, Aug. 6, 1858 cited, Clement to Barlow, Aug. 7, 1858 cited, Aug. 21, 1958 cited, Barlow Papers.

23. Thomson to Garrett, Feb. 8, 1860 cited, B&O Papers; *14th PRR Annual Report*, four times cited.

Chapter 7

1. Thomas Weber, *The Northern Railroads in the Civil War, 1861-1865* (New York, 1952), p. 100.

2. Thomson to Cameron, Apr. 27, 1861, *War of the Rebellion: A Compilation of the Official Records of the Union and Confederate Armies*, Ser. 1, 2: 606 (hereafter cited as *OR*); Thomson to Peters, Sept. 19, 1861 all citations, Nellie Black Papers.

3. Thomson to Peters, Sept. 19, 1861 all citations, Nellie Black Papers.

4. Cameron to Thomson, Apr. 17, 1861, Thomson to Cameron, Apr. 17, 1861 cited, *OR*, Ser. 1, 51, pt. i: 327.

5. Kamm, "Tom Scott," p. 26; George P. Kane to Charles Howard, Apr. 19, 1861 cited, *OR*, Ser. 1, 2: 630.

6. Thomson and Felton to Cameron, Apr. 19, 1861, Winfield Scott (Orders), Apr. 21, 1861, Felton to Cameron, Apr. 24, 1861 cited, *OR*, Ser. 1, 2: 578, 584, 598; Kamm, "Tom Scott," fn. 69, p. 33.

7. Cameron to Whom it may concern, Apr. 27, 1861, Cameron to Thomson, Apr. 27, 1861, *OR*, Ser. 1, 2: 603-04.

8. Thomson to Cameron, Apr. 27, 1861 cited, ibid.; Thomson to Officers

and Agents of the United States, Apr. 25, 1861, Magee to Palmer, May 10, 1861 cited, Palmer Papers.

9. Kamm, "Tom Scott," pp. 69-80; *14th PRR Annual Report*, p. 110; *15th PRR Annual Report*, p. 89.

10. Kamm, "Tom Scott," pp. 72-73.

11. *15th PRR Annual Report*, pp. 15, 21; Franciscus to Enoch Lewis, Sept. 28, 1861 cited, A. Taylor to Franciscus, Sept. 28, 1861, Carnegie to Lewis, Oct. 5, 1861 cited, Carnegie Papers, Library of Congress.

12. PRR Board Minutes, Oct. 9, 1861; W. Wilson to Lewis, Oct. 15, 1861 cited, Carnegie Papers, Library of Congress.

13. *15th PRR Annual Report*, p. 12; *16th PRR Annual Report*, p. 24; *17th PRR Annual Report*, p. 27; PRR Board Minutes, June 18, 1861, Feb. 12, 1862, May 13, Dec. 9, 1863, July 6, 1864, June 7, June 25, Sept. 20, 1865.

14. R. H. Lamborn to Palmer, June 11, 1862, Palmer Papers; *17th PRR Annual Report*, pp. 12-13, 41; *18th PRR Annual Report*, pp. 9, 10 cited, 28, 39; *19th PRR Annual Report*, p. 41; *20th PRR Annual Report*, p. 26.

15. *16th PRR Annual Report*, p. 13; Weber, *Northern Railroads*, pp. 131-32; *18th PRR Annual Report*, p. 41 cited; *20th PRR Annual Report*, p. 26.

16. *18th PRR Annual Report*, p. 6 cited; PRR Board Minutes, Aug. 18, July 3, Sept. 24, 1862, Feb. 8, 1865.

17. *14th PRR Annual Report*, p. 76; *17th PRR Annual Report*, pp. 6, 10; *19th PRR Annual Report*, pp. 9, 11; PRR Board Minutes, Apr. 17, Oct. 16, 1861, Apr. 16, Oct. 17, 1862.

18. *17th PRR Annual Report*, p. 10; PRR Board Minutes, June 10, 1863, Feb. 15, 1864, Apr. 1, 1863.

19. *19th PRR Annual Report*, p. 16 cited.

20. PRR Board Minutes, June 24, Sept. 2, 1863; *17th PRR Annual Report*, p. 19; Lamborn to Palmer, July 22, 1863, Palmer Papers; Kamm, "Tom Scott," p. 156.

21. Kamm, "Tom Scott," pp. 149-58; C. A. Walborn to Stanton, June 28, 1863 cited, Thomson to Abraham Lincoln, June 30, 1863 cited, Peter Watson to Stanton, July 5, 1863 cited, *OR*, Ser. 1, 27: 391, 435-36, 552-53; *17th PRR Annual Report*, p. 19; PRR Board Minutes, July 3, 1863.

22. Lamborn to Palmer, May 22, 1862, June 11, 1862 cited, July 21, 1862 cited, Palmer Papers; unidentified newspaper clipping, Lavinia Thomson's Scrapbook, Thomson Foundation.

23. PRR Board Minutes, May 14, 1862; Homer T. Rosenberger, *The Philadelphia and Erie Railroad: Its Place in American Economic History* (Potomac, Maryland, 1975), p. 406; Burgess, *Pennsylvania Railroad*, pp. 154-56.

24. PRR Board Minutes, June 17, July 5, July 24, Oct. 9, Oct. 12, Nov. 11,

1861, Feb. 1, 1862, Jan. 14, 1863; Rosenberger, *The Philadelphia and Erie*, p. 44; Burgess, *Pennsylvania Railroad*, pp. 159-60; *18th PRR Annual Report*, pp. 5, 7.

25. *15th PRR Annual Report*, pp. 23, 31; *16th PRR Annual Report*, p. 14; *19th PRR Annual Report*, pp. 33, 37.

Chapter 8

1. *Report of the Investigating Committee, 1874*, pp. 115, 167, 183; *27th PRR Annual Report*, p. 34.

2. PRR Board Minutes, May 3, 1869; *28th PRR Annual Report*, pp. 48, 159-61.

3. James J. Stewart to Garrett, Aug. 26, 1869, B&O Papers.

4. Burgess, *Pennsylvania Railroad*, p. 313.

5. PRR Board Minutes, Apr. 27, 1870; Burgess, *Pennsylvania Railroad*, p. 341.

6. *19th PRR Annual Report*, pp. 19-21; *18th PRR Annual Report*, p. 8; *20th PRR Annual Report*, p. 50; *21st PRR Annual Report*, p. 9; *26th PRR Annual Report*, p. 54.

7. PRR Board Minutes, Dec. 22, 1869, Jan. 26, Feb. 23, 1870; *24th PRR Annual Report*, p. 11; *26th PRR Annual Report*, p. 13.

8. Julius Grodinsky, *Jay Gould: His Business Career, 1867-1892* (Philadelphia, 1957), pp. 58-59.

9. PRR Board Minutes, Nov. 28, 1866; *19th PRR Annual Report*, p. 20; *20th PRR Annual Report*, p. 11; *21st PRR Annual Report*, p. 16; Schotter, *Pennsylvania Railroad*, p. 77.

10. Burgess, *Pennsylvania Railroad*, p. 196; PRR Board Minutes, Apr. 1, Dec. 16, 1868; Grodinsky, *Gould*, p. 60.

11. PRR Board Minutes, Jan. 11, 1869.

12. Schotter, *Pennsylvania Railroad*, p. 81; *22nd PRR Annual Report*, pp. 16, 17; PRR Board Minutes, Mar. 31, May 3, 1869.

13. Grodinsky, *Gould*, pp. 63-65.

14. PRR Board Minutes, May 21, May 27, 1869; Schotter, *Pennsylvania Railroad*, 79; *23rd PRR Annual Report*, p. 16 cited.

15. *24th PRR Annual Report*, pp. 18, 21; PRR Board Minutes, Mar. 18, 1868; Burgess, *Pennsylvania Railroad*, p. 205.

16. Grodinsky, *Gould*, p. 65; PRR Board Minutes, Feb. 23, 1870; Schotter, *Pennsylvania Railroad*, pp. 81-82.

17. Watkins, *Pennsylvania Railroad*, p. 12; Schotter, *Pennsylvania Railroad*, pp. 88-90; PRR Board Minutes, Jan. 25, Feb. 1, 1871, Mar. 26, 1870.

18. PRR Board Minutes, July 5, Sept. 4, 1867.

19. *24th PRR Annual Report*, p. 23 cited; Julius Grodinsky, *Transcontinental Railway Strategy, 1869-1893: A Study of Businessmen* (Philadelphia, 1962), p. 19; John F. Stover, *The Railroads of the South, 1865-1900: A Study in Finance and Control* (Chapel Hill, 1955), pp. 101-119; *25th PRR Annual Report*, p. 20 cited; *27th PRR Annual Report*, pp. 34-35; *Report of the Investigating Committee, 1874*, p. 76; Inventory and Appraisement of the Estate of John Edgar Thomson, 1874.

20. *24th PRR Annual Report*, p. 26; Schotter, *Pennsylvania Railroad*, p. 61.

21. Roger A. Barton, "The Camden and Amboy Railroad Monopoly," *Proceedings New Jersey Historical Society* 12 (1927): 405; Burgess, *Pennsylvania Railroad*, p. 238; *25th PRR Annual Report*, p. 15.

22. PRR Board Minutes, May 15, May 18, June 12, Oct. 2, 1867, Feb. 1, Feb. 9, Feb. 18, Mar. 16, 1871.

23. PRR Board Minutes, Apr. 26, 1871; *25th PRR Annual Report*, pp. 14 twice cited, 15, 26-28; Schotter, *Pennsylvania Railroad*, pp. 95-97.

24. Schotter, *Pennsylvania Railroad*, pp. 115, 193; *24th PRR Annual Report*, p. 11; *26th PRR Annual Report*, p. 13; *27th PRR Annual Report*, p. 16; *28th PRR Annual Report*, p. 28; Garrett to Thomson, June 24, 1865, B&O Papers; *19th PRR Annual Report*, p. 22; *20th PRR Annual Report*, pp. 27-28; Rolland Maybee, *Railroad Competition and the Oil Trade* (rpt., Philadelphia, 1974), pp. 114-18.

25. "Proceedings of the Railway Meeting," May 22-23, 1866, King to Garrett, June 28, 1866, June 28, 1866, "Resolutions of Trunk Line Meeting," Dec. 31, 1866, Thomson to Garrett, Jan. 29, 1867, Garrett to Thomson, Feb. 2, 1867, B&O Papers; *21st PRR Annual Report*, p. 9; PRR Board Minutes, June 26, July 5, May 4, Nov. 2, 1867; *23rd PRR Annual Report*, p. 19; *24th PRR Annual Report*, p. 10.

26. Maybee, *The Oil Trade*, p. 289.

27. Allan Nevins, *John D. Rockefeller: A Study in Power*, abridgement William Greenleaf (New York, 1959), pp. 42-43; Maybee, *The Oil Trade*, pp. 354, 391.

28. Schotter, *Pennsylvania Railroad*, pp. 114-15; *26th PRR Annual Report*, p. 26; *27th PRR Annual Report*, p. 14.

29. *Report of the Investigating Committee, 1874*, p. 22.

Chapter 9

1. Inventory and Appraisement of the Estate of John Edgar Thomson, 1874.

2. Thomson to Bell, Nov. 13, 1847 cited, Dec. 8, 1847 cited, June 12, 1848

cited, Bell Papers; Samuel N. Stayer, "James Martin Bell: Ironmaster and Financier, 1799-1870" (unpublished Ph.D. dissertation, Duke University, 1970), p. 170.

3. Thomson to Carnegie, Dec. 12, 1871 cited, Carnegie Papers, Library of Congress.

4. Inventory and Appraisement of the Estate of John Edgar Thomson, 1874 all citations.

5. Jackson to Palmer, June 28, 1866, Palmer Papers.

6. Lamborn to Palmer, Aug. 6, 1867, Charles Hinchman to Palmer, Oct. 31, 1867, ibid.

7. Lamborn to Palmer, Aug. 6, 1867 cited, Miller to Palmer, Nov. 5, 1867 cited, ibid.

8. Henrietta Larson, *Jay Cooke: Private Banker* (Cambridge, 1936), p. 249 cited.

9. Lamborn to Palmer, Oct. 4, 1868 cited, Palmer Papers.

10. Larson, *Cooke*, pp. 271-72, 330-32; Lamborn to Palmer, Sept. 8, 1869, Palmer Papers; Inventory and Appraisement of the Estate of John Edgar Thomson, 1874.

11. Larson, *Cooke*, pp. 333-34; Lamborn to Palmer, Sept. 8, 1869, Smith to Palmer, Nov. 25, 1869 cited, Palmer Papers.

12. Larson, *Cooke*, p. 336.

13. Taylor and Neu, *The American Railroad Network*, p. 17; H.V. and H.W. Poor, *Poor's Manual, 1889* (New York, 1889), p. 40; Thomson to Covode, July 7, 1868 cited, Covode Papers.

14. Smith to Palmer, Nov. 25, 1869, Palmer Papers; *Poor's Manual, 1889*, p. 40.

15. Smith to Palmer, Dec. 3, 1866 cited, Lamborn to Palmer, May 27, 1866 cited, Palmer Papers.

16. Lamborn to Palmer, Dec. 3, 1866 cited, Palmer to Lamborn, Dec. 6 1866 cited, ibid.

17. David M. Pletcher, *Rails, Mines and Progress: Seven American Promoters in Mexico, 1867-1911* (Ithaca, 1958), pp. 46-49.

18. Ibid., pp. 50-51, 60-66, 68 cited; Goary? to Palmer, n.d., Palmer Papers.

19. Haupt to Thomson, Dec. 9, 1861, Haupt Papers, Box 3; Haupt to R. M. Maguire, May 13, 1852, Haupt Letterbook, 1852, The Historical Society of Pennsylvania, Philadelphia; Haupt to Cameron, Aug. 27, 1854, Sept. 5, 1854, Allegheny Coal & Railroad Co., Circular, Sept. 4, 1854, Harrisburg Cameron Papers; Allegheny Coal & Railroad Co. Circular, Nov. 2, 1858, Haupt Papers, Box 2.

20. Howard N. Eavenson, *The First Century and a Quarter of the American Coal Industry* (Pittsburgh, 1942), p. 195; Ethel Armes, *The Story of Coal*

and Iron in Alabama (Cambridge, 1910), p. 403; Palmer's Diary, Mar. 18, 1857, Palmer Papers.

21. Carnegie to R. D. Barclay, Jan. 9, 1868, Agreement Between Carnegie and Scott, Feb. 18, 1868, Joseph Wall Collection of Carnegie Papers, Grinnell College, Grinnell, Iowa; Jackson to Palmer, Oct. 17, 1868, Palmer Memo, 1869 cited, Palmer Papers.

22. *The Manufactories and Manufacturers of Pennsylvania of the Nineteenth Century* (Philadelphia, Pa., 1905), p. 209; John Scott to Palmer, May 27, 1861, Prospectus of the Pittsburgh & Youghiogheny Coal Company, Apr. 11, 1856, Palmer Papers; Memo of Agreement between Scott and Carnegie, June 1, 1858, Wall Collection.

23. Palmer's Report on the Coal Valley Mines, Nov. 10, 1857, Palmer Papers.

24. *Poor's Manual, 1889*, p. 21; *Report of the Investigating Committee, 1874*, p. 132; Hinchman to Palmer, Apr. 16, 1868 cited, Jackson to Palmer, Apr. 21, 1868 cited, Palmer Papers.

25. *Manufactories of Pennsylvania*, pp. 411-14; Inventory and Appraisement of the Estate of John Edgar Thomson, 1874.

26. Hinchman to Palmer, June 30, 1866, Lamborn to Palmer, June 28, 1866, Palmer Papers; *Manufactories of Pennsylvania*, p. 324; Joseph Wall, *Andrew Carnegie* (New York, 1970), p. 178.

27. Palmer to Lamborn, Dec. 6, 1866 cited, Palmer Papers; Inventory and Appraisement of the Estate of John Edgar Thomson, 1874.

28. Lamborn to Palmer, Oct. 21, 1865, June 15, 1867, Palmer Papers; PRR Board Minutes, Nov. 1, Nov. 13, Sept. 13, 1865, Apr. 17, Dec. 11, 1867, Apr. 14, Nov. 24, 1869, May 24, 1871; *22nd PRR Annual Report*, p. 47; *23rd PRR Annual Report*, p. 30; *Manufactories of Pennsylvania*, pp. 343-44, 392; Inventory and Appraisement of the Estate of John Edgar Thomson, 1874.

29. Wall, *Carnegie*, pp. 254-55, 262 cited; Thomson to Carnegie, Jan. 1, 1871, Apr. 29, 1867, Carnegie Papers, Library of Congress; Carnegie Memo, Sept. 6, 1867, Wall Papers; *Manufactories of Pennsylvania*, pp. 367-68; "Certificate of Acceptance by Keystone Bridge Company of Provisions of a Certain Act of Assembly," Apr. 1, 1872, Wall Papers.

30. Carnegie to Thomson, Oct. 30, 1872 cited, Thomson to Carnegie, Nov. 14, 1872 cited, Wall Papers.

31. Haupt, "Reminiscences," p. 19; Haupt to Henry Cartwright, Aug. 11, 1857, Haupt Papers, Box 1; Memo. of Settlement with H. Haupt & Co., Mar. 17, 1875, Haupt Papers, Box 18; Kamm, "Tom Scott," p. 7; PRR Board Minutes, Sept. 30, 1863; Scott to Palmer, Feb. 27, 1858, Palmer Papers.

32. Palmer to Clothier, Sept. 14, 1859 cited, in Clothier, *Palmer Letters*, pp. 43-45.

33. Wall, *Carnegie*, pp. 270-72; Carnegie's Account with Scott, 1871, Wall

Papers; Thomson to Carnegie, Sept. 11, 1873, Carnegie Papers, Library of Congress.

34. Lamborn to Palmer, Aug. 6, 1867 cited, Palmer Papers; Inventory and Appraisement of the State of John Edgar Thomson, 1874.

35. Carnegie to J. S. Morgan, Apr. 21, 1873, Carnegie to Thomson, Jan. 24, 1871 cited, Wall Papers.

36. Charles Tracy to Palmer, Dec. 4, 1859, Palmer Papers; Wall, *Carnegie*, pp. 279-80; Carnegie to Thomson, Mar. 25, 1869, Carnegie note, Mar. 18, 1869, Carnegie to Thomson, Apr. 12, 1869 cited, Wall Papers; Inventory and Appraisement of the Estate of John Edgar Thomson, 1874.

37. Carnegie to Thomson, Nov. 8, 1871, Wall Papers.

38. Wall's notes from the Carnegie Davenport & St. Paul File, Wall Papers; Wall, *Carnegie*, pp. 289, 296-97; *New York Times*, Feb. 13, 1884.

39. Carnegie to Thomson, May 24, 1873 cited, June 6, 1873, Wall Papers.

40. Unidentified newspaper clipping, Lavinia's Scrapbook, Thomson Foundation; Inventory and Appraisement of the Estate of John Edgar Thomson, 1874.

41. Wall, *Carnegie*, pp. 138-43, 199-200.

42. Ibid., pp. 206-09; Carnegie to Pullman, Feb. 22, 1869, Carnegie to Scott, Jan 21, 1870, Thomson to Carnegie, Sept. 18, 1870, Carnegie to Thomson, Mar. 29, 1872 cited, Wall Papers; *Report of the Investigating Committee, 1874*, p. 126; PRR Board Minutes, Apr. 22, 1874.

43. PRR Board Minutes, May 18, Sept. 4, 1867; Wall, *Carnegie*, pp. 212-15.

44. Wall, *Carnegie*, pp. 216-20; Carnegie to ? Orton, June 3, 1873, Wall Papers; Inventory and Appraisement of the Estate of John Edgar Thomson, 1874.

45. Inventory and Appraisement of the Estate of John Edgar Thomson, 1874; *Manufactories of Pennsylvania*, p. 415.

Chapter 10

1. Charles N. Glaab, *Kansas City and the Railroads: Community Policy in the Growth of a Regional Metropolis* (Madison, 1962), pp. 103, 121; Britt A. Storey, "The Kansas Pacific Seeks the Pacific," *Journal of the West* 8 (July 1969): 402; Alan W. Farley, "Samuel Hallett and the Union Pacific Railway Company in Kansas," *The Kansas Historical Quarterly* 25 (Spring 1959): 3, 9; William R. Petrowski, "Thomas C. Durant and the Union Pacific, Eastern Division 1864-1866," *The Kansas Historical Quarterly* 36 (Summer 1970): 58-59, 60; A. C. Anderson to J. B. Anderson, Jan. 19, 1865, John Perry to J. B.

Anderson, Mar. 10, 1865, Scott to J. B. Anderson, July 14, 1865, Anderson Family Papers, Kansas State Historical Society; Lamborn to Palmer, Aug. 2, 1865, Palmer to Jackson, Aug. 7, 1865, J. W. Smith to Palmer, Aug. 23, 1865, Palmer to Jackson, Aug. 25, 1865 cited, Palmer Papers.

2. Palmer's Diary Aug. 2-7, 1865, Palmer to Hinchman, Sept. 2, 1865 cited, Palmer Papers.

3. Lamborn to Palmer, Sept. 14, 1865, Aug. 4, 1866, ibid.; Petrowski, "Durant," p. 63; William R. Petrowski, "The Kansas Pacific Railroad in the South west," *Arizona & The West* 11 (Summer 1969): 138; Ames, *Union Pacific*, pp. 161-62.

4. Hinchman to Palmer, July 24, 1866, Lamborn to Palmer, May 27, 1866 cited, June 14, 1866 cited, June 28, 1866, Palmer Papers.

5. Storey, "William J. Palmer," p. 166; Thomson to Palmer, Oct. 6, 1866 cited, Palmer Papers; *Commercial & Financial Chronicle*, June 5, 1869, June 7, 1873; W. Preston Smith to Palmer, n.d., Gilead Smith to Palmer, Nov. 17, 1866, Palmer Papers.

6. Lamborn to Palmer, Dec. 3, 1866, Palmer to Lamborn, Dec. 6, 1866, Lamborn to Palmer, Mar. 2, 1867 cited, Reiff to Palmer, Aug. 8, 1867, Palmer Papers; Petrowski, "The Kansas Pacific," p. 141; Storey, "The Kansas Pacific," p. 411; Lamborn to Palmer, Oct. 4, 1868 cited, Palmer Papers.

7. Thomson to Palmer, Nov. 1, 1868, Jan. 17, 1869 cited, Lamborn to Palmer, Dec. 15, 1868, Palmer Papers.

8. Perry to Palmer, Mar. 15, 1869, Reiff to Palmer, Apr. 23, 1869, Perry to Palmer, May 22, 1869, ibid.; Storey, "William J. Palmer," pp. 155-58, 160, 203-04; *Commercial & Financial Chronicle*, June 15, 1872; Perry to Palmer, May 24, 1869, Palmer Papers.

9. Reiff to Palmer, July 24, 1869, Aug. 16, 1869, Palmer Papers; Storey, "William J. Palmer," p. 200; Reiff to Palmer, Aug. 30, 1869 cited, Sept. 6, 1869, Lamborn to Palmer, Sept. 8, 1869 cited, Guarantee for Payment of Contractor, Nov. 1869, Palmer Papers.

10. Storey, "William J. Palmer," 230-35, 241-43, 246, 249; Inventory and Appraisement of the Estate of John Edgar Thomson, 1874.

11. *Colorado Springs Gazette*, n.d., Lavinia's Scrapbook, Thomson Foundation.

12. Larson, *Cooke*, pp. 258-59, 282-86; Thomson to Cooke, Mar. 22, 1871, Cooke Papers; Lamborn to Palmer, Sept. 8, 1869, Sept. 14, 1869 cited, Palmer Papers.

13. Gilead Smith to Palmer, Nov. 17, Nov. 25, 1869, Lamborn to Palmer, Jan. 24, 1870 cited, Palmer Papers.

14. Larson, *Cooke*, pp. 287-89, 327, 348; Grodinsky, *Transcontinental Railways*, p. 11.

15. Larson, *Cooke*, pp. 365, 396-97; Jay Cooke to Henry Cooke, Feb. 14, 1873 cited, Cooke Papers.

16. Carnegie to Thomson, Nov. 8, 1871 cited, Wall Papers; Wall, *Carnegie*, p. 287 cited.

17. Ames, *Union Pacific*, pp. 175-76, 404; U. S. Congress, House, *The Disposal of the Subsidies Granted Certain Railroad Companies*, 44th Cong., 1st Sess., 1876, Misc. Doc. 176, Pt. 1, pp. 48, 63; U.S. Congress, House, *Affairs of the Union Pacific Railroad Company*, 42nd Cong., 3rd. Sess., 1873, Rpt. 78, pp. 529, 650-51.

18. *Affairs of the UP*, p. 528; Ames, *Union Pacific*, p. 416; Carnegie to L. B. Boomer, Jan. 27, 1871 cited, Wall Papers.

19. PRR Board Minutes, Jan. 2, 1871; McCandless to Carnegie, Apr. 15, 1871, Wall Papers.

20. Wall, *Carnegie*, p. 289 cited.

21. Maybee, *The Oil Trade*, p. 301 cited.

22. Thomson to Carnegie, Jan. 1, 1871, Carnegie Collection, Library of Congress; *Affairs of the UP*, pp. 531, 650; McCandless to Scott, Aug. 19, 1871, Carnegie to Barclay, Nov. 3, 1871, Carnegie to Thomson, Nov. 8, 1871 cited, Wall Papers; *Disposal of Subsidies*, p. 48.

23. Thomson to Carnegie, Sept. 11, 1873 cited, Carnegie Collection, Library of Congress.

24. *Autobiography of Andrew Carnegie* (Boston, 1920), p. 165 cited.

25. C. Vann Woodward, *Reunion and Reaction: The Compromise of 1877 and the End of Reconstruction* (New York, 1956), pp. 73-81; Grodinsky, *Transcontinental Railways*, pp. 19-20, 45; Thomson to Carnegie, Oct. 3, 1873, Carnegie Collection, Library of Congress; *Philadelphia Ledger & Transcript*, Nov. 5, 1873.

26. PRR Board Minutes, Aug. 18, 1873.

27. Thomson to Carnegie, Nov. 14, 1872 cited, Wall Papers; Grodinsky, *Transcontinental Railways*, pp. 45-46; *Philadelphia Ledger & Transcript*, Nov. 5, 1873.

28. Thomson to Carnegie, Oct. 3, 1873 cited, Jan. 1, 1871 cited, Carnegie Collection, Library of Congress; Carnegie, *Autobiography*, pp. 173-74 cited.

29. Inventory and Appraisement of the Estate of John Edgar Thomson, 1874; *Philadelphia Ledger & Transcript*, Nov. 5, 1873.

30. PRR Board Minutes, Nov. 7, 1873.

Chapter 11

1. Burgess, *Pennsylvania Railroad*, pp. 306-07.

2. PRR Board Minutes, July 1, July 2, Oct. 22, Nov. 7, Nov. 26, 1873, Feb. 2, May 15, 1874.

3. Ibid., Dec. 4, Dec. 24, Dec. 30, 1873, Jan. 28, Feb. 25, Apr. 22, May 2, May 15, 1874.

4. *27th PRR Annual Report*, pp. 6-8.

5. PRR Board Minutes, May 15, 1874 cited.

6. *Report of the Investigating Committee, 1874*, pp. 163, 169, 194-95.

7. Thomson to Carnegie, Apr. 29, 1867 cited, Carnegie Collection, New York Public Library, N.Y.; Thomson to Bell, Dec. 22, 1868 cited, Bell Papers, Thomson to Palmer, Jan. 17, 1869 cited, Reiff to Palmer, Aug. 30, 1869 cited, Palmer Papers.

8. Walter T. K. Nugent, *The Money Question During Reconstruction* (New York, 1967), pp. 80-84; "John Edgar Thomson," *The Penn Monthly* (July 1874): 492; Thomson to Covode, Jan. 30, 1868 cited, Covode Papers.

9. *The Philadelphia Republic*, Dec. 6, 1868, cited; "Thomson," *Penn Monthly*, p. 492; McClure, *Old Time Notes*, 2: 226.

10. Reiff to Palmer, Aug. 30, 1869 cited, Palmer Papers.

11. Carnegie to Thomson, Jan. 29, 1874 cited, Wall Papers.

12. Inventory and Appraisement of the Estate of John Edgar Thomson, 1874; James A. Ward, "J. Edgar Thomson and Thomas A. Scott: A Symbiotic Partnership?" pp. 64-65.

13. John Wyeth to Haupt, Mar. 16, 1905, Haupt Papers; PRR Board Minutes, Apr. 22, 1873; Anna J. Reynolds, "The John Edgar Thomson School: The Past and the Present," in Thomson Foundation, p. 1; Thomson's Will, pp. 2-4.

14. Unidentified newspaper clippings, Lavinia's Scrapbook, Thomson Foundation; *Philadelphia Evening Telegraph*, June 1, 1874 cited; Reynolds, "The Thomson School," p. 2.

15. Unidentified newspaper clippings, Lavinia's Scrapbook, Thomson Foundation; PRR Board Minutes, June 3, 1874.

16. Thomson's Will, p. 1 cited; Unidentified newspaper clippings, Lavinia's Scrapbook, Thomson Foundation; *New York Times*, Feb. 13, 1884.

17. Reynolds, "The Thomson School," pp. 1-7.

18. Ibid., p. 7; "Thomson Foundation," *Savings Bank Journal*, pp. 42-44; "Mr. Thomson Aids Railroaders' Daughters," *Penn Central Post* (June 1974): 3.

Epilogue

1. Max Ways, "A Hall of Fame for Business Leadership." *Fortune Magazine* 91 (January 1975): 64-73, 71 cited.

2. Herbert G. Gutman, "Trouble on the Railroads in 1873-1874: Prelude to the 1877 Crisis?" *Labor History* 2 (Spring 1971): 217-25; PRR Board Minutes, Dec. 24, 1873.

3. Joseph Daughen and Peter Binzen, *The Wreck of the Penn Central* (New York, 1971); Richard Saunders, *The Railroad Mergers and the Coming of Conrail* (Westport, 1978); Harry L. Eddy to author, November 2, 1970, in author's possession.

SELECTED
BIBLIOGRAPHY

Manuscripts

Anderson Family Papers. Kansas State Historical Society. Topeka, Kans.

Baltimore & Ohio Railroad Papers. Maryland Historical Society. Baltimore, Md.

Barlow, Samuel. Papers. The Huntington Library. San Marino, Calif.

Bell, James Martin. Papers. Duke University Library. Durham, N.C.

Black, Nellie Peters. Collection. University of Georgia Libraries. Athens, Ga.

Cameron, Simon. Papers. Library of Congress. Washington, D.C.

Cameron, Simon. Papers. The Historical Society of Dauphin County. Harrisburg, Pa.

Carnegie, Andrew. Papers. Library of Congress. Washington, D.C.

Carnegie, Andrew. Papers. Manuscript Division, New York Public Library, New York, N.Y.

Coryell Papers. The Historical Society of Pennsylvania. Philadelphia, Pa.

Covode, John. Papers. The Historical Society of Western Pennsylvania. Pittsburgh, Pa.

Georgia Railroad and Banking Company. Minutes of Stockholder Meetings. Office of the Georgia Railroad Bank and Trust Company. Augusta, Ga.

————. Minutes of the Board of Directors. Office of the Georgia Railroad Bank and Trust Company. Augusta, Ga.

Grant, Lemeul P. Papers. The Atlanta Historical Society. Atlanta, Ga.

Haupt, Herman. "How J. Edgar Thomson Became President of the Penn. Railroad Co. (in 1852)." Association of American Railroads, Economics and Finance Library. Washington, D.C.

———. Letterbook 1852. The Historical Society of Pennsylvania. Philadelphia, Pa.

———. Papers, 1824-1905. Yale University Library. New Haven, CT.

———. "Reminiscences of Early History of the Pennsylvania Railroad Company." Hill Railway Library Collection, University of Wisconsin. Madison, Wisc.

Palmer, William Jackson. Papers. Colorado State Historical Society. Denver, Colo.

Pennsylvania Canal Commission, Reports and Documents. RG-17, W2C-20. The Pennsylvania Historical and Museum Commission. Harrisburg, Pa.

Pennsylvania Railroad. Minutes of the Board of Directors. Office of the Secretary of the Penn Central Railroad, Philadelphia, Pa.

Reynolds, Anna J. "The John Edgar Thomson School: The Past, Present, and Future." John Edgar Thomson Foundation. Philadelphia, Pa.

Thomson, John Edgar. Collection. John Edgar Thomson Foundation. Philadelphia, Pa.

———. Letterbook 1852. The Pennsylvania Historical and Museum Commission. Harrisburg, Pa.

———. Letters. The Historical Society of Pennsylvania. Philadelphia, Pa.

Thomson, Lavinia. Scrapbook. John Edgar Thomson Foundation. Philadelphia, Pa.

Wall, Joseph. Collection of Carnegie Papers. Grinnell College. Grinnell, Iowa.

Books, Articles, Dissertations, Reports, Government Documents, and Newspapers

Adler, Dorothy. *British Investment in American Railways, 1834-1898*. Charlottesville, Va.: The University Press of Virginia, 1970.

Aldrich, Mark. "Earnings of American Civil Engineers, 1820-1859." *The Journal of Economic History* 31 (June 1971).

Ambrose, Stephen E. *Duty, Honor, Country: A History of West Point*. Baltimore, Md.: The Johns Hopkins Press, 1966.

American Railroad Journal, 1850-1860.

Ames, Charles E. *Pioneering the Union Pacific: A Reappraisal of the Builders of the Railroad*. New York: Appleton-Century Crofts, 1969.

Armes, Ethel. *The Story of Coal and Iron in Alabama*. Birmingham, Ala.: Chamber of Commerce, 1910.

Athens (Georgia) Southern Banner, 1834-1847.

Autobiography of Andrew Carnegie. Boston, Mass.: Houghton Mifflin, Co., 1920.

Barton, Roger. "The Camden and Amboy Railroad Monopoly." *Proceedings of the New Jersey Historical Society* 12 (1927).

Bishop, Avard L. "The State Works of Pennsylvania." *Transactions of the Connecticut Academy of Arts and Sciences* 13 (Nov. 1907).

Black, Nellie Peters., ed. *Richard Peters: His Ancestors and Descendants*. Atlanta, Ga.: Foote & Davies Co., 1904.

Bogue, Allan G. *From Prairie to Corn Belt: Farming on the Illinois and Iowa Prairies in the Nineteenth Century*. Chicago: The University of Chiago Press, 1963.

Boorstin, Daniel J. *The Americans: The Colonial Experience*. New York: Random House, 1958.

Brooks, Terrence. *The Pennsylvania Railroad: The Early Days*. Los Angeles: Trans-Anglo Books, 1964.

Bruce, Alfred W. *The Steam Locomotive in America: Its Development in the Twentieth Century*. New York: Bonanza Books, 1952.

Burgess, George H. and Kennedy, Miles C. *Centennial History of the Pennsylvania Railroad Company, 1846-1946*. Philadelphia, Pa.: Pennsylvania Railroad Co., 1949.

Calhoun, Daniel H. *The American Civil Engineer: Origins and Conflict*. Cambridge, Mass.: Harvard University Press, 1960.

Clark, Thomas D. "The Montgomery and West Point Railroad Company." *Georgia Historical Quarterly* 17 (March 1933).

Clothier, Isaac. *Letters, 1853-1868: General William J. Palmer*. Philadelphia, Pa.: Ketterlinus, 1906.

Cohen, Henry. *Business and Politics in America from the Age of Jackson to the Civil War: The Career Biography of W. W. Corcoran*. Westport, Ct.: Greenwood, 1971.

Cumming, Joseph B. *A History of Georgia Railroad and Banking Company and its Corporate Affiliates, 1833-1958*. Augusta, Ga.: N.p., 1971.

Cumming, Mary G. *Georgia Railroad & Banking Company, 1833-1945*, Augusta, Ga.: N.p., 1945.

Davis, Patricia. *End of the Line: Alexander J. Cassatt and the Pennsylvania Railroad*. New York: Neale Watson Academic Publications, 1978.

DeBow, J. D. B. *Statistical View of the United States, A Compendium of the Seventh Census*. Washington, D.C.: Beverley Tucker, 1854.

Doster, James F. "The Georgia Railroad & Banking Company in the Reconstruction Era." *Georgia Historical Quarterly* 48 (March 1964).

Eavenson, Howard N. *The First Century and a Quarter of American Coal Industry*. Pittsburgh, Pa.: Privately Printed, 1942.

Farley, Alan W. "Samuel Hallett and the Union Pacific Railway Company in Kansas." *The Kansas Historical Quarterly* 25 (Spring 1959).

Farnham, Wallace D. "The Pacific Railroad Act of 1862." *Nebraska History* 43 (Sept. 1962).

Fishlow, Albert. *American Railroads and the Transformation of the Ante-Bellum Economy.* Cambridge, Mass.: Harvard University Press, 1965.

Glaab, Charles N. *Kansas City and the Railroads: Community Policy in the Growth of a Regional Metropolis.* Madison, Wisc.: The University of Wisconsin Press, 1962.

Goodrich, Carter. *Government Promotion of American Canals and Railroads, 1800-1890.* New York: Columbia University Press, 1960.

Grodinsky, Julius. *Jay Gould: His Business Career, 1867-1892.* Philadelphia, Pa.: University of Pennsylvania Press, 1957.

————. *Transcontinental Railway Strategy, 1869-1893: A Study of Businessmen.* Philadelphia, Pa.: University of Pennsylvania Press, 1962.

Gutman, Herbert G. "Trouble on the Railroads in 1873-1874; Prelude to the 1877 Crisis?" *Labor History* 2 (Spring 1971).

Harrison, Eliza Cope. *Philadelphia Merchant: The Diary of Thomas P. Cope, 1800-1851.* South Bend, Ind.: Gateway Editions, 1978.

Heath, Milton S. *Constructive Liberalism: The Role of the State in Economic Development in Georgia to 1860.* Cambridge, Mass.: Harvard University Press, 1954.

————. "Public Railroad Construction and the Development of Private Enterprise in the South Before 1861." *The Journal of Economic History,* Supplement 10 (1950).

Hill, Forest G. "Government Engineering Aid to Railroads Before the Civil War." *The Journal of Economic History* 11 (Summer 1951).

Hull, Augustus L. *Annals of Athens, Georgia, 1801-1901.* Athens, Ga.: Athens Banner Job Office, 1906.

Jackson (Mississippi) *Flag of the Union,* 1850-1854.

"John Edgar Thomson." *The Penn Monthly,* July 1874.

Kamm, Samuel R. "The Civil War Career of Thomas A. Scott." Ph.D. dissertation, University of Pennsylvania. Philadelphia, Pa., 1940.

Lambie, Joseph T. *From Mine to Market: The History of Coal Transportation on the Norfolk and Western Railway.* New York: New York University Press, 1954.

Larson, Henrietta. *Jay Cooke: Private Banker.* Cambridge, Mass.: Harvard University Press, 1936.

Livingood, James W. *The Philadelphia-Baltimore Trade Rivalry, 1780-1860.* Harrisburg, Pa.: The Pennsylvania Historical and Museum Commission, 1947.

Livingood, James W. and Govan, Gilbert E. *The Chattanooga Country, 1540-1962: From Tomahawks to TVA.* Chapel Hill, N.C.: University of North Carolina Press, 1963.

MacGill, Caroline F. *History of Transportation in the United States Before 1860.* Washington, D.C.: Carnegie Institution of Washington, 1917.

The Manufactories and Manufacturers of Pennsylvania of the Nineteenth Century. Philadelphia: Galaxy Publishing Co., 1875.

Martin, John Hill. *Chester (and its Vicinity) Delaware County.* Philadelphia, Pa.: W. H. Pile, 1877.

Maybee, Rolland H. *Railroad Competition and the Oil Trade, 1855-1873.* Reprint. Philadelphia, Pa.: Porcupine Press, 1974.

McCain, William D. *The Story of Jackson: A History of the Capital of Mississippi, 1821-1951.* Jackson, Miss.: J. F. Hyer Publishing Co., 1953.

McClure, Alexander K. *Old Time Notes of Pennsylvania.* Philadelphia, Pa.: The John C. Winston Co., 1905.

"Mr. Thomson Aids Railroaders' Daughters." *Penn Central Post,* June 1974.

Nevins, Allan. *Study in Power: John D. Rockefeller, Industrialist and Philanthropist.* New York: Charles Scribner's Sons, 1953.

North, Douglas C. *The Economic Growth of the United States, 1790-1860.* Englewood Cliffs, N.J.: Prentice-Hall, 1961.

Nugent, Walter T. K. *The Money Question During Reconstruction.* New York: W. W. Norton, 1967.

Pennsylvania Railroad. *Annual Reports of the Directors to the Stockholders,* nos. 1-30. Philadelphia, Pa.: 1847-1877.

Petrowski, William R. "The Kansas Pacific Railroad in the Southwest." *Arizona & The West* 11 (Summer 1969).

————. "Thomas C. Durant and the Union Pacific Eastern Division, 1864-1866." *The Kansas Historical Quarterly* 36 (Summer 1970).

Philadelphia Evening Bulletin, 1857-1860.

Phillips, Ulrich B. *A History of Transportation in the Eastern Cotton Belt to 1860.* New York: The Columbia University Press, 1908.

Pletcher, David M. *Rails, Mines, and Progress: Seven American Promoters in Mexico, 1867-1911.* Ithaca, N.Y.: Cornell University Press, 1958.

Poor, Henry V. *History of the Railroads and Canals of the United States of America.* New York: J. H. Schultz & Co., 1860.

————. *Manual of Railroads of the United States 1869-1870.* New York: H. V. and H. W. Poor, 1869.

Poor, H. V. and H. W., *Poor's Manual, 1889.* New York: H. V. and H. W. Poor, 1889.

Report of the Investigating Committee to the Stockholders of the Pennsylvania Railroad Company. Philadelphia, 1874.

Reports of the Directors, and of the Engineer-in-Chief, of the Georgia Rail Road and Banking Company to the Stockholders . . . 1840-1854. Athens and Augusta, Ga., 1840-1854.

Ringwalt, J. L. *Development of Transportation Systems in the United States.* Philadelphia, Published by Author, 1888.

Rosenberger, Homer T. *The Philadelphia and Erie Railroad: Its Place in American Economic History.* Potomac, Md.: The Fox Hills Press, 1975.

Rubin, James. "Canal or Railroad? Imitation and Innovation in the Response to the Erie Canal in Philadelphia, Baltimore, and Boston." *Transactions of the American Philosophical Society* 51, Pt. 7 (Nov. 1961).

Russell, James M. *Atlanta, Gate City of the South, 1847 to 1890.* Baton Rouge, La.: Louisiana State University Press, forthcoming.

Russell, Robert R. "The Pacific Issue in Politics Prior to the Civil War." *Mississippi Valley Historical Review* 12 (Sept. 1925).

Russell, William H. "A Biography of Alexander K. McClure." Ph.D. dissertation, University of Wisconsin. Madison, Wisc., 1953.

Saunders, Richard. *The Railroad Mergers and the Coming of Conrail.* Westport Ct.: Greenwood Press, 1978.

Schotter, H. W. *The Growth and Development of the Pennsylvania Railroad Company.* Philadelphia, Pa.: Allen, Lane & Scott, 1927.

Stayer, Samuel N. "James Martin Bell: Ironmaster and Financier, 1799-1870." Ph.D. dissertation, Duke University. Durham, N.C., 1970.

Storey, Brit. A. "The Kansas Pacific Seeks the Pacific." *Journal of the West* 8 (July 1969).

———. "William Jackson Palmer: A Biography." Ph.D. dissertation, University of Kentucky. Lexington, Ky., 1968.

Stover, John F. *American Railroads.* Chicago: University of Chicago Press, 1961.

———. *The Railroads of the South, 1865-1900: A Study in Finance and Control.* Chapel Hill, N.C.: University of North Carolina Press, 1955.

Taylor, George Rogers and Neu, Irene B. *The American Railroad Network, 1861-1890.* Cambridge, Mass.: Harvard University Press, 1956.

Temin, Peter. *The Jacksonian Economy.* New York: W. W. Norton & Co., 1969.

Thomson, J. Edgar. *Before Railroads: A Contemporary View of the Agriculture, Industry, and Commerce of the South in the Forties.* Nashville, Tenn.: n.p., 1928(?).

Thomson, John Edgar. *Report to the Commissioners on the Nashville and Chattanooga Rail Road.* Nashville, Tenn.: J. G. Shepard, 1847.

"To Care for those in Need: Pennsylvania Railroad Family Served by the John

Edgar Thomson Foundation." *The Savings Bank Journal* 20 (Jan. 1940).

Tolles, Frederick B. *Meeting House and Counting House: The Quaker Merchants of Colonial Philadelphia, 1682-1763*. Chapel Hill, N.C.: University of North Carolina Press, 1948.

Travelers Official Railway Guide of the United States and Canada, June 1868. Reprint. Ann Arbor, Mich.: National Railway Publication Co., 1968.

U. S. Congress, House. *Abstract of the Returns of the Fifth Census*. 22nd Cong., 1st sess., 1830, Doc. No. 269.

U. S. Congress, House. *Affairs of the Union Pacific Company*. 42nd Cong., 3d sess., 1873, Rept. 78.

U. S. Congress, House. *The Disposal of Subsidies Granted Certain Railroad Companies*. 44th Cong., 1st sess., 1876, Misc. Doc. 176, pt. 1.

Wall, Joseph. *Andrew Carnegie*. New York: Oxford University Press, 1970.

War of the Rebellion: A Compilation of the Official Records of the Union and Confederate Armies. 128 vols. Washington: U.S. Government Printing Office, 1880-1901.

Ward, James A. "A New Look at Antebellum Southern Railroad Development." *The Journal of Southern History* 39 (Aug. 1973).

————. "J. Edgar Thomson and Thomas A. Scott: A Symbiotic Partnership?" *The Pennsylvania Magazine of History and Biography* C (Jan. 1976).

————. *That Man Haupt: A Biography of Herman Haupt*. Baton Rouge, La.: Louisiana State University Press, 1973.

Watkins, J. Elfreth. *History of the Pennsylvania Railroad Company 1846-1896*. Philadelphia, Pa.: N.p., 1896.

Weber, Thomas, *The Northern Railroads in the Civil War, 1861-1865*. New York: King's Crown Press, Columbia University Press, 1952.

Wilson, William B. *History of the Pennsylvania Railroad Company: With Plan of Organization, Portraits of Officials, and Biographical Sketches*. Philadelphia, Pa.: Henry T. Coates & Co., 1899.

Wilson, William H. *Reminiscences of a Railroad Engineer*. Philadelphia, Pa.: Railway World Publishing Co., 1896.

Wood, W. K. "The Georgia Railroad and Banking Company." *Georgia Historical Quarterly* 57 (Winter 1973).

Woodward, C. Vann. *Reunion and Reaction: The Compromise of 1877 and the End of Reconstruction*. Garden City, N.J.: Doubleday, 1956.

INDEX

McClellan, George B., 133
McClure, A. K., 80
McCrea, James, 108
McManus, John, 161, 195, 206
Macon & Western R.R., 43
Magee, James, 90, 127, 171, 172
Marietta and Cincinnati Railway, (M&C), 106
Marshall, Thomas A., 57, 58
Maximilian of Austria, 169, 170
Meade, George, 133
Memphis Railroad and Steamboat Company, 42
Merrick, Samuel V.: PRR board struggle, 79-80, 86-90; PRR president, 71, 72, 75, 95; and Thomson, 76, 78
Mexican Railroad ventures, 169, 170
Middle Branch R.R., 34
Mifflin, Samuel, 3
Miller, Edmund, 165
Miller, Edward, 83
Missouri, Iowa and Nebraska R.R. (MI&N), 181
Mohawk and Hudson R.R., 22
Monroe R.R., 26, 33, 41, 47
Montgomery & West Point R.R. (M&WP), 30, 33, 41, 47, 72; GRR takes over, 51-54
Moon, Sam S., 155
Moran, Charles, 121
Morgan , John Pierpont, 4, 162, 221
Morgan , Junius, 162

Napoleon III, 166, 169
Nashville & Chattanooga R.R. (N&C), 51, 55-56, 67, 88
National Land Improvement Company, 168, 193, 196
New York Central R.R. (NYC), 94, 139, 140, 155, 203; merger, 223, 224; postwar competition, 142,

149, 153; western competition, 101, 104, 118
Norfolk and Western R.R., 223
Norris, William, 22, 74, 75-76
Norristown and Mt. Carbon R.R., 22
Northern Central Railway (NC): in Civil War, 123, 126, 128, 134; and PRR, 116, 117, 150, 201, 210
Northern Pacific R.R. (NP), 159, 165, 167, 170, 193, 208; Thomson investment, 197-200
Ohio and Indiana R.R. (O&I), 104
Ohio and Mississippi R.R. (O&M), 59, 106, 121, 122, 133, 142
Ohio and Pennsylvania R.R. (O&P), 104
Ohio Valley R.R., 106
Oil Creek R.R., 130
Oxford R.R., 21

Palmer, William, 127, 134, 162, 180, 190, 212; coal firebox, 100-1; coal investments, 172, 173; Mexican ventures, 169, 170-71; railroad investments, 178, 191, 193, 194, 195
Pan Handle R.R. See Pittsburgh, Cincinnati and St. Louis R.R. (PC&SL)
Parker, William, 3
Patterson, Robert, 174
Patterson, William: PRR board struggle, 79, 86-88, 90; PRR president, 80, 81, 83, 84, 85, 95, 112
Penn Central R.R., 151, 224
Pennsylvania Company (PC), 150, 151, 210, 222
Pennsylvania, Poughkeepsie and Boston RR, 183
Pennsylvania Railroad (PRR): accountability, 139, 144, 146; and B&P, 154; board formed, 71;

About the Author

JAMES A. WARD is a professor of History at the University of Tennessee at Chattanooga. His earlier writings include *That Man Haupt: A Biography of Herman Haupt* and *American History: A Brief View* (with H. L. Ingle).

Recent Titles in
Contributions in Economics and Economic History
SERIES EDITOR: *Robert Sobel*